PHARMFLUENCERS™

THE INSPIRING STORIES OF PHARMACY ENTREPRENEURS

Dr. Kimber Boothe, PharmD, MHA

www.Holon.co

ISBN#: 978-1-955342-55-1 (Paperback)
ISBN#: 978-1-955342-56-8 (Hardback)
ISBN#: 978-1-955342-57-5 (eBook)

Published by:

Holon Publishing & Collective Press
A Storytelling Company
www.Holon.co

I would like to dedicate this book...

TO MY PARENTS,
for encouraging me to dream big and be myself;

TO MY HUSBAND & CHILDREN,
for making life fun and supporting my career passions;

AND TO ALL PHARMFLUENCERS,
for your desire to influence and impact pharmacy through entrepreneurship.

CONTENTS

INTRODUCTION

I have always been incredibly inspired by hearing individuals share their stories. There is something empowering about taking hold of one's life and sharing that narrative with the world. When I first began my entrepreneurial journey, it was the stories of other entrepreneurs that motivated me to get to work and make my own career goals a reality. This is what always drew me to attending conferences and reading business anthologies, the opportunity to hear how others built joyful careers for themselves.

I know far too many pharmacists who are experiencing burnout from working within the healthcare industry, who find themselves unable to achieve the level of financial freedom they want, who believe they can do more than what they are allowed within the confines of their job. I want you to know it doesn't have to be this way. You deserve a career that is engaging and joyful, that allows you to grow and challenge yourself, that gives you financial freedom and invigorates rather than exhausts you. This book is specifically designed to inspire you to make that career a reality, to not only advance the pharmacy practice but to become your own business owner.

I am at a place in my life where I love the work that I do. Helping other pharmacists find meaningful careers to advance pharmacy entrepreneurship, and intrapreneurship is my passion. Therefore, it was important to me to create a platform in which I could pass along the inspiration by sharing my story and in which other pharmacy entrepreneurs could share theirs.

My goal for the "Pharmfluencer Summit: Influence, Monetize, Impact Pharmacy Through Entrepreneurship" was to assemble a group of Pharmfluencers, including myself, to share their entrepreneurial journey. My definition of a Pharmfluencer is a pharmacy influencer, someone who is impacting pharmacy through entrepreneurship. They are monetizing their knowledge and influencing the field. The event had 450 registrations and proved to be such a success. I decided my next task would be to write a book accumulating all the knowledge, advice, and personal experiences that were shared during the summit.

The Pharmfluencer contributors have all been incredible partners whose values align with mine and who are working to advance pharmacy through their businesses.

Each contributor's chapter is divided into subsections that address:

- Their entrepreneurial journey
- Methods in which they are monetizing their knowledge
- A specific topic on which each contributor has elected to share their knowledge
- Their advice for aspiring entrepreneurs.

The goal was to help inspire and inform people who are interested in entrepreneurship and looking to have a larger impact on the pharmacy profession. I wanted to gather all the Pharmfluencers out there and make their stories accessible to you! I wanted to provide a blueprint and business model as to how aspiring Pharmfluencers can monetize their knowledge.

What is an influencer? About seven years ago, I participated in a program called Experts Academy with Brendon Burchard. The terminology we used then was "expert" or "thought leader," but since then, that concept has developed to be encompassed by the umbrella term of "influencer." The defining characteristic of an influencer is both to be an expert in your field but also to monetize that knowledge in order to develop your business and have an impact.

Monetizing your knowledge could look like offering an online course, live course, or hosting webinars or webcasts that people pay for. You could host a conference or seminar both in-person or virtual. You could offer an ongoing membership where people pay a monthly or annual fee to access the information you are providing. You could write a book and sell it, offering both hard copies and ebooks. You could speak at events, provide coaching, or work as a clinical patient consultant. You could work as a business consultant; the opportunities are truly limitless.

If you're feeling a little overwhelmed by the possibilities, no worries. A trick I use is to identify my zone of genius. This is to say, identifying the areas in your field that make you happy and how you can zero in on those areas to develop your business. What do I enjoy doing? What do I want to learn more about? What do people naturally come to me for? Answering those questions is how you start to identify your zone of genius. This book will not answer those questions for you, but it will offer you a variety of perspectives you can use for reference so that by the time you finish, you can begin to identify it for yourself.

SETTING INTENTION: WHY YOU ARE HERE

There are a multitude of reasons why this information may be of use to you. But I have identified a few key reasons people in pharmacy seek entrepreneurship.

- Experiencing Healthcare Burnout: Seeking opportunities to influence change
- Desire for Financial Freedom: Want additional income and security
- Made for More: You feel this and believe you could have more impact
- Craving a Joyful and Engaging Career Through Entrepreneurship.

Whatever your reasons, learning how to become a Pharmfluencer can meet all of these needs and give you a new outlook on your career.

I met with somebody recently who was working in pharmacy but wanted to develop an entrepreneurial career outside the field. And while that is perfectly fine, I was surprised by how many people don't realize how ripe pharmacy is for entrepreneurship. The two are in no way mutually exclusive. The key is, once you know how to monetize your knowledge, you can apply that to any field, healthcare or otherwise. This book, however, is going to focus on pharmacy because I believe entrepreneurship can actually help advance pharmacy practice. My goal has always been to create more positions in the pharmacy practice. There are a whole host of unmet needs that can be met through your entrepreneurial practice.

The themes of this book are to:

- Influence
- Monetize
- Impact

INFLUENCE	MONETIZE	IMPACT
Why explore entrepreneurship and the influencer model	Learn the many methods to monetize your knowledge	Understand the business foundation and opportunities in pharmacy practice

We will be exploring: what is the influencer model, how you can have influence through entrepreneurship, how you can monetize your knowledge, and impact pharmacy practice by sharing your gifts with the world. By the end of this book, you will understand the steps to build an entrepreneurial business and how to develop a strong foundation for that business. Whether you are starting as a side hustle and moving toward a full-time entrepreneur, or you already have an entrepreneurial business and are looking to expand, this book will help you impact your industry in ways you may never have imagined.

Although taking this leap can often be frightening, it is also extremely rewarding. I'm also a wife and mother. I've been married for 13 years and have three kids; I know how high the stakes are when you are trying to make this leap while supporting a family. And while it is not all roses, and it may not be perfect for everybody, I truly believe the impact you can have in entrepreneurship is much greater than continuing to work in a job that is not satisfying you. Use this book as an opportunity to entertain your hopes and ambitions. Truly think about what your mission is, whom you want to support, and what your life would look like if you could have the kind of impact you have been dreaming of.

I have been a full-time entrepreneur for two years, and I cannot express strongly enough how great it feels to be in control of my career. My motto is that pharmacy can do more with more. I started my business to focus on helping advance pharmacy through intrapreneurship, innovative practice within organizations and health systems and supporting people in the profession who are looking to make an impact as an entrepreneur. By helping people through both avenues, I have been able to help advance the profession as a whole. Before becoming an entrepreneur, I have worked in varying capacities, mostly in hospitals and health systems. It was through these experiences that I realized the potential the industry held for entrepreneurs. I began my journey as an entrepreneur seven years ago and have never looked back.

I know there may be people reading this who are not even sure if they want to be an entrepreneur, but I cannot emphasize enough how wonderful a career choice it is. I'd like to tell a brief story about my first entrepreneurship venture, which I started when I was in college. I've always loved doing nails; as a student, I would do my friend's nails. I would go all out; I would even put fake nails on people and do designs with crystals. Well, I got to thinking about it and thought, "Why not? Why don't I make this into a real business?" I posted an ad in the college newspaper and ended up getting a nice letter from the university saying, "If you don't stop running this business out of your dorm room, you will be expelled."

That admittedly cut my entrepreneurial journey short. But I've had this entrepreneurial bug for a long time, and I've considered it within many different avenues. Early on, right after I finished my residency, I was doing consulting with pharma companies in which I was the cardiology specialist. It was from that position that I recognized the value of having a business because I had to deduct my business expenses. Even way back then, I had lots of different ideas about what it meant to run a business.

Seven years ago, I came across this entrepreneurial expert thought leader model; some people call it a knowledge expert or knowledge entrepreneur model. It was very appealing to me because one thing it emphasized was that you didn't need a physical space in order to be an entrepreneur. That really opened my eyes in terms of what it would mean to create a startup.

There is so much wisdom that can be gained from this book. You will hear entrepreneurs discuss taking the leap to follow your dreams, the value podcasting can bring to your business, the power of storytelling, and how medical writing can be a great role for pharmacists to play as a gig job or even a full-time career. Our Pharmfluencers will teach you how to use your strengths and stay true to yourself in business, how to take risks and make educated choices, how to seek valuable mentorship, and that is only the tip of the iceberg.

A recurring thread you will see throughout this book is the power of mindset. Mindset is incredibly important; I emphasize that in both my courses and the teaching that I do. You have to have a mindset of action; sometimes, that can be a messy action, but it is worthwhile.

William Jennings Bryan once said, "Destiny is no matter of chance. It is a matter of choice. It is not a thing to be waited for; it is a thing to be achieved."

I truly believe this. Whatever your reasons for picking up this book, you have made a choice to be here and to explore entrepreneurship as an opportunity. I'm so happy you're here.

—Kimber Boothe

Use this QR code to access the Pharmfluencers Workbook. Alternatively, you can find it online at **www.pharmfluencersbook.com**

THE PHARMFLUENCER BUSINESS MODEL

OVERVIEW

The purpose of this chapter is to provide you with new concepts to support your foundational knowledge while hearing the inspiring stories of pharmacy entrepreneurs. The contributions you will hear throughout this book are designed to inspire you and plant the seeds of action so you can begin or continue to expand your business. In this chapter, however, I want to address some of the key areas you will encounter and want to be prepared for throughout your entrepreneurial journey.

I include key points from my Pharmfluencer Business Course, which is composed of seven modules, and while I cannot go in-depth into each one, I do include a summary of each and what it contains. My hope is that this provides you with a general framework you can use to inform the development of your business. The seven modules are:

- Welcome & Overview
- Entrepreneurship & Business Models
- Methods to Monetize Your Knowledge
- Pharmfluencer Business Foundation
- Pharmacy Profession Strategies
- Acceleration & Growth
- Celebration

There are a number of reasons why people have sought out The Pharmfluencer Business Course, but I have identified three key factors that have led people to seek out new and valuable opportunities in entrepreneurship.

Influence. People who joined the course are seeking ways to further influence the industry than their current positions allow. They are passionate about building community. They are exploring having a part-time side hustle or how to be a full-time entrepreneur serving in their zone of genius.

Monetize. As much as we may wish to offer our knowledge and services for free, there is a saying that says, 'no margin, no mission.' Many people understand they have a sought-after body of knowledge, or they can provide meaningful services to the people around them, but they don't know how to monetize their knowledge. Finding creative and innovative ways to monetize your knowledge is what distinguishes a hobbyist from an entrepreneur. And while you may feel like your knowledge is too niche to attract an audience, you will be surprised at how willing people are to pay for a service when you offer it in a comprehensive and effective way.

Impact. The Pharmfluencer Business Course teaches you the foundational steps to building a career in entrepreneurship and how to impact pharmacy practice. By following these steps, you ensure your business is sustainable and can create value and impact for years to come.

There are some questions I want you to think about as you read. You don't need to have definitive answers for them, but I have found that keeping them in mind can be very helpful in developing your vision for your business:

- **Influence:** What is your zone of genius? What topic would you choose to be your focus?
- **Monetize:** What methods to monetize your knowledge do you like the most? What is your target annual income to feel financial freedom?
- **Impact:** What is the impact and level of influence you want to have? What would your life look like if you had the freedom to run an entrepreneurial business? What areas of pharmacy practice do you want to advance?

As Walt Disney once said, "All our dreams can come true if we have the courage to pursue them." Whatever your motivation is, I fully support you. While this chapter is only a brief and abridged look at what is covered in The Pharmfluencer Business Course, if it proves helpful to you, I highly recommend looking into taking the course in full. The course also includes access to tools and templates to support your journey. All information is available on my website at kimberboothe.com.

■■■

ENTREPRENEURSHIP & BUSINESS MODELS

When thinking about where my clients are on their entrepreneurial journey, I can usually sort them into five different places along a spectrum:

- Have not considered entrepreneurship
- Have some ideas
- Actively planning
- Current side hustle/part-time entrepreneur
- Full-time entrepreneur

Think about where you might be along this spectrum; this should inform the actions you take moving forward.

Before we get into the types of business models, I'd like to cover some basic statistics. The Small Business Administration (SBA) Office of Advocacy defines small businesses as those with fewer than 500 employees.[1] By this definition, over 99% of businesses in the United States are small businesses. Startups are firms that are under a year old; nine out of ten startups are very small, with only one to four employees. A side hustle, on the other hand, is a business that is not the primary source of income but is done in addition to the full-time job.

I want to cover these basic statistics so you can understand that our ideas about small businesses are often actually misconceptions. Rather than a dying industry, small businesses make up the overwhelming bulk of the American economy and carry tremendous weight. Not only that, but the majority of small businesses continue to thrive and survive. If you want to be an entrepreneur but imagine it to be a hostile climate or too difficult to accomplish, think again!

Before you can become a successful entrepreneur, you must have a successful business model. Focus on the basics, which include matters such as:

- Your 'why'
- Entrepreneur vs. Intrapreneur
- Business Models
- Your Topic
- Ideal Customer Avatar

Firstly, what is entrepreneurship, and what are the potential business models you can use to guide your practice? It is important to understand the frameworks you will inevitably be operating within. Many of us are not trained in entrepreneurship, this is not covered in our pharmacy school curriculum, so it is a critical place to start. This will also

---

1 Accessed February 23, 2022. Survival Rates and Firm Age [Infographic]. (n.d.). SBA Office of Advocacy. SBA Office of Advocacy. https://www.sba.gov/sites/default/files/SurvivalRatesAndFirmAge_ADA_0.pdf

help answer your 'why' and ground you in your purpose. I like to use the term *Ikigai*, which is a Japanese word referring to the topic that aligns with your ideal customers. This is the process of harnessing all of the different ideas in your head and bringing them together. You have to be strategic about what you are going to focus on, especially if this is your first business or the first service you are providing. It doesn't mean you can't do other things in the future, but you need to harness these ideas and narrow them down to what is the best fit for you. This is not just any business; it is your starting business.

After you choose your topic, you will go deeper on identifying the traits of who you serve by defining your ideal customer avatar (ICA).

There are many types of Business Models, but they can be boiled down to selling a product or service. The Influencer/Expert Business Model is a viable and flexible model that I am personally fond of. All the contributors in this book use the influencer business model as their main model.

■ ■ ■

METHODS TO MONETIZE YOUR KNOWLEDGE

Within the context of the Pharmfluencer Course, Methods to Monetize Your Knowledge makes up the bulk of Module 3. It is a key model in the program designed to teach clients the methods available to them for monetizing their knowledge. There are 14 lessons, one for each of the most common methods. It is important to emphasize that this is your method to monetize your knowledge. These are the products and services that you will provide for your ideal customer avatar (ICA). The goal in providing these services is to help them solve their problems and achieve their ideal goal and transformation.

I wanted to provide an abridged version to readers that could inform them in making these critical decisions. When considering how best to monetize your knowledge, there are a number of things to keep in mind.

This is an opportune moment to reflect on your Ikigai. What product or service exists at the intersection of your personal interests while also meeting the needs of your clients? Consider: What is the method most likely to get my ICA their desired outcome and transformation?

Another question to consider, simply enough, is, what do I like? You are going to want to select a method that you enjoy and prefer. Keep this in mind as you begin to design your product.

The 14 most common methods to monetize your knowledge can be seen in the graphic below:

Apps/Tools	Books/eBooks	Courses	Coaching
Consulting	Clinical Services	Live Seminar/Conference	Master-mind
Member-ship	PDFs	Physical Products	Speaking
Virtual Seminar/Summit	Webinars/Webcasts		

Methods to Monetize Your Knowledge

It is not all-inclusive, but hopefully, it will inspire you to find the method that is most effective for you. There are many ways you can share your knowledge and be paid for it. It is important to understand that these options are out there so you can prioritize your preferences and be aware of the choices you are making. For example, I have known for years that I wanted to write a book about pharmacy and entrepreneurship, but I knew that a book was not the best product to begin my journey with. Instead, I started by offering courses and coaching and worked my way up to writing the book. You should select your method in accordance with what is the best fit for you, both in terms of your personal preferences and how you want to share your knowledge, but also what is most impactful for your customers.

It may be helpful to reflect on a time you purchased one of these products or services for yourself. What was your experience with this product? What did you like or dislike about it? If there were things you disliked, was it a concern with the actual method, or just how that person implemented it. If the latter, what can you do better if utilizing this method?

I like to have my clients select their top three methods and then decide on which one they want to move forward with. As I stated earlier, you can always select more than one method down the road, but initially, it is best to start with one specific product or service. Throughout the model, students receive the following relevant information to each of the specific methods of monetizing knowledge.

- Description
- Characteristics
- Details
- Examples

You will be inspired by the multiple methods that our Pharmfluencers are utilizing to monetize their knowledge. I refer you to the summary table at the end of the book to identify which contributors are using the methods you are most interested in.

■ ■ ■

PHARMFLUENCER BUSINESS FOUNDATION

Once you have planned your business model, it is important to get to the basics of the business. It is in places like this where I recommend utilizing the Small Business Association and really focusing on the basics. This module covers content such as:

- Administration/Business
- Branding/Website
- Marketing/Launching
- Networking/Collaborating
- Social/Blog/Podcast
- Insurance/Healthcare
- Mindset

These are all really important elements to consider, and I recommend all my clients spend time planning each component to ensure their entrepreneurial project has a strong foundation. Think of them as a checklist of parts of your business you will want to establish and plan for. While you may not have to do all of them from the beginning, like a blog or podcast, they are a core part of a successful business.

Another element I would like to emphasize is mindset. It is important to be conscious of your mindset, especially when starting a business. Let's face it, most of the time, we are our own worst enemies. By taking the time to surround yourself with like-minded people, you are ensuring you have a support network in place that will keep you going through the tough times and remind you of your strength in moments of doubt. I can say without a doubt that I would not have had the degree of success I have experienced were it not for surrounding myself with peers who were both current and aspiring entrepreneurs.

Having the mindset of an entrepreneur is very important. The moment where I truly felt like an entrepreneur was when I began the marketing for my first course, Pharmovation. To see it listed on my website with "For Sale" next to it made me feel like a real business owner. Up to that point, I had been coaching people and had started projects, but always as a side hustle. I had been running my business against other competing priorities: moving, a new job, etc. It wasn't until that moment that I thought of myself as a real entrepreneur. I remember when the first sale came in when the first person bought that course, it really was a big moment for me.

Taking the time to understand these topics will ensure that you have the right foundation set up for your business.

■ ■ ■

Pharmacy Profession Strategies

I cannot overemphasize how important the pharmacy community has been to me on my journey. For me, the joy in this work has always been the community of other pharmacists. If I had seen other pharmacists becoming entrepreneurs when I was on my journey, it would have motivated me to move faster. I followed many entrepreneurs, but all of them were in other industries. That is why having this community now is important to me and why I want to share it with you.

If I had access to a book about pharmacists who were entrepreneurs, I would have wasted no time in reaching out and networking with them; I would have sought out the peer support that I needed. And as grateful as I am for the entrepreneurs who gave me support, their being in other industries made their journeys seem less daunting than my own. Marketing to marketers is a very different beast than marketing to pharmacists. These stories would have been incredibly inspiring to me; they would have been a peer group in which I could network. And although they have become that for me over time, I want to establish that network for you to be able to walk into without having to build it from scratch the way I had to.

Module 5 of the course is made up of all things pharmacy and hopefully is designed to familiarize you with all of the pharmacy professions opportunities available to you. This module covers:

- Pharmacy Landscapes
- Pharmacy Entrepreneurs & Innovative Leaders
- Pharmacist Marketing Strategies
- Pharmacy Stages

Obviously, this section is very unique to pharmacy; you won't see it discussed in other books on entrepreneurship. But as this book is geared towards entrepreneurs that are advancing pharmacy and healthcare, I think it is important that we understand the landscape we are working in and the needs we should be addressing. As I stated earlier, this community is everything. I want you to know about the movers and shakers who are entrepreneurs or innovative intrapreneurial thinkers, as well as some of the specific stages and organizations within pharmacy that you can rely on.

It was attending the Medipreneurs Summit that enabled me to niche down my business and begin catering to pharmacists. To have been asked back to speak on their stages is such a meaningful opportunity, as well as to be able to return the favor and promote their conference to people in my world. It is such a win-win when that happens.

I am a firm believer that all boats rise together. We should be collaborating and supporting one another to meet the needs of our industry. I have seen so much success happen when pharmacists come together to support and promote one another.

■ ■ ■

ACCELERATION & GROWTH

This module includes support systems that you will want to have in place whether you are just getting started or in the process of growing and developing your business. Having these networks in place is important to the success of your business because it allows you to enable an entrepreneurial mindset. In addition, having people around you who you trust and feel are on your team. Having people in your corner also eases the transition from being a solopreneur to hiring and filling positions, whether they are full-time or contracted work.

- Peer Group/Mentor/Coach
- Team/Hiring/Virtual Assistant
- Efficiencies
- Success Path

For me, this was my biggest learning curve. In retrospect, I should have hired a full-time virtual assistant much sooner than I did. Trying to run the entire business myself, both when it was a side hustle and full time, really slowed my growth. In the same way I tell pharmacists how to practice at the top of their licenses, it is important as entrepreneurs you practice at the top of your abilities and that you are utilizing technology and hiring out in areas that are not your zone of genius. That way, you can excel faster and focus your energy on what is most important.

This, more than anything, was a mindset shift. Even once I had hired a virtual assistant, I was not giving them enough work, even though there was work to be done. I had to get rid of the attitude that it would be easier to do everything myself. Once I understood that I am the CEO of my business, and there are things I am uniquely qualified to do, I was able to free myself up to actually do those things.

This concludes the Pharmfluencer Business Course Summary. If you are interested in taking the course, you can learn more on my website at kimberboothe.com.

Now for some inspiration from our fantastic contributors!

PHARMFLUENCERS

GREGORY ALSTON

Biography

Greg Alston is the only pharmacist in the country who has the unique experience of serving in a senior-level position in three different market segments in the pharmacy industry. He spent 15 years in corporate drug store management for three different chains. He owned and operated an independent high-volume drug store for an additional 15 years. And then, he served as a Professor and Dean at two colleges of pharmacy for 13 years. Greg is a serial entrepreneur who has owned and operated drugstores, DME companies, a chain of Halloween shops, an internet publishing business, a real estate investment business, and a vacation rental business. He's penned four best-selling books on Amazon and written multiple peer-reviewed articles and chapters on pharmaceuticals and business skills. He has trained thousands of new pharmacists on how to monetize their professional skills, and he is currently the CEO of RXVIP Concierge, a pharmacist-based clinical services company.

Entrepreneurial Journey

I received my K-12 teaching credentials before I started my career as a pharmacist at Sav-on Drugs in Southern California. I was working as a pharmacy manager when my regional manager came to me and said, "Hey, we need somebody in the corporate office to be a training manager. Can you do that?" Because he knew I had a teaching background. Within three years of getting out of school, I'm running all the training for a drug chain on the west coast. A few months later, their marketing guy quit. My boss says, "We need somebody to do marketing. Can you do marketing?" I did that for a year. And then Sav-on Drugs got purchased by the Jewel Company. My new boss at Jewel said, "Hey, we're looking to put pharmacists in general management. We want to train you to be a vice president. On Monday, we'd like you to be a buyer."

I said, "Okay." But I know nothing about buying.

I'm a pharmacist on Friday, and on Monday, I'm buying patio furniture, ice chests, barbecues, and everything the company needs to supply the stores. I'm running around trying to figure out how to do this. And it took about two years, but I finally got really good at it. I was a rising star in the company.

Then the Jewel company got purchased, and everyone I had worked hard to impress got fired. New management came in and changed everything. Then they changed ownership three times in four years. The company was finally integrated into Osco Drugs of Chicago. The new management wanted me to move to Chicago. I did not want to move my family; I left the company and purchased a drugstore.

I really enjoyed owning my own drugstore. It was a huge store. I worked my tail off, but the business was great. This was right around the time when Health Maintenance Organizations (HMOs) were created. The HMOs came through Southern California and took all of our customers. There were no "any willing provider laws" yet; they killed a lot of retail pharmacies by taking all their customers.

Undaunted, I went back to work as a pharmacy director for two different chains. At that time, I had several hundred direct reports. I left Thrifty Drug because they got bought out by a utility company that had no clue how to run drug stores. I took over as the California director of pharmacy for Smith's Food and Drug in Southern California. I helped them grow to forty stores. But they ended up selling the Southern California Division, and the new owners wanted to move me out to Salt Lake City. I had no interest in living in Utah.

I've learned over the years you can't trust that your interests and those of your employer are aligned. You can't trust employers to act in your best interest. My wife and I decided to take all our knowledge and open a one thousand-square-foot pharmacy in Sun City,

California. We built it into a $10 million business by early 2006. It was doing really well. We're helping people. I love treating senior citizens. And then the state of California decided they wanted to do many stupid things and make it very difficult to operate a business in their state. I sold the retail operations and moved to North Carolina to become a professor and assistant dean at Wingate University School of Pharmacy. I wanted to teach pharmacy students the business skills needed to monetize their degree and provide value to patients.

Through this journey, I realized that you can't let other people define your value. If you let other people determine what you're worth, you end up having to live with their choices. Corporate executives don't give a damn about how their decisions affect you. That may sound harsh, but I have 45 years of experience that support my opinion.

I wrote a book a few years ago called *Own Your Value: The Future of Pharmacy Practice*. It talked about how we need to get our ambulatory care clinicians out of hospital systems and get them into the community. That's where they belong. That's where people need our help. Well, I took flack in academia for saying things like that. But I really believe the patients need the care where they live. That's where the care should be provided. I stand by that even more since the COVID Pandemic. Today we have people who are afraid to leave their homes which means that their chronic conditions are not being treated.

If you became a pharmacist to make a difference, then you should be serving patients directly. The best way to serve them directly is now Telehealth. At my new company RXVIP Concierge, we exist to provide for the chronic care needs of our patients. They need our care more than they ever have. Essentially, I believe that if you don't stand for something good, then you stand for nothing at all. At RXVIP, we are building a TelePractice Toolkit that allows any pharmacist with the passion for serving the platform to excel. We are constantly upgrading the technology to improve the ability of individual pharmacists to launch their own clinical practice.

Methods to Monetize Your Knowledge

There are only three ways that you make money in a clinical consultant business. You can do some kind of insurance billing, which currently means partnering with a physician to do incident to billing. That requires meeting a physician that is willing to work with you. And then you do the billing on their behalf and share the revenue with them. There is a whole legal process to do this correctly.

Another way you can go about it is by offering service directly to patients. There are a lot of patients out there who want to problem solve and will pay for your service.

The third avenue is probably the least well-known; we do have some clients who do it, though. There is a lot of money dedicated to health disparities and rural health deficits. There is a lot of grant money dedicated to solving those issues. You can apply for those grants and use the funds to serve people that can't afford to pay or don't have insurance. My service offers the tools to guide you in any of those three methods.

How to Create Your Own New Revenue Streams by Capitalizing on Changes Due to COVID

I am always thrilled to meet new young people in the pharmacy industry, and while you may not think of yourself as young, I have been in this field for 45 years. I graduated in 1977, y'all, probably before some people reading this were even born. But I don't disregard the younger generation because they have so much enthusiasm, a lot of great ideas, and energy. Often, when I meet these inspiring young people, I think to myself, what can I add to this conversation?

And the reality is I have watched the major decisions and changes that have altered the path of the profession. I am a big believer that life is about the decisions you make. Well, I am here to tell you that we as a profession have made some pretty stupid decisions over the years. I see students come in with a certain set of assumptions: they plan their career and expect to make X a year, and that paycheck will get higher and higher. Every year new students come in and see their future as a rising line, going straight up. And I have to tell them that is not how the world works.

As a young person, I believed—and I see my students believe this too—that if I work hard and do my job well, no one will ever get rid of me. But that's just not true. It's happened to me five times, including at pharmacy schools. I was doing my job, running the self-study, and getting all the faculty accredited. The next day they fired me.

The only real job security you have is the security you create for yourself. You keep moving forward. And I had realized by working with students that you don't learn by studying. You don't learn by reading textbooks and taking courses. You learn by having first-hand experience. I started offering virtual Advanced Pharmacy Practice Experiences (APPEs) and supervised over 400 students in our program at RXVIP. And I realized that school hadn't taught them how to engage with humans. They can memorize guidelines, but that doesn't translate into patient care. Realistically, a patient doesn't want to work with an intelligent pharmacist; they want to work with someone who helps them reach their health goals. My clinical faculty didn't like me saying that, but it's true.

Many students don't know how to listen to patients. They end up not even treating the patients but rather treating an algorithm guideline that is inaccurate by design. The guideline doesn't work for everyone. Students have only been trained to implement guidelines; they are unable to meet patient needs. I realized that we needed to reeducate young pharmacists on how to create value for people. That is what we started delivering at RXVIP. Care, compassion, and empathy are the currency of clinical excellence.

I learned all of this through trial and error. It's an expensive way to learn because you make mistakes along the way. Taking courses is helpful because the course content gives you the meat of the material. But you also need to have that human interaction with a patient to help you interpret the information and apply it to each scenario.

When I wanted to launch a brand-new line of business at the drug-store in long-term care, I went to a friend of mine's pharmacy that was already doing it, and I spent a week with him learning how he did it. The practical nature of the field is just as, if not more important. It isn't just about the material. We offer courses that cover a bunch of material, but the interaction with patients and other experts in the field is crucial because that gives you clarity; you get your misconceptions corrected.

There are plenty of avenues for you to pursue, plenty of unmet needs. The COVID-19 pandemic has done several things. It has put people at a lot of risk health-wise; it's locked them in their homes, it has shut them away from other humans. People haven't been treated for chronic conditions because they can't go to hospitals. People are afraid, and they're depressed; they're not getting their medication refilled. You have a situation where doctors are losing money because patients are scared to go in. And the healthcare system has handled chronic care terribly forever, but in the last year, they haven't handled it at all.

We're looking at a huge explosion in emergency room visits and hospitalizations. This year, people are dropping dead because they're not getting care. We need to fix that. I got tired of it. We put together a pathway where physicians can use software tools to remotely monitor people's diabetes, hypertension, and weight. Those are the three big things that cause people to die too soon. We rent out this software for $15 per month per patient, which is less than a lunch at Applebees. This way, doctors can have that tool in their hands and start treating patients again.

But keeping in mind what I said earlier, you actually have to interact with people too. How do you do that if people aren't leaving their homes? Well, the virtual care system sets appointments, sets reminders, lets you check insurance eligibility. And it allows you to bring other caregivers on the call within the Health Insurance Portability and Accountability Act (HIPAA) compliant format.

Let's say you have an older patient and may have trouble taking care of themselves. You recommend the son or daughter take care of mom and refill her pill pack every day. Well, the daughter lives in Ohio, and mom lives in Florida. Guess what? You can bring them on the same call using telemedicine. You can bring them together so the child can be active in mom's care. And it's only a few dollars a month. You can treat a thousand patients with it if that is what you want.

We also embedded a tool in our remote patient monitoring platform that allows you to do genomic testing because you can't do med reconciliation without genomic review. It's a matter of the standard of care. If you don't do it, that's considered malpractice. Now you have a tool where you can put all the medication in, and the system will review it and say, none of these drugs is a risk. Or it will say, these four drugs need to be changed.

What can you do with that? You can go to doctors and say, "I can help your patients get better outcomes. I can do this in a way where there are no out-of-pocket costs to you, doc. And when you get paid by Medicare, you pay me what my fair share is." Or you can take it directly to the patient. People will pay to have their parents or loved ones monitored by the system and have visibility for their results. It's amazing.

I wonder why we don't use this all the time. This is what we assembled. And if people don't have the tech brain to do all this, we have tools in place that are very simple to use. If you want to know more about that, you can check out my free course, and the details are all in there. The system is called Remote Patient Monitoring; it allows you to connect through either a cellular or Bluetooth device. We can connect blood glucose meters, weight scales, and blood pressure cuffs.

We designed this because although similar systems exist, they're not designed for the pharmacist. Ours has artificial intelligence built into it. Let's say you're looking at a patient, and after lunch, their glucose levels are always low. The system will recommend lowering their morning insulin, and it will bring up the clinical guidelines to explain why. You can look at it and say, "Oh wow, we've got to do this," and go ahead and make a change in the care plan. If you're going through a doctor, forward it to the doctor, and they can sign off on it. The typical diabetic patient goes to the doctor maybe once every 90 days; how can you manage that disease in the interim?

The answer is you can't, but we've found in working directly with the doctor's offices that 40% of the information on the doctor's chart about what the patient is taking is wrong. They've got drugs in there that they're not taking. They've got drugs in there that they think they're taking, but the patient can't afford. The American medical system is a mess; it's the most unorganized system on the planet. Doctors are guessing what patients are taking; they're guessing at the treatment. They say, "Let's try this for 90 days."

That didn't sit right with me. What we offer is a system where you can go to the doctor and say, "Look, we're going to monitor the patient, and we'll give you the data so you can make a real informed decision based on that data." We've even had patients who take the initiative, who take it to their doctor because they know they need better care.

We've had four calls with physicians in the last two weeks, and when we tell them about it, they're all like, "Why aren't we doing this already?" And if other pharmacists are still reluctant, we have a training package for $97 with all the information on how to use it. But the important part is you get direct access to it. We have found that even with the knowledge of what this system does, some people are still reluctant. And it's not about the system itself as much as their hesitancy to start something new. So, realistically, life is about the choices you make.

The choice that you have to make now is either, "Hey, this is not interesting. I don't want to do it. I'm going to trust my employer's going to take care of me. Good luck." Or you can decide, "I'm not quite sure. Let me go do the free mini-course and see what it's all about." That's fine. Or you can identify a practice that you think might be interesting. We'll even make the sales pitch for you because that is a big fear for many people. How do I talk to the doctor? Or you can start by getting the tool and trying it for 60 days with a couple of family members and take your time in understanding how to use it.

We're really trying to remove all the barriers. We don't want to keep this for ourselves. We could do it. I could add two practices a month. And at the end of the year, we'd have 24 practices. But I believe if we put this tool in the hands of everyone, we could have a thousand practices by next year. The reality is patients need us now more than ever. We can't wait for permission; we have to act, start delivering care. That is what we're all about, putting the tools in the hands of pharmacists.

Many people tend to think that if they run everything themselves, it'll be better, but there aren't enough hours in the day, you can't do everything. By selecting great partners and working with them, you can expand your capabilities. Why would I want to build something that already exists? What we do instead is we buy master licenses, it costs a lot of money, but then I can rent out sub-licenses at affordable prices. That way, you don't have to pay $15,000 or $20,000 for a license. We're doing it for you so you can get started. This is our belief that by doing this, we can expand the capabilities of pharmacists faster.

The field is ripe for entrepreneurship. It's just a matter of getting started. But if you want to start a business solely to make money, you're going to fail. If you want to start a business so you can solve problems for people, you're going to find yourself making money. As a grey-haired older person, I grew up in a family with eight kids; six boys, two girls. My whole life, I was able to say I came from a big family, and sadly I can't say that anymore.

Three years ago, my oldest brother died of a massive heart attack at age 73. He was in the military; he went to the doctor every year for checkups for active duty. And I can't figure it out. What the hell did they miss? Just last week, my 64-year-old baby brother died of a massive heart attack as well. He had a heart valve problem. I spoke to him a month ago when he got diagnosed, and I told him, "You need to get this taken care of."

Well, guess what happened? The insurance company got involved, and he had to go through all this rigamarole to get approval on the treatment he needed. They scheduled the surgery six weeks from now, and he passed before he could get it. I believe the insurance company took their time on purpose because they saw how severe the problem with his valve was. Is that true? I don't know. But I don't trust that the insurance company had my brother's best interest at heart. We need to advocate for our patients. We need to help people get the care they need.

What often happens in the United States is to get the care you need, you have to demand it. Too often, patients don't know enough to demand it. That is where we come in; that is our responsibility.

All of this is explained on my website RXVIPconcierge.com. Use it as a method for monetizing your knowledge to provide direct patient care. Or, if that's not part of your plan, share this knowledge with others.

Advice for Aspiring Entrepreneurs

What I would tell you as entrepreneurs and aspiring entrepreneurs is to learn how to simplify. Stop overthinking and cut your method down to what is really important. Can you identify a problem that needs to be solved? Can you build a solution to that problem? And can you offer it to people and adjust it until it works? Because guess what, no matter how well you plan, your method likely will not work on the first people you try. You have to improvise, adjust, and accommodate.

The reality is, if you're not solving a problem, you're never going to get paid. I teach young pharmacists three things: you need to know how to be a good pharmacist, you need to know your method will make things better for patients, and if you simplify your process, you can be a lot more helpful to people.

You have to let the patient decide their path and help guide them through their journey. People want simplicity. They're overwhelmed; they're confused. There's so much misinformation. Just simplify it for them. That's what we do. We're trying to simplify the business offers for pharmacists as well. Teach them how to get started in their own business.

CONTRIBUTOR
CONNECTION

Gregory Alston, PharmD

🌐 www.rxvipconcierge.com

in www.linkedin.com/in/greglalston

ANNE ARVIZU

Biography

Anne Arvizu, PharmD, FASCP, PCC, is a pharmacist, transformational coach, philanthropist, entrepreneur, and former fortune 500 global biotech executive. As a published author, podcaster, professional speaker, and coach trainer, Anne's core mission is to bridge the gap between healthcare and healing. In 2022, as an advocate for women's health, disease awareness, and patient education, Anne is spearheading the creation of the world's first and only non-profit foundation for women with endometrial cancer and their caregivers. Dr. Arvizu and her team work with patient-centric healthcare leaders, healing professionals, and leading organizations delivering coach training programs, retainer consulting, content creation, and inspiring keynotes. Past advisory engagements include Pfizer, Shire, Merck, Teva, Alnylam, Ipsen, Servier, IQVIA, Kindred Health, the YMCA, the DIA, Pepsi, Wells Fargo, and others. Anne is the honored recipient of the prestigious Healthcare Businesswomen's Association (HBA) 2020 Luminary Award.

Professional work in the pharmaceutical industry includes service in key senior executive roles such as the Global Head of Medical Information/Knowledge Management at Baxter, Baxalta, and Shire Pharmaceuticals, as well as Regional Head, Latin America for Medical Communications/Medical Information at GlaxoSmithKline.

Philanthropic leadership roles include Chair Emerita of the Board of

Directors of the South Florida YMCA; past Officer of the American Medical Writers Association, Regional Board of Directors; past Meeting Chair and Program Advisor for the Accreditation Council of Medical Affairs (ACMA), Dynamic Global Events (DGE) and the Drug Information Association (DIA).

Anne holds degrees from The University of Florida (PharmD), The University of Sciences in Philadelphia (BSPharm), Villanova University (BA), and Erickson College International (PCC).

Entrepreneurial Journey

I will never forget the breathtaking scene: I opened the blinds and stepped on the balcony with my coffee to gaze out at the ocean at sunrise. I was regional director of Medical Information at GlaxoSmithKline (GSK) on a business trip to train my new-hire PharmD when the 'download' came. I rushed back into the hotel room, grabbed a pen and journal, and scribbled out twenty-two pages of notes. On the next page, I gave the baby a name (RxER Communications). Finally, I sketched out the logo and wrote the tagline: *The right drug, for the right patient, at the right time*®. When I returned home to Miami, I vetted my new business model with someone at a top 5 consulting firm and learned that it was rock solid. The vision was so crystal clear that I knew I was meant to create this company. Over the next eighteen months, it percolated on the backburner. I loved my international corporate job, my lifestyle, and my status at this multi-billion-dollar global icon. I had risen through the ranks of clinical research and development roles to become regional director of various medical affairs functions. My leadership role jetted me all over Latin America, to our headquarters in London and to speaking engagements, congresses, and investigator meetings, domestically and internationally. I was in my mid 30's, full of energy, and still enamored with the fast pace of corporate life. I quickly climbed the ladder to be one of approximately 200 top women leaders in a post-mega-merger 150,000-person global entity. I could have easily stayed at GSK for the duration of my career.

One day after a working lunch, my colleague headed back up to our office. I sat for a few more moments, savoring a Cuban coffee at an outdoor café in Coral Gables, FL. I remember watching the breeze rustling the palm fronds, set against vivid blue skies. I was grateful. I loved my job, my dream boss, and my corner office. I even loved the green carpet we had. Then, that moment turned strangely surreal, and inaudibly I heard the words, "Everything is about to change."

In the Spring of 2003, Dream Boss got promoted to Senior VP, and in walked He-who-shall-not-be-named. Over the next year, our office staff was pitted against each other by manipulative power plays. Our voices were silenced to upper management, and the office was repainted and recarpeted to make it as austere as possible. We were made to office swap, and I lost my beautiful corner space for a smaller one...closer to Nightmare VP. Then, as the storm clouds of a South Florida summer rolled in, the weather in our office also grew dark.

Suffice to say, as the pressure at work mounted, the possibility to leave and finally start my own business surfaced. I prayed for the right timing to leave and the resources to cover start-up expenses.

Then, I made the leap from corporate to freedom.

I started my first company, RxER Communications, officially in late 2004 and had instant success. In our first year, we grossed $386,000 in patient-centric contracts—a number I will never forget and am proud of to this day. Here's a part of that story I never usually tell. I had a hand-cut paper' business card' and a white 3-ring binder that I filled with images of patient-centric medical affairs programs that I could create. In other words, I did what I could with what I had, cast vision, and struck while the iron was hot. If you do your best and believe that it's enough, it will pay off.

I got that first contract, hired other pharmacists, and set up a medical information contact center. I also created two (clinical and MSL) preceptorship programs for Shenandoah University pharmacy students interested to fast-track into the pharmaceutical industry. Also, during those first few years, I learned all I could about entrepreneurship, business, and life coaching. I became a certified professional coach, NLP practitioner, Ericksonian hypnotherapist, and coach trainer. It was a great time of growth and flow.

Eventually, beginner's luck wore off, as it always does in entrepreneurship, and I had my first major entrepreneurial test. 2008, much like our 2020 pandemic, was a harsh time for business. The pharmaceutical industry landscape in FL was made up of small companies like Ivax and Kos. And, as one client after another sold out to Big Pharma, our fully staffed contracts were cut short, our company savings dwindled, and all our business development attempts were thwarted. I stopped my own pay to take care of my team and help them find new jobs.

Simultaneously, my husband (a pharma physician) lost his job. His company was purchased and closed, and he was made redundant. So, for many months, I was the incumbent breadwinner. My husband finally found a new job with Wyeth, but it required a relocation to Pennsylvania in the middle of winter. We also lost my mother-in-law, our schnauzer, then my beloved cat, all in the same year.

Externally, the economic bubble burst, the housing market crashed, and my business flatlined right before our move. My family seemingly lost everything that year, our house, our car, our condo, retirement savings, and our 401K. It seemed unfair after a decade of hard work.

Just when I thought it couldn't get worse, I went through a significant personal health crisis and began the irreversible process of early menopause/premature ovarian failure and eventual infertility.

It was 2009. I was grieving, exhausted, and physically depleted when I found myself in a supermarket grabbing a cheap bottle of face lotion. The label on the bottle says, "for dull, tired skin," and I chuckled to myself, thinking, "I need to pour this all over myself." I never really shared my internal struggles with anyone; I just kept going and restarted my company and my life. I coached myself using many of the personal development materials I'd acquired during seminars I'd done all over the globe between 2004-2007.

During those early profitable years, I had steeped myself in motivational events and extreme challenges. I walked on fire, raced cars, jumped off trapezes, bungee jumped, and went cliff diving—loads of what I call "Mountain Dew Moments." The purpose was to become the CEO I was meant to be in the face of adversity. I had also earned multiple professional certifications, including a degree in coaching, coach training, and multiple certifications in consulting, speaking, business management, and leadership. I became an avid 'life-long learner' in the personal development space, consuming all the transformative methodology. As a scientist, I loved that it was anchored in cognitive functional neuroscience and psychoneuroimmunology, which was the basis of not just professional coach training but positive psychology and cognitive therapy. And I met, was mentored by, and learned directly from the best in the field: Tony Robbins, Dr. Deepak Chopra, Gabrielle Bernstein, Ali Brown, Sage Lavine, Marci Shimoff, Lisa Garr, Dr. Sue Morter, John Maxwell, Jeff Walker, and others.

But, as I poured over the many various 'work-life balance' models leftover from my start-up years, I realized none of them really showed you how to get back up when you're down. Every coaching life-balance model had the same philosophical flaws, in my humble opinion.

They could show me where the gaps in life were, but none told you how to fix those gaps and recalibrate freedom. Nor could they show you how to lead from your strengths because that theory also fell short and didn't work in many scenarios.

They *did* tell me how to rate the areas of my life on a 1-10 type scale—mental, financial, vocational, physical, social, etc. Ever the optimist, I was giving almost every area of my life a 2 or 3 at the time, except spirituality. It was my only saving grace, and I ranked it an 8. I pondered all this, and I remember the day I distinctly made the choice to let it go and "make my own sunshine." I got my first small contract and was back in business. Then larger ones trickled in. Not too long after that decision of the heart came an extraordinary, unexpected moment.

I was at my desk pecking away at a spreadsheet for a corporate biotech client, and then—BOOM—it came to me. A massive, instantaneous 'download' that went beyond words. An interruption I could not ignore.

Before I could comprehend the full extent of the idea, I could feel that it would redirect the course of my life as an entrepreneur—and show me how to rise, recover, and stay strong no matter what. I stood up in obedience to this incoming idea, walked across my 1100 square foot basement office to my whiteboard, and I drew it out.

It took about 10-15 minutes to perfect and extract all that I was seeing. It was the first C-O-R-E WHEEL, a solution for balancing your life, rebounding when you're down, and attaining victory over the more difficult situations in life. I sat down at the conference table right next to the whiteboard, and I looked up and said, "Wow, Thank you, God."

I stared at it in awe, thinking, 'I know this idea is divine because I could not have thought of this simple solution on my own.' When my husband came home from work, I showed it to him and explained the foundation of this new methodology. I said, "I know I will teach this, in one form or another, for the rest of my life."

Since that destined day, thirteen years ago, I've continued to teach, publish, test, and expand my C-O-R-E theory and framework, evaluating it in my own life every day. I became its 'client zero' and have benefited from it ever since. Just a few years after working with my wheel, I reached 7-figure revenues in only four months based on the business-specific version of this model. But the most rewarding part has been witnessing the transformative effect it has had in the lives of my individual and corporate clients that I've had the honor of teaching it to. When I coach my clients to the center of my wheel, that's when the truth comes out, and the tears flow.

2021 brought with it a profound shift for me. A diagnosis of endometrial cancer sucker-punched me two days before the weekend of the first Pharmfluencer Summit. Todd Eury, a trustworthy friend and advocate spoke in my stead thanks to Kimber's support. I endured two major surgeries, including a total hysterectomy in the summer of 2021. I won't go into details now because that is still news in the making, as we form our not-for-profit entity, which will fill an enormous gap for this patient population. My new *why* is crystal clear. And for me, a major reframe I did was to ask myself this, "What if cancer didn't happen to me? What if it happened for me?" With research, I realized this type of foundation doesn't exist, is needed, and given my pharma background and contacts I can leverage, I seem to be the perfect person for the job. After a little firsthand experiential understanding of the disease, my whole life's work seems to be diverging for my legacy play. As it's been said, it's in moments of decision that your destiny is shaped. I can tell you this for sure; my C-O-R-E life coaching method became my best friend again this year. It is the lens through which I find the way to true healing, mind-body-spirit wholeness, and well-being, and the method I use to teach others to unleash their core power. I am more convinced than ever of its value, worth, and place in teaching it to other healthcare leaders and healing professionals. Recently, I ordered an endometrial cancer survivor tee shirt on Amazon. It said this, "The devil whispered in my ear, 'You're not strong enough for this storm.' I whispered back into the devil's ear and said, 'I AM THE STORM.'"

Methods to Monetize Your Knowledge

Just because you can do something or teach something doesn't mean you have to. Sometimes, the more experienced and knowledgeable, the more confused you can become. I see so many people self-sabotage or never even get started because they overthink everything. In this analytical scientific crowd, that is almost a guarantee. Choose something you love to do, and feel called to do, and do it well. Once you master that, other avenues can branch off from there. A great majority of the information on how-to-do entrepreneurship that you will find online is over-rated and confusing.

I built a 7-figure sustainable business and have been featured on a prime-time TV show, the news, and across the media and have been corporately and publicly awarded. I have enjoyed some of these unsolicited accomplishments with using minimal social media and by always focusing on my clients and the solution my team could create for them as their business consultant and content provider. Their success was my goal, and therefore my team and I were compensated. It was easy for me to pitch realistic contracts and get us paid. With time and connections, word-of-mouth referrals took over as my primary business development source. I don't burn bridges; I keep relationships going and don't let things bother me. And all of this is a learned skill set. So much of this kind of real 'social proof' is relational and trust-based, and the ultimate key is mindset. Learn to master your mindset, and the relationships you build will become your supporters because they believe in your passion. Therefore, if you want to monetize your expertise and you believe in yourself, then others will believe in you. In that sense, almost any method or form becomes viable. Don't get stuck in the word 'how.' Stick with your *why,* and you can make any *how* happen. The key to making money really is that simple.

What is the Best Business Model?

I love this question in light of the fact that I teach business modeling and consult on the best model to choose when working with my clients. After vetting over 50 global business models personally, I have landed on about 20 that work, but it depends on your intention, offering, and scale plan. I believe entrepreneurship is a calling, and it's important to say that because you shouldn't dive into business without that calling. I also believe that a vision for healing and well-being always comes first. So, using myself as an example, after I already had an established business (with a consulting firm B-2-B model), I created the Corepreneur brand and a podcast, and a learning platform with multiple courses (D-2-C model). Then I had to choose how to execute that model.

Let's look under the hood at one of my brand evolutions: I developed Corepreneur University as a transformational business incubator, guiding an elite group of healthcare entrepreneurs using the business and life coaching framework I created in 2009 to promote mission-centric productivity, personal life-balance, and coach training and certification to core-value driven entrepreneurs, or Corepreneurs®. This 16-week course for leaders, mostly women, who want to leave their corporate jobs and craft their 7-figure business plan using their expertise through coaching & consulting.

Because I know my clients, the schedules they keep, the kind of flexibility they need, and the pricing models from spending years in the space, I chose my model based on market knowledge and International Coach Federation guidelines. Then I beta-tested the first version of it with both a small group and a large group in 2010 to see which was more sustainable. Small groups were far more successful, and, for me, preferable, we tweaked it each year until 2015 when a global commitment took precedence for me, and I set it aside for my full-time company for a while. I don't throw courses together and slap a price on them. Once I know my customer and my market space, I create a training program for them and deliver it in a way that I enjoy and am gifted to do. If you are video-shy, don't use a video course just because someone else is. Execute in a way that will be sustainable long term for you.

Advice for Aspiring Entrepreneurs

First, focus on one or at most two main offerings. Just because you can do something, or create something, or teach something, doesn't mean you have to or should. My friend Carrie, who was one of my guests on the *Corepreneur Podcast*, is an amazing speaker grossing over a million a year in paid engagements. But she doesn't have a course or teach speaking just because she's mastered the art. What lights her up, besides her family, is inspiring women through speaking. Period. She's a great example of the old saying, 'do what you love, and the money will follow.'

Second, shift as needed, leaders lead, and sometimes when life circumstances help you change your mind, then do so without too much worry about what people will think. Change course when it feels right. TV shows do this all the time. It's the season and series finale, your favorite show is canceled, and you now just have to imagine the happily ever after. This year after a cancer diagnosis and treatment, I decided to consolidate two businesses back down to one, change the name, choose from our key offerings and focus only on that so that I have the time to create our non-profit. I'm a boat owner, and I can tell you that we've been caught in some pretty unexpected scary storms out at sea. Captains know when to turn their vessels or when to navigate through the dark storm clouds. Turn back or away when your boat is in true jeopardy, not just because you are weary and not achieving projected quarterly revenues just yet. In my book, *Affluent Minds: Core Expressions for a Rich and Wonderful Life*, I talk about the power of persistence, and that is what I am illustrating here. There is a great acronym, HALT, that I have used as a guide for many years. It represents not making decisions when you are *hungry*, *angry*, *lonely*, or *tired*. Something you learn over time is that your platform should grow and evolve as you do.

In almost 25 years of coaching businesses, I've met very few true business investors or 'serial' entrepreneurs. The definition of which is someone who builds a profitable business then removes themselves from leadership so it can sustain with minimal guidance. Then they invest in starting or funding another company. Most of the time, when I coach excited new entrepreneurs that want to start multiple endeavors too fast, what I hear between the lines is: "I'm a brilliant dabbler, with a lot of fabulous ideas but not enough focus, time, or resources to bring them to fruition." Once you have created a sustainable 7-figure success model, then free up your time by raising a successor, if that's your goal, and then creating another one.

I landed the first podcast on the topic of entrepreneurship on the Pharmacy Podcast Network because that space did not yet exist. I had hoped to share the vantage point of non-pharmacy or pharmaceutical businesses to showcase what is working in other industries, so we apply some of these pearls of wisdom to our own businesses. Key number three is anytime you create a new product or service, write out one to three key outcomes for your consumer and communicate that, and it will gain acceptance.

We all learn by example; I created the Corepreneur based on my C-O-R-E coaching method so that you could listen in to me and my guests share not just success stories but the stories of rising strong through adversity. That's the C-O-R-E in Corepreneur. It stands for being centered, open, resilient, and energized. Secondly, I wanted to pioneer the first podcast on entrepreneurship on the Pharmacy Podcast Network because that space did not yet exist. Lastly, I wanted to share the vantage point of non-pharmacy or pharmaceutical businesses to showcase what is working in other industries, so we apply some of these pearls of wisdom to our businesses. The pearl here is that anytime you create a new product or service, write out your two or three key outcomes for your consumer and communicate that, and it will be a sure hit.

In just 15 episodes, the *Corepreneur Podcast* hit over 35,000 downloads and was awarded one of the Top 20 Systematic Podcasts of 2021. And although positive metrics and unsolicited kudos are nice, the show's success was the by-product of delivering excellent content and stories that matter. A lot of my guests are friends and colleagues that I've met along my entrepreneurial journey, and we have bonded over business because business is challenging. Season 2 is kicking off in 2022 with a Corepreneur that created a wellness brand to the tune of $74 million dollars in annual revenue. We'll also have on a few pharmacists that have built noteworthy platforms, a prime-time television CEO, and a top business mentor who sold her business for a billion-dollar valuation. They share their ups and downs because if we are truthful, real life is messy and hard, no matter how easy some high achievers make it look. Finally, there is no time for jealousy, copying, or comparison, and I say that because sadly, that's a thing that I've encountered from others not being happy for my success. We all have doubters and downers around us, but we can choose a mindset of abundance and celebrate each other's success. If you find yourself comparing yourself to others, or worse, jealous or envious, you are still operating at much lower-level energy and from wrong core values, and it will eventually weigh you down. That's a universal truth. You can't fake it spiritually. As an entrepreneur, you are a leader; just lead. Don't compare yourself to others. Be happy for and supportive of the accomplishments of others, and success will happen for you. Get your heart and motives right. I just stay in my swim lane and create excellent content that my ideal audience needs. That's it. You can do that too, and we can make the world a better place in the process.

Remember that shift I talked about? As my soul is led toward building a national non-profit organization, I will be following my own advice that I gave previously. As healthcare professionals, your wellness and happiness come first. I shared a personal story of a major health challenge that I went through. Any major crisis, such as illness, death of a loved one, divorce, caregiving, etc., will have a significant impact on your business. When life's circumstances come knocking, make sure your health comes first and give yourself the grace of not needing to be all things to all people, and change course as needed. Even though I used my brand above to illustrate some keys for business, I am currently in the process of deprioritizing one brand and repurposing and rebranding other content based on market research as my new initiative scales. That's evolution in business. A river flows effortlessly around all the rocks it encounters. Put your health and happiness first, align with your core values, and your business will keep flowing also.

CONTRIBUTOR
•••
CONNECTION

Anne Arvizu
PharmD, FASCP, PCC

🌐 www.annearvizu.com

in www.linkedin.com/in/annearvizu/

ALEX BARKER

Biography

For a time, he was a burned-out clinical pharmacy specialist; Alex Barker is now the head coach at The Happy PharmD© and helps pharmacists create fulfilling lives and careers. Alongside his team, he creates classes to help over 750 pharmacists find and create new career paths. He recently published the book, *Indispensable: The Prescription for a Fulfilling Pharmacy Career*. His goal is to help 500 pharmacists transition to new jobs by January 1st, 2022. When he's not working with pharmacists, he spends time with his wife Megan and two lovely girls: Izzy and Addie.

Entrepreneurial Journey

I started my pharmacy career in 2012. After graduating, I did a residency and began my practice. But as soon as I began practicing, I noticed something felt a little off for me. I began reflecting, read a lot of self-development books, took some classes, and realized that I wanted to do something more than just pharmacy. I began dipping into entrepreneurship on the side.

If I could reach it, I would grab it. I sold stickers on Amazon and Etsy; I sold baby strollers; I did podcasting for a while; I got into a franchise;

I created content for websites; I did a lot of different things and eventually landed on coaching. I had hired coaches myself to guide me through this process, and a few of them suggested I try coaching for myself. I was ambivalent, but I gave it a shot. I took some classes and helped a few people. And I discovered that helping other people achieve their dreams was what made me feel the most fulfilled.

I started the Happy PharmD in 2017, really out of shame, honestly. After trying for four years in different businesses, I felt like a failure. I was frustrated that I was not seeing the progress I wanted. From there, the business really took off. Over the past four years, we have grown exponentially. We now have a staff of 20 people, and I have been full-time since 2018.

It's been wild; as any entrepreneur can tell you, the experience is a rollercoaster. You have highs and lows. That has been my journey to entrepreneurship.

Methods to Monetize Your Knowledge

Specifically, in the last year, we have done a deep dive into labor economics as a business. I know that sounds super sexy and exciting—it's not. What it means is as a business, we are jumping into the job market, understanding trends, trying to predict what markets will see growth and what markets will not. And while we don't specifically sell this knowledge, we use it as a value-added service to our current clients. Everything else we do is centered around courses.

This strategy is actually one of the easiest ways you can monetize your knowledge. It's something I've done multiple times in past courses, create study guides, those kinds of materials. It's very easy to make these things as long as there is a market and demand for them. You can market to your audience and sell your knowledge and information that way.

I offer both individual and group coaching sessions. And I don't want to make a generalization, I don't want to say all pharmacists are private people, but you find it's very personal when discussing your career and the things going on in your life. Not everyone is willing to share that kind of information in a group setting. However, once pharmacists make the transition to entrepreneurship, I have found that they become more open and more willing to share.

I have my own mastermind group, we meet every Tuesday, and I share my soul with them. Sometimes it's ugly, sometimes great, but it gives you a space to share your wins, which I think is important too. It creates a community.

How to Choose & Scale Your Business Model

If you're reading this book, I am going to assume you are either considering starting over in terms of your career or currently are in the process of starting over. Some of you may be balancing entrepreneurship with other careers, some of you may be doing it full time. No matter where you are on your journey, the most critical component to your success is choosing the right business model.

Nobody wants to jump headlong into something. Nobody wants to try various things and just hope they work. That's what I did for four years. For four years, I tried different things, hoping the next one would be my big break. Only one really made me any money; the rest were learning lessons at best. Most of the things I tried were based on what other people told me. I'd be listening to a podcast and think, "Oh, I need to try that because this guru told me to. This seems like a great idea."

I often talk about the concept of Ikigai. I discuss this more in my book *Indispensable*, but to put it briefly, Ikigai is a Japanese word meaning a reason for being. Ikigai is what wakes you up in the morning, it's what makes you excited, it's what gives you success, and it's what the world needs.

There are four main components of Ikigai: What the world needs, what you're great at, what you're curious about, and what you can get paid to do. This is also the essential step that I've seen many pharmacists fail to recognize when choosing the right business. We have to come to terms with who we are as a profession. We are a product-based business. We are not tied to services yet. I know that's changing; we're trying our best to provide services. But the truth is pharmacists are viewed by the public and within healthcare as being tied to a deliverable. When I see pharmacists trying to create a service-based business, that is a particular problem because they don't get it.

You need to be able to answer, why should I pay you as a pharmacist to do this? The role pharmacists play in communities is one of accessibility. You can just walk in and speak to them. So, of course, people are unwilling to pay a pharmacist for things they could get for free. It connects back to the third component of Ikigai: what you can get paid to do.

The business model you choose has to be based on what people are willing to pay for, and you can sneak in pharmacy along the way. Something that is very popular right now, pharmacists love helping with health—helping with healthcare, getting rid of medicines, getting rid of polypharmacy, things like that. And one way to do that as a pharmacist is to tell people, "This is what I'm going to do for you. I am going to be your health consultant."

People are willing to pay for health coaching, health information, anything about health. We all know the health industry is a multi-trillion-dollar business. We can work as experts on either disease, drugs, or whatever you feel you are knowledgeable in and curious about. Find what you're naturally good at, what you think the world needs more of, and most importantly, what people are willing to pay for.

As pharmacists, we are perfectionists. But you have the knowledge; you can get people to pay you for these services and form your business as you go. My motto with our team is Progress Before Perfection. Nobody will ever reach perfection anyway, but you can convince someone to pay you $50 and help them lose five pounds. It is being done all over the country.

I believe that the best way to find your business model is to get paid first. I cannot emphasize that enough. You don't have to wait until every element of your business is concrete before you start working with clients. I see so many people just waiting for the perfect thing to happen, waiting for the right opportunity, waiting for the money to come. And the thing is, business is messy, and you have to get messy too. You have to push away your pharmacist tendency, push away the thought that you can't make any mistakes.

Business is messy; it gets ugly sometimes. You have to be willing to sit in that ugliness to figure it out and move forward. You have to be willing to accept money to help someone. When you find Ikigai, money will come. I tried finding it for years only to realize I was running away from the thing I knew how to do best, which was coaching and helping pharmacists. That was my journey.

How do you scale your business? Let's say you have been hustling with your side business, and you want to make it your full-time job. Perhaps it's been your full-time job, and you're finally ready to hire someone to help you and start delegating. Whatever stage of the process you are at, there are two four main systems when it comes to business: marketing, sales, fulfillment, and operations.

Marketing is getting in front of people. And I think a lot of business owners assume marketing will solve their problems. They think, "I just need to get in front of enough people." "I just need more leads" "I just need enough people to think that I'm awesome and I'm going to make so much money!" But the truth is, it usually doesn't work that way.

Next is sales. Someone has to purchase something. They have to go to a website. They have to believe that whatever they are purchasing will help them solve their problems. Then they give you their credit card, and that's where we transition to fulfillment. Fulfillment means delivering on that promise. This is the most important thing; the way to scale is fulfillment.

These are all of the things that go on in the background: what you do as a founder, what your team does to help you deliver. The way to scale that is by doubling down on fulfillment and doing an amazing job at it. When you help one person, that first customer that you go above and beyond expectations with, you start down a path to making more money. When you exceed your customers' expectations, you make more profit; you make more sales, etc. The way to scale is to figure out what problems the consumer might be facing and how you can deliver on remedying those problems.

Once you have done that, it becomes much easier to sell them on the next thing. If you decide you want to become a health consultant, think about the most important problem clients face. Maybe it's that they want to lose five pounds. Great, buy this $5 toolkit. It's going to give you things that you can do to lose five pounds.

They buy it. Maybe now, instead of just giving the client information, you give them a complimentary phone call. "How did you like this product?" "What worked?" "What didn't work?" "What else is going on? What other problems are you having?" And that allows you to sell them on the next thing. Maybe it's a three-month-long contract; maybe it's more information. Maybe it's how to lose 15 more pounds.

Whatever it is, it gives you an opportunity to fulfill the service you have promised. And fulfillment is typically what pharmacists are really, really good at. We're not great at sales and marketing, but we thrive at fulfillment. By doubling down on fulfillment, I promise you can make more sales.

Whenever we have a business coaching client, we always look at how much they make a month. Okay, you made $5,000 this month. That's great. And what they typically want to do is get into this business cycle where they start thinking, "I have to get more sales." "I have to get more leads."

And I will tell them, "No, wait. Let's look at what your past customers are doing." Let's catch up with them. Research shows that when a business tries to sell to their current clientele, they are 85% more likely to make a sale than the 35% who make a sale with someone brand new. My point is to double down on fulfillment, particularly with your current client. Do a great job. That is how you scale.

Operations is another thing I am eager to talk about. It's hard to come to terms with this, but if you're working as an entrepreneur on the side, you can't do everything. I know you want to. And I know many people have trust issues when it comes to giving up power and control. Nobody wants to give someone else the thing you've been doing so well.

This was a real struggle for me when I hired my first pharmacist coach, Jackie Boyle. She is now our lead coach. She's amazing. And in truth, I was scared. I hired someone before Jackie, and she totally screwed me over. She took all of my information and ran and started her own coaching business. Getting screwed happens in business, and there are certain steps you should take to protect yourself. I didn't have an NDA, which I absolutely should have.

But the way to scale is by doubling down on fulfillment and hiring other people to help you along the way. What this does is it frees up your time to use your brain to focus more on the strategy, vision, and operations.

The transition to being an entrepreneur full-time is actually fairly straightforward. The key is to replicate your expenses. Now I know pharmacists, and I know we like to make a lot of money, and this comes down to a lifestyle decision. If you go to thehappypharmd. com, we have a budget sheet where you can insert your income. And if you put your expenses into this Excel spreadsheet, and then you put in your business revenue and some other parameters around your business, you'll be able to calculate how much income you need to quit your job.

In 2017, at the beginning of the year, I launched Happy PharmD and made a very hard goal, which is what I'd recommend everyone do. Now, if you really want to move into your business full-time, establish a goal. Say, "I want to be at least able to pay myself a salary within 18 months. And if I were able to pay myself $6,000 a month for three months in a row, then I'll have the confidence to transition to my full-time job."

That's essentially what I did, not $6,000, but in October of 2017, I was able to pay myself a salary to pay off my living expenses. And I took my day job income that I was making, and I pretended it didn't exist. I saved it. I think I was paying off the last parts of my debt at that time. And I did this month after month after month. And I remember telling my wife, "This is real. This is happening. I'm able to do this. I don't need my day job because we're paying our bills with my business."

Shortly after that, in March of 2018, I made my intentions known. I was going to quit. I stayed for another five months because my partner at the time had a baby. And I just didn't feel right leaving at the time. But in August of 2018, I was able to quit. The best way for you to transition safely and securely is to grow your business. Scale it to the point where you can pay yourself consistently, use that money and pretend your day job doesn't exist. Save that money, put it in the stock market, use it to pay off debt, but don't use it to pay your bills because you need to prove that you can take care of your daily costs with the money from your business.

If you're married, you also need to have a challenging conversation about making that transition. My wife doesn't work; we didn't have medical insurance outside of my job. You need to be really aware of what you're walking into. The best way to do that is to make the transition slowly over time.

Advice for Aspiring Entrepreneurs

If you want your business to be successful, you have to go at it full time. Plan it out and give yourself that time limit and use that limit to be bold. Because if you don't say, "In 18 months, I'm going to quit my job and do this full time," then you don't have the motivation to give it your everything. You have to say with certainty that you really tried. And even if you fail, you will know that you gave everything you had, and you can learn from it and move on to the next business idea.

That happened to me time and time again for four years. I tried, I failed, I didn't move forward. And now we've got this business with an amazing, world-class team of pharmacists. My hope for you reading this book is that you feel motivated to start your business, and you go on to hire other pharmacists because that's how we fix this job crisis.

CONTRIBUTOR
CONNECTION

Alex Barker, PharmD

www.thehappypharmd.com

www.linkedin.com/in/alex-barker-pharmd/

HILLARY BLACKBURN

Biography

Hillary Blackburn is the voice of women in leadership when it comes to pharmacy topics. She is a clinically business-trained pharmacist who has been practicing for almost a decade in a variety of healthcare settings. She has experience in healthcare strategy, business development, formulary development, and management consulting. She has established a number of successful medication access programs. In her current role, she serves as the Director for Pharmaceutical Services at the Dispensary of Hope, a national non-profit medication distributor hosted by Ascension. There she leads their pharmacy team and oversees their reviews formulary, leads-based research initiatives, and manages their network of volunteer pharmacist strategic advisors. She was elected to serve in a national leadership position for the American Pharmacist Association Academy of Pharmacy Practice and Management (APHA-APPM) committee. She has also served as the co-chair of the advocacy committee for the APhA Care of the Underserved Special Interest Group. She precepts at Belmont University and serves on the Dean's external advisory committee. She's a graduate of the University of Mississippi School of Pharmacy and postgraduate year one (PGY1) pharmacy residency at the University of Mississippi. She is passionate about promoting the pharmacy profession and delivering expert patient care. She hosts the *Talk to Your Pharmacist Podcast*, with over 200 episodes, and is the author of a book on women in leadership, *How Pharmacists Lead.*

Entrepreneurial Journey

I grew up in a small town in Mississippi where my high school's motto was, "Excel with all your heart." That's something I've tried to follow to this day. Growing up in a small town, I was able to try many different things staying busy with multiple sports, academics, and volunteer activities, which helped make me a really well-rounded person. During my childhood, I always knew that I wanted to follow in my parents' footsteps and find a profession where I could serve others—a career in pharmacy has helped me to reach that goal. My mother was a teacher, and my dad worked for the government. While my mother encouraged my academics, my dad helped coach me in sports (soccer, basketball, etc.) They also instilled in me the importance of being involved in our community. I think they led a very fine example and helped me to pursue my goals.

Upon graduation from high school, I attended the University of Mississippi School of Pharmacy as an Early Entry pharmacy student and even represented the School of Pharmacy and Associated Student Body. I then interned in Washington, DC, on the Hill, which really helped shape my life and further my interest in policy and advocacy. While I was in pharmacy school, I chose a variety of rotations to get a broad experience and even served as an intern during two summers with the Health Resources and Services Administration (HRSA) 's Office of Pharmacy Affairs in Washington, DC. During one of these summers, I even attended APhA's Summer Leadership Institute. The OPA oversees the 340B program, a program to support the hospitals and clinics across the country serving the safety net. This HRSA internship was a unique experience to explore public health and how to operationalize a national program and ultimately provided me insight into the importance of caring for the safety net or underserved population. As we all have heard many times, pharmacy is a small world, and I was able to intern at Health Resources & Services Administration (HRSA) with the Office of Pharmacy Affairs (OPA), since a University of Mississippi alum was the director.

After graduation from pharmacy school, I completed a PGY1 residency at the University of Mississippi Medical Center and really loved clinical care. I loved being in the ER and in the ICU, rounding with the internal medicine team, even being in the ambulatory setting, and just really loved all of the preceptors there. But when I moved to Nashville, there were not as many hospital jobs open—it is a competitive market as a highly desired place to live with three pharmacy schools! So I changed my path a little bit and have had some experiences in the independent pharmacy setting working for a family friend, working for a health plan and specialty mail-order pharmacy, and where I am now, which has been just a wonderful fit is at the Dispensary of Hope.

Since 2015, I've served as the Director of Pharmaceutical Services at Dispensary of Hope which is a charitable medication distributor. The Dispensary of Hope (www.dispensaryofhope.org) is the nation's leading charitable medication distributor. Since 2012, Dispensary of Hope has assembled a collaborative of most of the largest drug manufacturers in the generic pharmaceutical space and most of the largest health systems serving the uninsured. The work of the Dispensary of Hope is to acquire donated medication in large volume and then, in turn, ship that to communities across the US. This donated inventory is stocked in free clinics, FQHCs, charity pharmacies, and health system outpatient pharmacies, where it is provided in a consistent fashion to the safety net population. Dispensary of Hope has seen significant national growth over the past few years, counting large health systems as partners—many of which are utilizing Dispensary of Hope as a component in their population health strategies. The Dispensary of Hope serves over 200 medication access dispensing sites across the United States, supplying a consistent inventory of essential medications to serve the low-income population. Dispensary of Hope provides this service in partnership with 26 pharmaceutical manufacturers. Over the next ten years, Dispensary of Hope will grow to serve all 50 states and 1.3 million of our nation's most vulnerable uninsured patients.

As the Director of Pharmaceutical Services, I am responsible for providing clinical pharmacist expertise to support the organization as well as its network of pharmacies and charitable clinics. I consult with pharmacy leaders across the country, sharing expertise on affordable medication access for low-income patients. My work with health systems includes strategy development for identifying and implementing programs to address gaps in pharmaceutical care through the inclusion of the Dispensary of Hope program. In addition, I lead our research and formulary development and create tools for successful program utilization by the pharmacies and charitable clinics in Dispensary of Hope network. I have helped develop and maintain strategic partnerships with several external organizations, including The Advisory Board Company and Belmont and Lipscomb Colleges of Pharmacy.

This was a role that did not exist before I started in this position, which is why the importance of volunteering can sometimes lead to unique opportunities. Prior to joining Dispensary of Hope in this capacity, I served in a volunteer capacity to develop the Dispensary of Hope's formulary before joining full-time in November of 2015. And so, although I did not find the non-profit, I've had a chance to build it and to help create my own position. Starting out, I worked primarily as a consultant pharmacist and was on sales calls. Now, I lead the pharmacy department and wear a lot of different hats. Because my role has shifted away from direct patient care responsibilities and more into management, I went back to school to get my MBA through Western Governors University in 2019.

Beyond my "nine to five day job," I still try to be really engaged and involved with the community. I live in Nashville, and although it's not my alma mater, I've kind of adopted Belmont as my school here, although I work closely with some of the other schools as well. I serve on the Dean's External Advisory Council and serve as a preceptor with Belmont. This is one way I've chosen to spend my time and give back to the profession through investing in future students.

I believe it's very important to be involved in your state association, not only being a member but signing up for committees. I serve on the Tennessee Pharmacists Association's legislative and policy committee and then nationally with APhA. I've been a committee member for the Care for the Underserved Special Interest Group, which ties in nicely with The Dispensary of Hope, and serve on the APPM Executive Committee.

I truly believe as pharmacists, we are also community leaders. So it's important to be engaged and give back to your community. There are many different ways that my husband and I choose to do that. My husband, Chad, and I are very involved in the Nashville community through volunteering with the Nashville Ballet and Junior League. We also enjoy our church and spending time with friends and family. Being a volunteer, as I mentioned earlier, helped lead to my current role at Dispensary of Hope. As pharmacists, we are seen as leaders in the community and should be committed to being involved and serving others around us in and out of the pharmacy.

Methods to Monetize Your Knowledge

A few ways that I've been able to monetize my knowledge has been through obtaining sponsors for the *Talk to Your Pharmacist Podcast*, writing a book on women in leadership called *How Pharmacists Lead*, and speaking to groups about the topic of leadership.

Podcasting was my first entree into entrepreneurship. The *Talk to Your Pharmacist Podcast* celebrated four years in August 2021. It was a bit of a learning curve; the first episode was not perfect. But I believe it's important to get version 1.0 out there and learn as you go. It was scary because you're putting yourself out there, but it's been wonderful to get to connect with pharmacy leaders from across the country and share the story of over 200 pharmacy leaders. After reading many books and listening to podcasts myself, it lit my passion for leadership, particularly helping women get into leadership. I decided to write a book on that topic and share some of the stories of women leaders who were my role models. I wanted to share the stories of powerful women that other people could see themselves in.

Having those conversations and learning about these topics has really helped me become more knowledgeable about the industry. Hopefully, it has been able to help share with others what options are out there besides traditional pharmacy. Many times, if you ask a room full of people what a pharmacist does, they'll say, "Oh, a pharmacist fills my prescription." But the truth is there are so many things that pharmacists can do. These are just a few hot topics, but essential oils, opioid management, building your business model as a consulting pharmacist, podcasting, pharmacogenomics, gene therapies. There are lots of different things.

We've even made money through serving as hosts on Airbnb for our primary home. We love to travel, and we used our Airbnb to fund our travel. If we were traveling for the weekend or even on a trip to Cuba, Greece, or Thailand, we could open our home for rent and essentially fund our vacation. So there are lots of little entrepreneurial things you can do to make sure you have the life you want, pharmacy-related or not.

Advancing Women Leadership in Pharmacy

Women make up 80% of the healthcare workforce, but only 3% hold the title of CEO. Despite this, females now make up the majority of graduates and the health professions, including pharmacy. So even in the 2017, 2018 American Association of Colleges of Pharmacy (AACP) statistics, 60% of pharmacy degrees that were conferred went to females. With so many women in the healthcare industry, we really need female role models to inspire us and to represent us in leadership. That's the state of pharmacy leadership and why we need more female leadership.

What are some of the factors that contribute to a lack of female leadership? Many are personal factors such as mindset; there is still a mindset of the 1950s single-family earner where women stayed at home. And although much of that has shifted, women still tend to bear the brunt of housekeeping responsibility and the responsibilities of motherhood. I can really empathize with that, especially with the COVID-19 pandemic. A light was shone on how many responsibilities women have to balance. I do think that organizations are starting to notice that, which is great. But there are other barriers too. Many women often feel they don't have the qualifications to pursue a career, or they need to put their family over their career, and that's okay. Being a mother, I know there have been times in my life where I want to set my career aside and really focus on my family, and there have been times where I really want to come back to it and achieve my goals.

There are also organizational factors; I believe there are higher standards for women in leadership. The rigor is more intense; all of this contributes to a lack of female leadership. Even interpersonally, many women cannot visualize what it would be like for them to be in a leadership position. They may not have female mentors, or they may have been exposed to negative stereotypes. When you think of the C-suite, who do you think of? It's likely a man in a suit. Women, when applying for jobs, will read a job description and think, "I'm not qualified for that!" But I say, go ahead, put your name down, raise your hand, take charge. What's the worst that can happen? They won't call you back for that interview, okay, so what? No harm comes from raising your hand and putting yourself out there. Fortunately, a lot of these biases are being shattered, and we are starting to see more women in leadership roles. There are also a lot of benefits to female leadership. There have been numerous studies that highlight the importance of women in leadership. They have revealed that women can outperform men on several competencies. These competencies have been motivating others, fostering communities, producing high-quality work, listening, and building relationships.

In spring 2021, I interviewed four different female leaders, focusing on the hospital or health system perspective and how they led their teams during the COVID pandemic. It was really interesting to hear from them and how they lead their teams. It echoed a Harvard Business Review article and a Zenger Folkman study that came out. They said that having a diverse sense of leadership and having women on the board helps eliminate the homogenous point of view that often comes with an all-male board. Women tend to think differently and approach situations differently than men. McKinsey even produced an article showing that companies with more women do better financially and have higher corporate social responsibility standards.

With the majority of the workforce being female, it helps to have leadership that can relate to that workforce. It's exciting to see more and more chief pharmacy officer positions being created and given to women. We actually have more females taking on those positions in two of the biggest health systems: Hospital Corporation of America (HCA) is one of them, which is located here in Nashville. Karla Miller is a female Chief Pharmacy Officer at HCA, the largest for-profit health system in the country. Ascension as well, which is one of the largest non-profit health systems, and Lynn Eschenbacher is the Chief Pharmacy Officer there. So it's exhilarating to see women stepping up into those types of positions.

When I interviewed Mary Alice Bennet for the podcast, she shared a quote that I love. She said, "Grab all that you can while you can." I think about that a lot. Through different seasons of my life, my priorities have changed. I focused on my career for the first ten years that I was in the workforce, and then we decided to have a baby. For those first years, my husband and I wanted to make sure we could travel and focus on our career, get that out of our system before we decided to have a family.

It's important to think about what kind of assets you have and what you are willing to give up. So grab all you can while you can. Now, my husband and I are in a different season of life with a baby, but that doesn't mean you have to give up on your leadership skills. Maybe you're not the CEO, but you're a staff pharmacist, or you can serve as chair for your junior league; there are many different things you can do.

Advice for Aspiring Entrepreneurs

What I would give as advice to younger pharmacists is to let go of your plan. I know we are very big into planning, but sometimes you need to allow yourself to follow where your career will take you. I didn't know that I would be at the Dispensary of Hope, and now I have been for the last six years. So sometimes, letting go of your plan leads you to other things that you had no idea you would find— allowing yourself to be educated, whether it's going back to business school or just learning from books. I would say that reading and listening to podcasts has been instrumental in changing my mindset and allowing for a growth mindset to flourish.

I would also recommend you think outside the box. A lot of people are hesitant to claim leadership skills as something they possess. They think, "Gosh, that's not in my title," or, "I'm not a CEO, I'm not in the C-suite. I don't even have a forum to talk to the senior leaders at my organization." But there are so many ways people lead even when they are not in charge. What are your spheres of influence? What do you take responsibility for? Claiming those things can allow others to see you and appreciate you for all that you do.

Finally, finding ways to make your life more efficient so you can focus on building your career and leadership skills is possible, even if it's something as small as hiring someone to clean your home, or ordering your groceries online so you don't have to go to the grocery store.

**Hillary Blackburn,
PharmD, MBA**

CONTRIBUTOR

CONNECTION

www.hillaryblackburn.com

www.linkedin.com/in/hillary-blackburn
-pharmd-mba-67a92421/

ASHA BOHANNON

Biography

Dr. Asha Bohannon is the founder and owner of Patient Advocacy Initiative Wellness Group, LLC or PAI Wellness Group©. She is based in Raleigh, North Carolina, and is a holistic pharmacist, best-selling author, speaker, and business consultant. After starting her own wellness practice in 2017, she and her husband Eric partnered to create and launch a business consulting program to help other pharmacists do exactly what she's done. Dr. Asha's passion is helping pharmacists like herself get out of their traditional pharmacy jobs and fulfill their life dreams of running their own businesses and successful wellness practices. Dr. Asha helps pharmacists learn how to get out of their own ways, the right steps to starting a wellness practice, and mistakes to avoid.

Entrepreneurial Journey

My name is Dr. Asha Pai Bohannon, and I want to share some of my journey with you. After I graduated from pharmacy school, I completed a community/ primary care pharmacy residency. After that, I went into independent retail pharmacy. I worked full-time in that setting for seven years. I worked my way up to store manager, thinking this was exactly where I should be. But that entire time, I actually felt unhappy with what I was doing in my career.

My desire was to be more patient-centric and clinical, and I just wasn't feeling fulfilled. To be completely honest, I felt like I was feeding people's illnesses rather than helping them get and stay well. That was really difficult. I felt shackled to what I call the golden handcuffs. There was a degree of comfort that came with the job, and I knew I needed to stay there because Eric and I wanted to start a family. I stayed stuck. I don't know how else to put it.

After I had my first child, the waterworks really started coming. I was feeling miserable all the time, every single day. I wanted flexibility and less stress, especially considering amidst all of this, my health had begun to decline as well. I was like, "Where do I go? What should I do?" I had no idea. Finally, I began moving forward and looking at different entrepreneurship opportunities that came my way. That was when I realized that the first thing which needed to happen was a change of mindset. Believe me, I have gotten in my own way quite a few times and continue to do so today. We all do it.

I began learning about sales, which I had never formally done in the past. I was just throwing spaghetti at the wall and seeing what would stick. I came up with ideas and began thinking about different things. I went out and tried all of these different things, but nothing was sticking. I was frustrated, but I also knew that I wasn't approaching my career in the most efficient way. Finally, after lots of trial and error, I decided I really wanted to start a wellness practice.

I spoke to Eric, and it quickly became clear that even with my clinical mindset and the sales knowledge I was bringing to the table, I was only getting so far. Now Eric's job is helping create and launch million-dollar services to large fortune 50 companies. I realized that he might have the knowledge to help me out, we partnered together to start my wellness practice.

Methods to Monetize Your Knowledge

I am a certified diabetes care and education specialist, and I really wanted to focus my holistic wellness practice on diabetes education and management and medication management. These are the things I am passionate about. I am off on my own; I'm not billing with any insurance companies or anything like that. Everything I do is a fee-for-service, but I wanted to put that holistic element into it. I have an

East meets West kind of philosophy. That is how I choose to work with my clients.

As I was building my business, I encountered more and more pharmacists who were in the very same situation I had been in. They were trying to get out of a miserable situation. They were looking for answers and trying to break free of the golden handcuffs.

A few years ago, Eric and I went to Medipreneurs together. He's a great support system, and I'm really grateful for that. We got together, and people were asking me about all the different ways I had been monetizing my knowledge. At this point, I had started my wellness practice and written a book called *To Medicate or Not? That is the Question!* I was being asked these questions more from a business perspective, and as pharmacists, we are not taught the MBA side of the work. It is hard to understand that stuff. Eric and I came together and realized there was something missing in the way pharmacists create their businesses. We had this great value in clinical knowledge, which we are able to give as pharmacists, but we don't have the business sense as much.

We needed to combine these two areas of expertise together and create an end-to-end solution that walks pharmacists through the step-by-step process of how to create a business. This is how I understood being able to make an impact on the lives of pharmacists and, by extension, impact the lives of their patients as well. We wanted to help people live a life of passion, purpose, and enjoy the profession that they are in.

Another way I monetize my knowledge is a book we wrote called *Impact Pharmacist* on Amazon, and it is a very thorough guide to our course. We also work one-on-one with clients who want a little bit more hand-holding through the process. As recently as earlier this year, we also created an online program to make it more cost-effective and efficient. It's a self-paced program that people can take while still having our support along the way. And this is really designed to allow us to walk alongside our clients as they go along this journey. We provide a facilitated program in which clients can get the level of support they need.

Breaking Free from the Golden Handcuffs: Three Secrets to Starting a Successful Wellness Practice

I love talking about the golden handcuffs because I know as pharmacists, we are not the only people who feel this way. For those of us who have been in the same job for a number of years, it becomes a big thing. We begin to feel trapped and stuck. I want to help people understand they can achieve the life of their dreams; they can create a greater impact and build a legacy for themselves. That is what I struggled to figure out for many years. I went through trial and error and made mistakes, so I want to help people not to make those same mistakes.

For many years I was truly defined by these golden handcuffs. The handcuffs can be inflicted by your employer; they can be based on how long you have been here, what your pay is, and the bottom line. But what this is really about is self-infliction. I totally inflicted the golden handcuffs on myself, and it was because of comfort. Knowing what to do, having a steady paycheck, all of these things allow you to stay within your comfort zone. It is so hard to let go of your comfort zone, and I know a lot of my colleagues in the professional pharmacy arena can attest to this. You feel stressed and overwhelmed, but you stay where you are anyway.

The reason why I wanted to be a pharmacist to begin with was to help people. But it became the thing that stressed me out the most because I felt like I was never truly helping anyone. Trying to find the balance between helping patients and competing with the bottom line becomes really overwhelming. It started causing me more health issues and stress within my family. It threw me off balance: my health, my mindset, my family life. Everything was thrown completely off-balance, and I found myself struggling.

I did a couple of certifications and kept going back and forth, trying to find my way. I know there are a lot of people out there who are in that same space. You're probably thinking, "What certifications do I need to get? What do I need to do? How do I do this?" But I realized all of those extra things I was adding in order to find my direction just added to the confusion. It wasn't helping me understand what my strengths and interests were. It wasn't telling me what I was passionate about. It just became another certification to get, another piece of spaghetti to throw at the wall.

I did this for two to three years. I want to help you to not do the same thing. Because what I didn't realize was that I wasn't truly looking for another job. I was looking for freedom. When I say freedom, I mean all kinds of freedom, financial freedom, and freedom to fulfill my passion and my purpose. I think most people can attest to this, too. I wanted to be able to leave a legacy and have an impact on patients' lives, pharmacists' lives, and my family's lives. I wanted to be able to impact the people I encounter every day.

I was trying to understand how to put together the pieces of the puzzle. That was the moment when I enlisted Eric's help. I could go out and talk clinical all day long, I could talk about diabetes all day long, but that doesn't bring patients in, and it doesn't bring money in. It didn't have the impact that I wanted. It was when we combined our areas of expertise, my clinical and his business strategy, that I realized I could break free of the golden handcuffs. That was how I could find freedom and get to the pot of gold at the end of the rainbow. That is what we decided to do.

We partnered together to create the Impact Pharmacists Online Program—this is an incredibly valuable tool we really want people to have access to. One of the things this program teaches is what we call the top three secrets to start your own successful wellness practice.

Number one, getting out of your own way. Getting out of your own way is all about your mindset. You must have the right mindset to get into entrepreneurship and leave the comfort of what you know behind. Like I said earlier, it's easy to stay comfortable, but we need to be able to leave all that behind.

Number two, after getting out of your own way, is something called analysis paralysis. Analysis paralysis means overthinking a situation past the point of action. It means you are stuck in a loop of analyzing to the point where you are paralyzed. I have gotten stuck in this loop so many times. As pharmacists, I know for a fact that we all sometimes suffer from analysis paralysis because when we feel uncertain or like we don't know the answer, we overthink. We might be creating a pros and cons list; we might be listing out all of the research we need to do or certifications we might need. And while this may seem productive at the moment, it is actually stopping you from moving forward. I am not saying that all of the tasks you are listing are completely unnecessary, but the act of writing them out and analyzing your strategy is often used to procrastinate actually getting them done.

Instead of accomplishing what you set out to, now you are paralyzed. You're stuck in a loop of analyzing everything to death. But I think it is also important to say that this is not a fault of your own. This is how we were trained! We were trained to be jacks and janes of all trades, not to be specifically focused on one thing. As pharmacists, we tend to know a little about a lot, but not a lot about a little. It makes it really difficult to think outside of the box when you're stuck in a spinning hamster wheel.

When it comes to starting our business, we tend to think we don't know enough. We're not taught a lot about running a business; even with an MBA, it is still a difficult task. We get stuck again. We think, "I need another thing, another thing, another thing." It creates paralysis. It is a kind of fear of missing out when it comes to certification. We want to accumulate all this knowledge that we think will help prepare us, but we don't actually look for answers on how to start a business. You don't look for the tools that would actually benefit you.

I am here right now, telling you that you have everything you need to start a wellness practice. There is nothing extra that you need to go off and do clinically speaking (until you figure out what niche you want to target). You are a clinical practitioner as you stand, and you will always be able to go out and discover what you want to do with that. Once you find out what you want to do, nothing will teach you better than actually doing it. It will save you time; it will save you money and a whole lot of emotions. You just have to get out of your own way. Then you can learn the steps it takes to create your business in the right way, without putting the cart in front of the horse.

The third secret I teach is the four pitfalls that we see most startup entrepreneurs fall into. This is the secret to thriving rather than simply surviving. When thinking about starting your business, you need to think about it kind of like a puzzle, and you need to identify the pieces you need. Eric is always saying that "entrepreneurs are risk-avoiders, not risk-takers." If you can identify these four pitfalls and focus on them, so you know how to avoid them, you will succeed.

The first pitfall we often see is that when people think they have a great idea for a product or service, they will assume that everyone wants it. What they find from talking to consumers is that only a few actually like it or are willing to buy it. And in truth, that's not bad. You still have got a couple of people, but you haven't quite met the customer's needs. They discover in the end that after putting in all of this time and energy, they have designed the wrong service.

They go out and talk to tons and tons of people, but now they don't have a target customer. This is the second pitfall; they keep experiencing these moments of failure. Their target market is not the people they are talking to; they haven't found the right customer.

The third pitfall occurs when they actually do have the right product, and they may be talking to the right people. Customers are hearing about the product and buying into it. But two things can happen that allow it to go wrong. Either they are overpricing the product because they keep getting such positive feedback yet only a few buyers, or they are underpricing it because they are talking to tons of people and it is being bought, but they do not see any profit or return. It becomes a matter of the right pricing model. I have seen many people fall into the trap of not having the right pricing model.

Finally, the fourth pitfall is having the right messaging. The entrepreneur might have identified the right service, the right target market, they've got the correct pricing structure, and they're talking to the ideal customer. They have all these things going for them; what else is left? Somehow they fail to articulate what the customer will get out of the product or service; they can't tell the customer what is in it for them. And when this happens, it usually means their marketing is off too. No matter how good their product is, they are not going to sell if they can't explain *why* it is a good fit for the client.

Once you address these four pitfalls, you have the target market, the right product, the pricing structure, and your messaging; you will be successful in starting your business. These are the four things that you really need to be thinking about when starting your entrepreneurial journey or creating a wellness practice within the pharmaceutical world.

Once you have addressed these, the next question is, "How do I thrive in this?" You have addressed the four pitfalls. You have a service in hand. You know what you're doing, and clinically you are ready to go. That's great, but what comes next? I like to think of it as having a handful of ingredients that guarantee your business will have the secret sauce.

I'm going to share a little secret. And in truth, it's not really a secret; having bypassed all of the four pitfalls is amazing, but what you really need is harmony between them. What do you need to guarantee harmony? The first thing is passion. You have to be passionate about what you are doing. Finding out what you want to do, being passionate about it, and not sticking yourself into the hole of what you think you should be doing.

Number two, you need money. It takes money to make money. I think about that a lot. You have to put the time and energy into building a new business. A lot of people think if they just create the business, it will be wanted; people will come to me. And if that happens, it's great, but you have to put in the time. You have to talk to the right people and learn how to market yourself. You have to put the commitment in. When I began this process several years ago, I was heavily committed to it and to being consistent with it. You can't just do a little bit here and a little bit there. It takes a consistent daily grind to build the legacy you want for yourself.

Last but certainly not least is the sales and growth mindset. You have to really get yourself into the sales mindset. You have to be constantly thinking about how you can grow. Without that constant growth, it is really easy to get paralyzed again.

Once again, harmony is tying together all of those four pitfalls. That harmony is what is going to allow you to thrive in your business. Now there are a lot of objections out there. I can hear them already. You'll say, "I don't have time," "I don't have the right knowledge," "I don't have the money," "I don't know where to start." I hear these over and over again. But the truth is, time is the thing we want the most and use the worst. We all have the same amount of time allotted to us every single day, but we don't always use it well.

We waste precious time looking for the perfect moment to start a business, but there is never going to be a perfect moment. All we have is right now. That is my favorite thing to say. Now is the perfect time, don't let anything stop you, don't make those excuses. There is always going to be an excuse to stop you from doing what you want and being who you want to be. But now is the time to forge past that. Now is the time to take action. You need to take action so you can understand what it is you really want and how best to move forward with that. There is no better opportunity than right now.

I like to use analogies to illustrate my points, so I'm going to give you one now. This was something that came to me when we were starting our Impact Pharmacist Program. Imagine building a house. Would you start with creating a blueprint, building a solid cement foundation, and then putting up the beams and the walls? Or would you start with the wooden beams and then go back afterward to decide if you want to lay a cement foundation?

Personally, I have done both. My personal opinion would be to actually do the latter; sometimes, it's better to get started without the knowledge and comfort of getting where you want to go. I really want you to think about demolishing those objections, figure out your next steps and think about how you can move forward and take action today.

I want you to take a minute and think about what parts of your life you are sacrificing at this very moment. Are you sacrificing your health? Are you sacrificing time spent with your family? Are you sacrificing your own personal fulfillment? I have done all of these. I am right there with you. But I also want you to think about the flip side. Are you ready to grab life by the reins? Are you ready to help people get what they want and deserve? Are you ready to get what you want and deserve? Ask yourself, are you ready? These are really important questions to ask as you begin your journey because you could be stalled right now and not even realize it. I have been exactly where you are. I have had butterflies in my stomach. I understand the nervous excitement that you are feeling because it is nerve-wracking, but it is also super exciting.

This is a very disruptive time in our profession, which is why it is also the perfect opportunity to be a trailblazer. It is a really exciting time, and I am excited to be part of it with you. Eric and I have spent the last two-and-a-half years working with other pharmacists trying to help them get to where they want to be. I think it is the best time to learn the processes the ways to go about starting a business to ensure success. We have a really great opportunity to make this work.

I am going to take a few moments to share with you about our Impact Pharmacists Online Program. We have worked to develop a cost-effective way to help you through this process. It is a self-paced online program divided into six sections and 14 modules, along with a bonus module about sales. Each section is designed to take about two weeks if you go straight through; it is about a three-month program. It contains video and audio content so that you can listen wherever you are, worksheets, templates, and everything you need. We really wanted to give you everything.

The material covers mindset, business development, marketing strategy, and all the tools and knowledge you would need to move forward in your entrepreneurial journey. We're excited to be walking alongside you on this path. We've had several people who have done the program give us some great testimonials, and I'd like to read one out loud. This is one from Plano, Texas: "Dr. Asha Pai Bohannon and Eric Bohannon have been a godsend. They have helped me dig deeper for my target audience than I had previously working with another coach. I was impressed with how specific you can go in clarifying your niche. I am more prepared to move forward with clarity and get paid what I am worth for my wellness practice."

That, folks, is the bottom line. Pharmacists are worth so much. We have so much knowledge and value. We are worth more than we give ourselves credit for or that anyone else is going to give us credit for. We have to go out and make it for ourselves. I am excited to see where this journey leads you.

The best way to reach me is through my website: ashapaibohannon.com. You can also connect with me on Facebook, Instagram, or LinkedIn at Dr. Asha Pai Bohannon.

Advice for Aspiring Entrepreneurs

My advice for aspiring entrepreneurs is twofold. Firstly, figure out the right way for you. Secondly, don't wait. This is the biggest piece of advice I can give you. The time you have right now is your opportunity to be a trailblazer, it is there for the taking. Don't wait!

CONTRIBUTOR
CONNECTION

**Asha Bohanon,
PharmD, CDCES, CPT**

www.paiwellnessgroup.com

www.linkedin.com/in/drashapaibohannon/

KIMBER BOOTHE

Biography

Dr. Kimber Boothe, PharmD, MHA, is a pharmacist, healthcare leader, and entrepreneur with decades of experience in health systems and the pharmaceutical industry. She is known as the 'Strategy Pharmacist' and Chief Connector & Pharmovator. Kimber is the founder and CEO of the Kimber Boothe Group, where she provides coaching, consulting, courses, and speaking on: Leadership & Career Development, Pharmacy Strategy & Innovation/Intrapreneurship, & Pharmacy Entrepreneurship. She is a graduate of the University of Connecticut and Medical University of South Carolina, the University of Phoenix Masters in Health Administration, and completed residencies at Virginia Commonwealth University. Kimber previously led the pharmacy services for a four-hospital community health system, where she drove innovative strategy for the pharmacy enterprise as System Director of Pharmacy. She was also the Director of Clinical Pharmacy Services at Yale-New Haven Health. She is passionate about spending time on the right things to develop others and deliver strategic, focused results by living her values of Lead, Inspire, Value, and Excel. Her motto is Pharmacy Can do More with More, and her goal is to support the addition of 100 new health system pharmacy positions annually. She is the recipient of the Connecticut Society of Health-System Pharmacists Meritorious Achievement Award, and her prior organization has been recognized with the Kentucky Society of Health-System Pharmacists Innovative Health-System Pharmacy Practice Award.

Entrepreneurial Journey

I help pharmacists strategically advocate for roles and resources to advance practice and have joyful engaging careers. This is my simplified 'why' statement like you will write for your business. My services extend to both what I like to call intrapreneurs, people working within organizations, and entrepreneurs following an influencer model to impact pharmacy.

A few fun facts about me: I moved from clinical practice into leadership early in my career. I did community pharmacy when I was in school and during my doctorate and residency, and then I worked at Yale-New Haven Hospital in different roles. I went into the pharmaceutical industry for ten years in various roles, including medical affairs, and then went back to health systems as a Director of Clinical Pharmacy Services. It was then that I became drawn to this influencer model and how I could shift my work. At the end of 2014, I formed my LLC and officially started my business, but I still wasn't ready to do it full-time, so I worked as an entrepreneur in a limited capacity.

My family relocated to Cincinnati/Northern Kentucky, and I got a wonderful position as a Chief Pharmacy Officer while working on my business as a side hustle. I was doing coaching training, working as a consultant and public speaker all part-time, and I had a multi-year plan to transition to focus 100% on my business.

When I do coaching, I try to emphasize to my clients that their careers are not the only important element of their lives. I am also a wife, a mother, and a daughter. My dad lives down in Florida, where I, too, lived for some years. I have family in Brooklyn and a brother in Connecticut. I want my clients to understand they have these vast networks outside of just their careers. I like to think of my life as a Venn diagram of four circles, each representing a different aspect of my life—Self, Family/Friends, Career, Community. I do this so that my clients and myself alike can understand that there is a need for balance and integration. It's important that we dedicate time to other parts of our lives besides our careers.

One of your circles is also your community. I am a big believer in supporting your community, whether through pharmacy organizations or volunteer organizations. I'm a big roller blader too, and one of the ways I volunteer is helping maintain multi-use trails in my area. I love spending time with my family, traveling, and making memories together. We love to go diving; we went to Jamaica when I was pregnant with twins and explored caves there. We love to go on cruises.

My entrepreneurial journey followed my intrapreneurial journey working within organizations. I was very interested in innovation within the safety of an organization. And so, as I was working within these organizations, I would justify my position and the work I was doing. In one organization, I wrote a business plan. I was working in cardiology and taking care of about 150 patients. And I needed another pharmacist so I could expand my services and not be stretched too thin. This was the year after my residency, and I wrote my first business plan. I created an organization for pharmacists at Bayer called Pharmacists at Pharmacists (PhAB).

When I moved from pharmacy to health systems, I worked as the director of clinical services at Yale-New Haven Health, and I was asked to focus on the pharmacy Practice Advancement Initiative (PAI). I began developing business plans in that capacity. In early 2015 when I formed the Kimber Boothe Group, I created a model for thought leaders and a course called Connector 101. I began coaching the following year and created 50 new positions through business plans to advance acute care services. I then went on to create another course called the Connector Academy, which was designed to be a deeper dive into leadership. In 2017 I was able to create 20 new positions and was just trying to be very bold about advancing the practice.

In 2018 I continued down this intrapreneur path to focus on innovating practice within existing organizations. Now living in Ohio, I was able to replicate the success I had previously and create 50 new positions within my new health system. Later that year, I attended a conference for entrepreneurs that really helped solidify what I wanted to do. I was having so much success in pharmacy strategy that I decided pharmacists would be my target customer.

When I had been doing coaching before, my reach was a lot broader. My first client was a soccer mom who also performed opera. I helped her get back into jobs on stage by strategically planning her career moves. But opera singers aren't really my passion; attending this conference helped me realize that pharmacists were who I wanted to cater to.

The following year, I created another business plan to expand ambulatory services, and I also created my course, Pharmovation. I launched them both at the same time, at the Medipreneurs conference. I used this as an accountability deadline for myself. I said to myself, "I cannot attend this meeting without being able to share that I launched my course." I launched the course and had about three students my first year. It wasn't huge, but it validated a lot of the work I had been doing.

At the end of 2019, I resigned from my position and became a full-time entrepreneur. I began working right before the pandemic with an expanded list of health system Pharmovation Consulting clients. I was making a lot of big decisions during this period, and the questions I asked myself to guide my journey were: *Where do you want to have an influence? What are your passions?* And I knew if I could find the intersection of my passions and where I wanted to have an impact, I would find the work I was meant to be doing.

Methods to Monetize Your Knowledge

Something I teach in the Pharmfluencer Business Course and that I find very helpful when you are getting started is interviewing people in your target audience. Asking them questions about what their needs are and identifying the most important things. When I held the Pharmfluencer summit, I had all the registrants fill out a survey upon registering. This helped me understand what their needs were, what they were hoping to get out of that experience. That way, I could tailor my materials to answer their questions and provide them with the information they need.

Realize that people will pay for your services, and if they won't, they're probably not your ideal customer anyway. And as you are transitioning into this process, you can offer discounts or scholarships for people who really cannot afford to pay because you do want to reach as many people as possible.

As we have covered, there are many methods to monetize your knowledge. To mention a fun one—I am currently helping my son launch a membership box service. These are incredibly popular right now, a monthly subscription where you receive a box of some kind in the mail. You may pay a monthly or quarterly amount to get a product shipped to you. He definitely inherited the entrepreneurial spirit. And I've realized that my training in pharmacy has allowed me to think very strategically. I am always thinking of ways to innovate and monetize. I am very proud that he has picked up on that from me.

When I began my consulting, I was very strategic with how I grew my client base and developed my business. I wanted to grow my business online, so I could reach more people with the services I provided. One of my goals is to help create a hundred new pharmacy positions every year. That is difficult to accomplish if I am only doing one-on-one consulting. I need to reach more pharmacists who create their own impact within their organizations or supporting entrepreneurs who are also supporting bold practice advancement.

I organize the methods I use to monetize my knowledge into a product matrix of topic areas and low to high tier offerings. The three topic areas I have grown into are leadership, intrapreneurship, and entrepreneurship. I began with one-on-one coaching and created my first course in my zone of genius: pharmacy strategy and innovation (intrapreneurship): Pharmovation® Course. I then added the high-tier consulting service. It was very validating because I now had contracts where I'm paid for the value I bring. I also wrote my first book, *Pharmovation*, which is considered my low tier. I also created virtual live events and summits to help educate and get my message out. All of which is part of my long-term strategy to continue building my business. In the topic area of entrepreneurship, I created a product line for Pharmfluencer™ with the summit, on demand course, this book, and a mastermind membership. In the 3rd topic area for leadership, my Connector brand, I serve through coaching and the Connector Leadership Circle™ membership.

Connecting Your Why to Your Impact Through the Pharmfluencer Business Model

I wore a specific necklace today. I wore it because it has a path going through the back, and it says, "Trust Your Journey." I wanted to start with that because, in many ways, it is the first step, trusting your own journey, trusting your heart. What this means to me is not letting fear take over. One of the biggest things that allowed me to transition into being an entrepreneur was trusting in my journey and not letting fear take over.

Although I haven't always been an entrepreneur, I have had entrepreneurial ideas for many years. When I was in college, I began doing nails out of my dorm room. I even advertised my business. Unfortunately, this was actually against university policy. I got a nice letter from the university saying I had to stop or I would risk being kicked out of school. Although I wouldn't qualify that venture as being successful, it began a pattern of entrepreneurial ideas I had.

Another idea I had when I was working in the pharmaceutical industry was to create a database for hospitals. I was working as a medical science liaison, and something I found was that the hospitals were always asking for proof of vaccinations. I thought there must be a way to create a database for this information. I put the idea in a folder and never got around to acting on it. And sure enough, now there are two major companies that make millions of dollars doing exactly that.

My reason for sharing this is that hopefully, it will motivate you to not just keep your big ideas in a drawer somewhere. If you're reading this book, I assume you have the entrepreneurial spirit, and you just may not know how to tap into it. The key is identifying your passions and where you want to have an impact. Who do you want to serve? What are the problems you are drawn towards solving? I'm a big fan of *Building a StoryBrand* by Donald Miller. It's a great book. And the idea in that book is that the people you want to serve are the heroes; you are the guide. You have the competency, skill, knowledge, and belief to teach them how to be successful.

Everyone has a passion for something, and it can be incredibly niche. Some people are huge war buffs. They have an interest in military history, strategy, or weaponry. Whatever it may be, they don't realize they can monetize their knowledge. For me, it was pharmacy and helping people become leaders. I was doing those innovative things. I was speaking, and I was getting paid for it.

The critical decision in making all of this happen was creating a limited liability corporation to protect myself. When I was transitioning from being an entrepreneur part-time to full-time, I also developed a phased timeline that would ensure I had enough business on the side so that I was comfortable enough leaving. I would always recommend that, just to ensure you are covered financially as you make that transition. It was important to me during that process that I remain independent and flexible. During that time, several pharmacy consulting firms reached out to me, asking me to join them as a partner or consultant. I declined those offers preferring to work with those organizations as a subcontractor rather than an employee.

Identifying who I wanted to serve who my clients were going to be, gave me the impetus and direction to begin working as an entrepreneur full-time. Once I had that realization, I knew I had made the right decision because it felt natural for me to focus on helping pharmacists.

I think this model of entrepreneurship is especially appealing because there are very few barriers to entry. You don't have to acquire a physical space; you are not selling physical products, there is no question of multilevel marketing. You can begin working out of your home. When I began, I had no website; I had nothing. My clients were people who lived in my town, and they paid me because I had the expertise. It's not as hard as you might think it is. If you have the knowledge and a sphere of influence, you are already there. The hardest part was charging people for my services, and I didn't charge a lot of my clients early on. This can be strategic; you may want to give your services away for free to a few people to gain testimonials. But pretty quickly, you need to begin charging people and realize that your services are worth money. People will pay for it.

Advice for Aspiring Entrepreneurs

There are key learnings that I want to share with you from my journey.

1. Inner Circle/ Network is Vital. One reason I am so passionate about conferences and summits is that it allows you to create this inner circle of like-minded people that you may not get the opportunity to meet otherwise. These networks are important when transitioning into running your own business. You never know who in the room might be your next client or could give you your next client.
2. Continuous Development in new entrepreneurship topics while continuing to develop your zone of genius is important. I would highly recommend becoming familiar with membership and marketing. I took a number of courses on that when I was making the transition. I had the knowledge to know how to run a successful business and was not just going in blind.
3. Start with one thing—product or service. I know I mentioned my product matrix, but it all started with one and was built over time.
4. If I could do one thing differently, I would have hired help earlier. A lot of people are hesitant to hire help when they are building their business, which is understandable. A lot of people believe you can't hire help until your business is booming. But I've found that the longer you wait, the harder it becomes to delegate those tasks and outsource some of the responsibility. I think if I had hired someone earlier, it would have allowed me to scale and grow more quickly while having more balance. It's a hard lesson to learn, but you really don't need to be practicing at the top of your capacity 24/7. It's okay to get some support. I've only done that in the last year-and-a-half.

When I was still working full-time, I had a cleaning service and some childcare support. I also had virtual assistants to do some of the administrative tasks. I thought when I transitioned; I would no longer need that support. But having a graphic designer, copywriter, and someone to help with marketing and social media is absolutely critical. If I could do it again, I would hire all of those people earlier. I look at my work and personal time to ensure I am "practicing at the top of my license" and focused on what I am uniquely qualified to do.

That is my story and how I developed my business. I hope this book gives you the motivation to pursue starting your own business. And if you are looking for more guidance in identifying your topic, your ideal customer, and how to build a path to success, I highly recommend my Pharmfluencer Business Course. It also goes deeper into what is being covered in this book: how to monetize your knowledge, building a business foundation, forming an LLC, branding and website decisions, and even what it means to launch a product.

When you're not working for somebody, there are important decisions and a specific mindset that are critical to the business foundation. I also go into pharmacy profession strategies. We looked specifically at the pharmacy landscape and where there are opportunities for business. I offer different options for the level of involvement as well as a student price. If this interests you, please explore the options at my website at Kimberboothe.com

The final thing I want to address before leaving you with the wisdom of my many fantastic contributors is how to find a coach, and more specifically, the right coach if you haven't honed your niche yet. There are many coaches out there who offer services similar to mine but more focused on general strategy. Don't think you need to wait until you have identified your niche in order to seek guidance. Having a coach can actually help you make those decisions that will lead to you identifying what your area is and who your ideal clients will be. Starting my business was one of the best decisions I have ever made, and I hope this book empowers you to develop a joyful and impactful career.

Final words of advice—Just do it!

**Kimber Boothe,
PharmD, MHA**

CONTRIBUTOR
CONNECTION

🌐 www.kimberboothe.com

💼 www.linkedin.com/in/kimberboothe

DEREK BOROWKOWSKI

Biography

Derek Borkowski, PharmD, is a pharmacist, software engineer, and the founder and CEO of Cosmas Health©. His background includes experience in community pharmacy, digital health, and the pharmaceutical industry. He is the creator and software engineer of Pyrls.com, a drug information website and mobile application for clinicians and student-clinicians. Additionally, he continues to practice community pharmacy. Derek is a 2018 Doctor of Pharmacy graduate from the University of Minnesota.

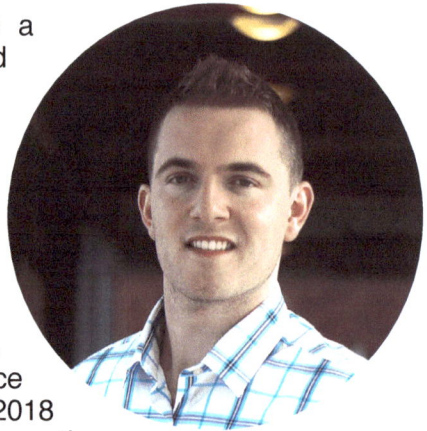

Entrepreneurial Journey

After forming my LLC, Cosmas Health, I actually only used it for freelance web development work. And it became apparent that having some knowledge of pharmacy and having some knowledge of web development was incredibly synergistic. I wasn't the best web developer in the world, and there are plenty of pharmacists who know more than me but having a combination of the two allowed me to do something unique.

Through freelance work, I was able to meet my first few clients. One was in medical practice, and they needed their website rebuilt. And because I was a pharmacist, I was able to relate to them on a personal level, as a colleague in the healthcare field, and I could also get the website development done. It was that combination that landed me my first client. Having that domain expertise, but also being able to provide a service.

Eric Christianson, who runs MedEd 101, is a friend and mentor of mine. I met him at a conference when I was still a student. We collaborated and built RxGrad.com, a NAPLEX preparation website. Eric provided the content, and I had the software engineering and design skills to build the website out as well as help review content. I can't stress enough how important it was for me to have these skills in addition to the knowledge of the pharmacy industry.

I then went on to start Pyrls.com, a medical information reference tool. I would compare it to a digital version of the top 300 drug study cards. It's for people who are learning about different medications and people in the outpatient setting. And every so often, I will have people ask me, "How are you going to compete with UpToDate or Lexicomp? They're going to crush you." I tell them what I'll tell you. A core tenet of my business model is that I have very little operating expenses because I am both the domain expert and the one who is taking the time to build these skills.

For a time, I was working two full-time jobs, and I know many people trying to start their own business are in this exact same position. We're all obsessed with building and doing interesting things. But because I wear multiple hats in the running of my company, I don't need to make $700 million a year in revenue to support all of the operating expenses that a major publishing house has. My costs for maintaining my website are low as well because I custom-coded the HTML and everything myself.

Methods to Monetize Your Knowledge

Creating apps and developing tools on the internet is definitely a way you can monetize your knowledge. I often get asked about Pyrls, what is it and what is Cosmas. Cosmas Health is my company where I work with others to build medical information products for clinicians.

The most popular feature of Pyrls, and what was a big inspiration for me in creating it, is wanting a better resource for counseling points. Users always praise the counseling points because it is such a valuable resource. I've learned when building a product to scope it as specifically as possible. If I were to start Pyrls over, I would probably have started with only diabetes drug reference because that's what people care most about. Pyrls is divided into four big sections, but right now, it seems that diabetes medication information is what most people care about. Focusing your scope is really important; the more specific, the better.

Two is Better than One: Build Your Product or Service

I knew after graduating that in the years that followed, I wanted to start my own company. The opportunity actually came sooner than expected, and that would not have been able to happen without something I want to talk about today: embracing technological skills, which melded perfectly with my pharmacy knowledge.

And the truth is, when it comes to being a pharmacist, I'm a 5/10. As a software engineer, I'm a 5/10. As a marketer or as a designer, I'm a 5/10. But by having knowledge of multiple fields, without being an expert in any singular field, I am able to do what I do now. Someone who is 10/10 when it comes to being a pharmacist but a 0/10 engineer could not do what I do, and vice versa. Embracing the variety of knowledge I have has been critical to my success.

Why is that? I'm a builder at heart. I'm sure many people reading this can resonate with that because those are the kind of people who will be attracted to a book like this. That's why you're trying to learn how to turn your passion into a business. What I mean when I say I'm a builder is that if I had been dropped in a different century, I would probably be a sculptor; I would be creative.

And creativity can be uncommon in our industry; we have to discover innovative ways to express our creativity. Website development is a passion of mine, and I got really deeply involved in it. And part of why I was so drawn to it was because of how fast the iteration cycle is. Anyone who has ever worked on their own website, no matter how you've done it, knows this. You're making changes to the page right in front of you. By embracing that technology, you can see your vision come to life right away. It's a positive feedback cycle.

That is an example of how I love to build. And I love to think of it as sculpting; you're creating a vision out of a block of stone. I love that.

Part of why I wanted to be an entrepreneur was so that I could tap into that creative side.

I really want to encourage pharmacists to embrace technological skills wherever they can. I would highly encourage you to do it yourself. There is nothing wrong with doing it yourself. There is nothing holding you back from getting out there and starting to build what you have been working on.

The traditional thinking is that you need a partner who knows how to do programming, or you need to hire a consulting agency to do it for you. We think of technology as a foreign skill. But no one bats an eye when they see a PharmD/MBA or a PharmD/JD or a PharmD/MPH or a PharmD/Ph.D. That's considered normal, whereas learning about programming is still thought to be impossible. But as pharmacists, many of us did dual degrees; technology is just another domain in which you can build your expertise.

Finding the best starting point for building technological skills depends on what you do. I own a website called Pharmacist.dev, and I wrote a blog post a little while ago that directly answers this question if you are interested in learning more. But the first thing is knowing what you want to do. Broadly speaking, there are three paths: website development, data analytics, or something else. You want to tailor what skills you learn to align with what it is you actually want to do.

For myself, I started learning website development, even though as a pharmacist, if you're trying to get a job in technology, data analytics is probably the best skill to learn. There are more careers in that area and people hiring for that specific skill set, whether it be pharmacy benefit managers, health systems, informatics. If you're trying to find a career in pharmacy, learning data analytics is likely the most helpful. But the same way there are subcommunities in pharmacy: community pharmacy or hospital pharmacy, there are subcategories in technology. But I knew from the get-go that I wanted to work in website development, so that is what I pursued. There were websites that I wanted to build, so I began learning the necessary skills.

I would say that if you're interested in learning, you should be honest about if you actually enjoy it. Don't spend all of your time coding if you don't find it fun. One really problematic thing for me in running my business is I can't stand keeping books; that is something I personally outsource, the financial side of things. So, by all means, pursue the things you enjoy but don't force yourself to do something you don't like when you can hire someone else to do it. Yes, develop the skills you need to do things yourself, but play to your strengths.

Advice for Aspiring Entrepreneurs

In terms of building your technological skills, there are a couple of ways I would think about it. There are different skills you can learn, all of which are really helpful—identifying what you want to learn more about, whether it's website or app development or data analytics. Even becoming really well-versed in a commonly used software program is a valuable skill. Being a Microsoft Excel wiz is really powerful. Truthfully, data analysts spend most of their time in Microsoft Excel or on a similar high-level program. Familiarizing yourself with these programs can be incredibly helpful.

My advice is to learn the skills to help you accomplish what you're trying to build, but it's equally important to feel like you're being productive with your time and learning things that you find interesting. You only have one life to live.

Even that can provide other challenges, too, however, especially when it comes to growing your business. I know for myself that I enjoy coding so much that I'm very hesitant to let it go. Learning how to be a manager is a challenge for everyone. I hired a few interns a few months ago, and I apologized in advance. I said, "You're going to help teach me how to be a manager and how to delegate responsibilities."

Everything comes with new and unique challenges, but whatever it is you want to do, launch it. There's a phrase in startups, "launch before you have your password reset page done." And the point of this expression is you should not build your password reset page until you're getting so many emails from people needing to reset their password that it's worth your time. There are so many more important things to be dealing with in creating a website; you don't have to wait until every little detail is perfected for you to launch.

**Derek Borkowski,
PharmD**

CONTRIBUTOR
CONNECTION

www.pyrls.com

www.linkedin.com/in/derek-borkowski/

DELON CANTERBURY

Biography

Dr. DeLon Canterbury is a Board Certified Geriatric Pharmacist. He founded GeriatRx, which is a telehealth-based Medication Deprescribing and Senior Care consulting company focused on advocating for older patients. GeriatRx combines pharmacogenomic testing, comprehensive medication management, drug cost savings to address social determinants of health, such as food, shelter, financial stability, and health literacy. He helps patients who are struggling to achieve their healthcare goals and improve their quality of life by reducing high-risk medication use and polypharmacy in seniors. GeriatRx not only provides 1:1 patient-centered concierge pharmacist services but teaches other senior care providers, clinicians, home health agencies, nursing homes, retirement living communities, and caregiver advocacy groups how to leverage their pharmacist and provide value-based care through his Deprescribing Accelerator program. He is an Executive Board member of the African-American COVID task force (AACT+) in Durham, North Carolina, a formulary committee member for Senior PharmAssist in Durham, and served as the Community Health Coalition telehealth director, serving low-income senior African-American patients with health, wellness, and reassurance checkups during COVID.

Entrepreneurial Journey

My story really began with my two parents, Stanley and Sandra Canterbury, who emigrated to the US from Guyana, South America, in the early 1980s. My Caribbean background sparked my initial interest in understanding natural medicine and herbal products extensively used in Guyana for healing a number of illnesses in my childhood.

Unfortunately, my entrepreneurial journey began with a point of pain and frustration with the direction of retail pharmacy. Working as a Walgreens Pharmacy Manager, I felt completely unfulfilled and depressed with my role at a high-volume store. I believed I wasn't helping patients the way our pharmacist license had meant for us to fully do. I wanted to have a lasting impact and instead grew tired, frustrated, and angry with our healthcare system, especially when it came to health barriers for Black, Latino, and senior populations. I never felt so hopeless within my entire career, and it was even more frustrating hearing what patients had to go through before getting to the pharmacy counter.

It was this feeling that pushed me to start GeriatRx, focusing on providing comprehensive care while emphasizing cost savings and medication deprescribing for overmedicated seniors. I constantly remain active within the Durham community by guest speaking and conducting a webinar series called "Drugs with Dr. DeLon," focusing on Medication Management and COVID updates for church panels, town halls, caregiver support groups, and senior care organizations locally and nationally while Helping seniors suffering in isolation.

This led to me becoming a paid guest speaker and being featured on international podcasts. I have had multiple news media features, and GeriatRx is becoming known as a caregiver advocate and supporter. I had no idea this journey would take me here. Pharmacists are so valuable, and we should be portrayed just as ubiquitously within the media. This could really impact care. I've met people who have con-tacted me through WhatsApp or GroupMe because of things I would post just to inform the public. You have to use your voice to serve; that is our secret power as pharmacists. Everything I do on a day-to-day basis is informed by servant leadership.

Methods to Monetize Your Knowledge

I monetize my knowledge in my business by offering coaching packages. This is an all-encompassing package; customers will have me on retainer for 90 days. It begins with an initial comprehensive medication review. From there, we incorporate genetic testing. It's also important to develop a rapport in regard to what the patient knows at baseline to assess gaps in their social determinants of health. We need to identify what they do and do not know. We start with patient education; we do a social determinants of health assessment. With that, we are looking to see; are there any financial barriers to this person's care? Are there any transportation issues? Are there health literacy issues? Do their caregivers have support? We really try to make it a holistic package.

The next steps are to communicate any areas that need improvement to the doctor and come up with a plan that is personalized for the patient's needs. It usually tends to take three months to get these things, and the patient can choose to continue our service after three months. My goal is to build a relationship with the providers so that they are all in accordance and can provide the team-based care that I feel healthcare is lacking. Every patient receives a customized retainer package that is based on their individual needs.

Why I Stepped Down from My 6-Figure Salary

I was working as a retail pharmacy manager, but what I really enjoyed was serving people, and I felt this was something I was lacking in my job. For example, I served at several career and health fairs at a local middle school in Henderson, NC., and helped to volunteer with local HIV Awareness community-based organizations. These were the events that really brought me joy. But day-to-day work was just not for me. I did not feel like I was doing what I was intended to do. I felt like I was a passenger in my own life.

I'm sure everyone at some point in their life has had that feeling of waking up Monday morning and not wanting to face the day. That was me every day, standing for hours with no break and no end in sight at the corner of depression and insanity. I was so disenchanted with our healthcare system. It just became incredibly apparent that we were operating as a part of an expensive and unsustainable health care model that has worse outcomes significantly for Black, Latino, and senior patients, and we pretend that medical racism and ageism doesn't exist within health care. Patients need pharmacists as they can't manage their own meds their side effects, all while trying to navigate this system.

It was this frustrating feeling that pushed me to launch GeriatRx. I truly believe that in our current healthcare system, we are overmedicated. I feel that costs are going up, and pharmacists have a valuable opportunity to be a liaison for patients and push health care to unfathomable heights when we work at the top of our pharmacist license! GeriatRx helps patients get off unnecessary medications focusing on reducing health care costs, preventing harm with medication deprescribing, and improving patient quality of life.

By the grace of God, we've been featured on ABC, Spectrum, PBS "Black Issues Forum," and WRAL NBC. A lot of that came from simply serving my community. I then began with my work on the African-American COVID task force (AACT+). About nine of us here in Durham, North Carolina, saw there was a need for easily accessible COVID testing and vaccinations in Black and Latino communities. Our reach expanded across neighboring counties helping to leverage our connections with Duke Hospital, University of North Carolina Health System, local non-profits, and interfaith communities to dispel COVID misinformation and conduct food drives along with health screenings. Unexpectedly, working in this space has opened up so many doors for GeriatRx and my network of strategic partners, who I am grateful for to this day!

What do we actually do at GeriatRx? We provide comprehensive medication reviews, and this doesn't mean a short MTM. We're talking about identifying social barriers to care. Does the patient have the health and, of course, financial literacy to access and manage their medications? We use pharmacogenomics at the forefront of our deprescribing methodologies along with deprescribing for senior patients. We also provide caregiver support. Caregivers are, unfortunately, some of the most unpaid health workers in our system. They are exhausted and don't have many who advocate for them. With our Deprescribing Accelerator, we look to improve the impact.

If I can leave you with anything, it would be the understanding that our healthcare system is broken. This may be an unpopular opinion, but I believe it is fundamentally true. I want to tell you about my grandmother, Mildred. Nearly 275,000 people die from medication mismanagement each year. And Mildred was very nearly one of them. We spend so much money on our health system that we waste half a trillion dollars due to mismanaged meds and suboptimal treatments.

When Mildred was sick, my parents struggled to figure out what was wrong. It turns out a nursing home prescriber had actually written an inappropriate prescription for behavior management. Unfortunately, the medication was intended for chemical sedation, and her initial mild cognitive impairment was exacerbated to totally severe. Once she was given that medication, she was inevitably kicked out of the very same nursing home that had written it, forcing my parents to take her in from Brooklyn to Atlanta, Ga. They were overwhelmed, completely stressed out, and didn't have anyone to advocate for them. All it took to fix the situation was one pharmacist in a community setting to advocate and fight back against this unnecessary prescription.

Thankfully, Mildred lived to see 90, that prescription was stopped, and her symptoms were resolved. Her trials are exactly what inspired me to start my company GeriatRx. Focusing on precision medicine, deprescribing, and most importantly, identifying social barriers to care has led to my success today with GeriatRx and servant leadership.

What is the point of being a pharmacist if you're not serving your community, your people, your patients? And I don't mean fake serving; I mean providing lasting impact. What is Pharmacy for, if not that? One of our hallmark cases was a patient who was struggling with being overprescribed. She was on 36 medications. We were able to get her down to 8 medications while also keeping her from being involuntarily committed to a nursing home. Not only that, but in doing so, we saved her well over $150,000 and helped her get her life back, just like my grandmother Mildred did.

I can't lie; I've done a lot of things wrong personally and in business. I thought for a long time that being a pharmacy manager, being a poison control pharmacist, getting my BCGP would be the end all be all. But I ultimately knew I wasn't putting myself first. I thought that achieving these career goals would equate to happiness in life, but it never did because, in truth, I wasn't living for myself. I was super depressed, super anxious, and worst yet, I hated myself. I wasn't doing something I loved. I started focusing on how I could serve my community.

Now, I do teaching and educational events with nursing homes, caregiver groups, dementia, and support groups across the triangle. A part of my toolbox that has made me successful in this area, which I would never have anticipated, is using the media, particularly when it comes to positioning yourself as an authority. Being fluent at mastering my own story, being bold, and not being afraid to share the work that I'm doing has served me best. When you're serving people from the heart, people know that you're not just clout chasing. I've learned how to brand myself and how to leverage my knowledge.

I've been featured on some amazing podcasts; I've worked with folks from The Happy PharmD. I actually just finished wrapping up an appearance on PBS. This is the second time I've been on PBS talking about COVID; learning how to leverage television as well has been helpful. What it really comes down to is building relationships. I can easily call the producer for the PBS show and say, "Hey, I've got someone for you." or "I can talk to your audience about this." They've actually agreed to have me on to discuss overprescribing in the near future, which is going to be great for building GeriatRx's brand.

I've also learned how to leverage health blog sites and got GeriatRx highlighted on several sites to discuss precision medicine, deprescribing, and caregiver advocacy. I've been on radio stations in NC and Chicago. This has been pivotal in working to dispel covid vaccine barriers and reaching marginalized communities. I always use these opportunities to tell my story, share my passion and inspire those by what happened to my grandmother, and unveil how there are still so many people dealing with this who don't know where to turn or who to ask.

I've written health blogs, posts, and news articles for known insurance companies. I've learned how to use my Alma Mater to become a highlighted alumnus. These are little steps I've learned along the way about how to maneuver the media. The most important thing I want to convey is that servant leadership has led to growing and building long-lasting relationships with amazing people along the way. The primary goal has always been to be a community advocate and a resource for those who may have questions, and that just so happened to be good for business.

GeriatRx has been featured at community health fairs, Lions Clubs, rotary clubs, church panels. It's about providing a service. When you lead with service, you are able to truly build a lasting impact, and to be completely honest, doors just open for you. That's something I never thought I would experience. I don't want any patient to fall victim to overprescribing as my grandmother did. I don't want anyone to feel the pain that my parents felt for four months when they didn't know where to turn. My grandmother passed away a month after her 90th birthday, after my last day of 4th-year pharmacy rotations, but she would not have lived that long had it not been for the pharmacist who advocated for her five years prior.

When I give talks, I tell people, "Not all medications are safe. You may have a family member, you may have someone you know who is dealing with this, and if you want an objective, unbiased opinion, you need to foster a relationship with your pharmacist. I'll be more than happy to take or make a referral to help any of your loved ones." More importantly, joining the Deprescribing Accelerator is one for others to excel in their deprescribing skills within senior populations.

Advice for Aspiring Entrepreneurs

Never be afraid to use your voice or your story when you're advocating for others. Pharmacists are simply brilliant, and we need to tap into our gift beyond just pharmacy but in healthcare as a whole. We often get stuck in our own little bubble listening to that little voice in our head, or we become camera shy, but we all have the power to leverage our voice and grow our profession. I want people to get comfortable using all types of platforms to leverage themselves; this is how you reach more people and build your business.

I would not be where I am today if it wasn't for the servant leadership mentality I've embraced as a part of my business model. My advice is simply to serve from your heart when working with your patients or clients. Serve your community, serve others, and when you become selfless, everything else just falls into place.

CONTRIBUTOR

CONNECTION

DeLon Canterbury, PharmD, BCGP

🌐 www.geriatrx.org

in www.linkedin.com/in/geriatrx/

KELLEY C. CARLSTROM

Biography

Kelley Carlstrom received her doctorate in pharmacy from the University of Colorado and completed her postgraduate residency training at Beth Israel Deaconess Medical Center and the Dana Farber Cancer Institute in Boston. She's a board-certified oncology pharmacist that has worked in a variety of traditional and non-traditional settings. This includes a large academic medical center, where she specialized in blood and marrow transplantation, a small community hospital, and as a consultant for a large electronic medical record implementation. Most recently, she has worked in the healthcare technology industry, helping build technology products for oncology clinicians and patients. Kelley is passionate about oncology and sees a growing need for more pharmacists to be trained in this specialty. She supports these pharmacists through unique oncology training opportunities because she believes every pharmacist deserves access to specialty training that can transform their career.

Entrepreneurial Journey

My pharmacy entrepreneurial journey started in 2018, but looking back, I realize I have had entrepreneurial experiences that I hadn't thought about since committing to pharmacy as a profession. After making a leap into a nontraditional role, I started recognizing there were oncology pharmacists that needed support in learning this complicated specialty. I had a lot of ideas but didn't know what to do with them or what my next steps were. Thankfully, I stumbled upon the Medipreneurs Summit and found a group of like-minded people. I didn't know what to expect when I showed up there, but as I talked to other passionate people, I started piecing together my ideas into something I could take action on. The journey to becoming an entrepreneur has been absolutely fascinating!

The big 'Why' of my business is about supporting pharmacists in oncology. There is elitism in our profession that tells us only residency-trained pharmacists can, and should, work in oncology. But that's complete hogwash because there are tons of pharmacists working in oncology without residency training, and I strongly believe any pharmacist can learn oncology with the right support—we are a profession of self-learners! Supporting these pharmacists on their oncology journey is why I created KelleyCPharmD.

Methods to Monetize Your Knowledge

I monetize my knowledge through oncology training programs. Pharmacists hire me to help them develop their baseline oncology knowledge to be more confident at work, to take better care of their patients, and to pass the BCOP exam.

I currently work with pharmacists in two ways that both include access to a robust eight-month online training program. My clients can elect a self-paced program where they have lifetime access to go through all the materials, including practice questions, or a support program where they get access to myself and other experienced oncology pharmacists to guide them on their journey. We have a community to interact with others in the program and regular office hours calls to answer questions on the course materials. Building a community of oncology pharmacists that is engaging and supportive is my north star.

Career Risk: Terrifying or Motivating?

Talking about career risk is important to me because although I've taken many risks in my career, I never thought that I would, and I wish

I had started sooner!

I have always been risk-averse, rightly so for patient care reasons. But in truth, being risk-averse in our career path is not a great quality to have in our field. Let's actually talk about what constitutes risk. Risk is defined as "a situation involving exposure to danger, or the process of exposing somebody or something to danger, harm, or loss." Now, this sounds pretty terrible. No wonder nobody wants to take risks! Well, I'd like to present a new definition of risk that better fits the context of this conversation. Risk is an action that makes you feel uncomfortable but exposes you to something new and potentially valuable. What this means is that risk is not universal; what may be risky to me is not necessarily risky to you.

For example, after graduating from pharmacy school in Colorado, I moved to Boston to do residency training. Some people might think moving halfway across the country and living on a resident's salary with a mountain of student loan debt was risky, but it didn't feel risky to me. I then moved from Boston to Cleveland for my first post-residency job. Even my dentist in Boston thought that was risky. I got a lot of, "You're moving to Cleveland? What's wrong with you?" That didn't feel risky to me either.

The first thing I encountered in my career that felt like a big risk was when I was recruited into a consulting role for an electronic medical record (EMR) implementation. It felt risky for a couple of reasons. First, I was leaving direct patient care and essentially giving up on the goal I had worked towards for ten-plus years. The second reason it felt risky was that it was pretty unstable. It was a job with few benefits, and it was project-based. Essentially, when I did good work and finished the project, I put myself out of a job. It was very different from the work an oncology pharmacist typically does.

One great thing that came out of me taking that risk was that I realized I had a love for oncology and technology that I never knew was there before. I didn't get to flex those skills enough in my patient care role, so when I was looking for a new full-time role, I specifically looked for that industry that would lead me to the world of startups, another risky sector!

In truth, I think I'm becoming a little bit addicted to career risk because I have found that there are so many good things that come out of it. This is what I really wanted to talk about. It is well known that the pharmacy profession is not the same now as it has been in the past. As a profession, it's fundamentally changed. We all need to find our own ways to adapt to this. I think there are a couple of things that pharmacists who have been successful in adapting have been willing to do. Now, I say "willing" here as a caveat. Willing does not mean that you're convinced of these things or even that you're at all confident, but it means you do them anyway.

You change and adapt. Those are common ones but important. Nobody wants to be the pharmacist who is white-knuckled, hanging on for dear life. You want to learn new skills, whether that's clinical skills, functional medicine, pharmacogenomics, oncology, or operational skills. Whatever it is, you want to learn new things that will bring value to your patients, to the clients you serve, and to the profession at large. And this involves taking risks. What I never realized before was that stepping off a cliff not knowing what is beneath you opens your eyes to doors you never saw before; you need that jolt of perspective to see a different reality.

You will not have all the answers, but nobody has all the answers. You need to start thinking of your career as a journey rather than a destination. You'll constantly be learning during every step you take. I want you to consider your situation. Are you risk-tolerant or risk-averse? Think about the context of your career but also your day-to-day life. Some people may be more risk-averse when it comes to work than they are to life. You may skip preventive visits to the doctor. You may occasionally text while driving. To some people, karaoke might be risky.

When it comes to making risky career moves, there are always reasons why you may not want to do it. Maybe your family situation makes it difficult, or you have limited location mobility, maybe you have limited free time. You could be caring for children or parents. What about your financial situation? Is it conducive to taking risks? Maybe there is no wiggle room for emergencies. Your ego can also get in the way of taking a risk.

I know a lot of pharmacists who refuse to change along with the industry. They think, "That won't happen to me," or "I don't need to change," or "I can wait it out until retirement." Or it could be the opposite; people doubt themselves and their ability to take those chances. "Who am I to do this thing?", "Who am I to start this business?", "Who am I to support XYZ?" The fear of the unknown is incredibly powerful if you let it be.

I encourage you to look at your current job situation and evaluate how happy or miserable you are. What are your career goals? Do you have a plan? Many people have one distant career goal they've held on to for so long that it makes it very difficult to pivot. What about expectations? Where are you supposed to be? What responsibilities do you have? That can come from family or colleagues.

I did my residency training, I got the job I was supposed to get, and I was supposed to be happy with it. But when I wasn't, I felt guilty. What about leaving behind coworkers or unfinished projects? I know a colleague who just left direct patient care in the middle of an EMR implementation. Leaving people hanging is not a great feeling, even if you are doing it for the right reasons. I want you to think about risk. If you took that risky move that you've been thinking about, or maybe that's been roaming around in your subconscious, what is the worst thing that could happen?

When I began thinking about my consulting role, the worst thing that I could think of was that I would get there, they would realize I had none of the skills they wanted, and I would get fired. And that outcome seemed plausible because the hospital I worked at had Epic, and I was hired to do a Cerner Implementation—I knew nothing about Cerner.

But in being able to identify that as the worst possible outcome, I could then ask myself what I would do if that happened. I would look for another job since I'm not independently wealthy. I could go back to my previous job, or I could find another job. I was able to talk through that and verbalize it. Yes, you may lose money, you may feel like a failure for a little while, there may be financial instability or embarrassment. But being able to name the risk stops it from being all-consuming and terrifying and allows you room to make a contingency plan.

We all have biases when it comes to making big decisions. A bias many of us have is assuming we can't fix the situation. We assume it's a one-way door, and once we make that decision, there is no going back. And that's just not true. The vast majority of the doors we walk through are two-way doors. We don't usually regret the things we did because even if we make a mistake, we can fix it. I could get another job in patient care. It's the things we don't do that we regret. These are the doors we truly can't go back through.

How can you get around these feelings of risk? You really have to think about what is going to make you feel more confident. We're each individual people, and walking off a risky ledge is challenging. One thing that can help is cleaning up your financial house. Having a strong sense of your finances and a plan for what to do with them can make an otherwise uncertain journey much easier.

Talk about your plans and ideas out loud. Oftentimes, if you leave the thought in your head, you can convince yourself it is ridiculous when it's not. I remember explaining my oncology training program idea, and someone responded, "It's like a virtual residency."

I said, "Yes. That's exactly what it is." Saying thoughts out loud can be really helpful.

In the pharmacy profession, we tend to run away from things we fear. I often get messages on LinkedIn from pharmacists who say, "I just want to do anything except what I'm doing right now." And the truth is, that is running away out of fear. That is not running towards something you want. In order to move forward, you need to shift the way you look at things.

I read an interesting article that talked about keeping your world small because it is so easy to get lost in the day-to-day of what needs to be done. For example, I have an upcoming launch of the next iteration of my program. I have 200 things I need to get done. And it's overwhelming to think even weeks into the future. Instead, I try to work in terms of day-to-day tasks. If even that is too much, I break it down into very tiny chunks. What is your most important next step? What can you get done today? What can you do in the next six hours to make your workload feel less overwhelming?

It's easy to get stuck in the planning and idea phases because when it comes to actually putting something out into the world, it's really scary. But you have got to do it, and you learn so much by doing it. Successful people have an inclination towards action.

I had a lot of ideas about how I wanted to support pharmacists in oncology. And because I myself am trained in oncology and knowledgeable about the field, I thought I would do it all myself. I developed this big course and worked on it by myself. And one day, months into the process, I realized, "Why would I do this all by myself?" Just because I can doesn't mean I should. That gave me the idea to reach out to other pharmacists in oncology who are looking for extra income. That made me realize that I'm not just supporting pharmacists wanting to learn about oncology but also supporting pharmacists in oncology by paying them to help me create content and deliver value to the pharmacists in my program.

You're not going to be good at everything, and you're not going to want to do everything. Figure out the things that you're not good at, or you don't enjoy and have other people do them for you. Follow your curiosity because the truth is there are so many amazing things that happen when you allow yourself to take risks, whether that is going into an entrepreneur business pathway or stepping into a new role. There are so many avenues you can take, and those will show themselves when you pursue your curiosities. You would be surprised at what asking, "I wonder what that's about," can lead you to. And of course, if one of your interests is oncology, I would love to support you in taking that leap.

Advice for Aspiring Entrepreneurs

I want to encourage all pharmacists to assess their risk tolerance and what they would need to feel comfortable taking on more risk. Perhaps it's having a bigger emergency fund or living close to family for additional support if needed.

I can see clearly now that the pivotal moment in my career was when I finally took a consulting role after three months of dragging my feet. It felt scary as hell. But I talked it through, and in all honesty, the benefits barely outweighed the risks. I could tell that this was one of those opportunities where I had no idea how many doors were going to open because of it; I saw potential.

The potential that role had was showing me how to solve problems from a business perspective. As a full-time employee, I took care of patients all day. I had never really considered my role in the broader issues of healthcare. It was taking that job that taught me how to think about value propositions. What value do I bring? It wasn't directly linked to my hourly wage. The value I brought in that role was getting their multimillion-dollar project completed faster. The amount of money I saved them was way beyond my salary.

What value can you bring to the world? Pharmacists are highly skilled professionals, and I can assure you there is something valuable hanging out inside your head. Whether that turns into a business idea or pushes you towards a new position that lights you up doesn't matter. It's a disservice to the profession not to let that value out. Let it shine!

CONTRIBUTOR
CONNECTION

Kelley C. Carlstrom, PharmD, BCOP

www.kelleycpharmd.com

www.linkedin.com/in/kelleydcarlstrom/

LAUREN CASTLE

Biography

Lauren Castle is a pharmacist and founder of the Functional Medicine Pharmacist Alliance© (www.fmpha.org). She received her Doctorate in Pharmacy from Ohio Northern University in 2013 and her Master of Science in Human Nutrition and Functional Medicine from the University of Western States in 2018. Lauren has also completed training through the Institute for Functional Medicine, the School of Applied Functional Medicine, and Functional Medicine University.

Entrepreneurial Journey

As far as being an entrepreneur, it's something I have always been fairly close to throughout my career in pharmacy. When I was 16 years old, I worked for an independent pharmacy, and my dream was to own my own pharmacy one day. After that, I decided to go to pharmacy school. As fate would have it, it was in pharmacy school that I met my husband. We ended up moving, and I had to get a job outside of the independent pharmacy I had worked at for all of those years. In doing that, I thought I would try something that was the complete opposite, just to gain experience.

That was how I ended up with a summer internship at Walmart, thinking I would probably hate it and go back to my dream of owning a pharmacy. But ten years later, I am still pursuing my entrepreneurial dreams. I know Pharmfluencers talk a lot about being an entrepreneur and an intrapreneur, and I can thoroughly say that I am both.

I think it is actually a very important point to remember if you are trying to look for a career in entrepreneurship or intrapreneurship: you don't have to pick a side. You can definitely do both. There is truly a spectrum of opportunities available in pharmacy and in the field of functional medicine. So for me, working as a pharmacist at Walmart was actually how I got started in functional medicine. I was working in the middle of the Flint Water Crisis and seeing patients come in with lead toxicity. I had no idea how to treat that as a pharmacist; lead toxicity wasn't a topic covered in school.

That is really what sparked my journey into functional medicine: learning about these new concepts and pursuing the education that I did not get in pharmacy school.

Methods to Monetize Your Knowledge

After discovering functional medicine and learning about it, I was trying to connect with other pharmacists who were in this space because it was so new. I didn't know anyone else who was interested in it, or doing it, or trying to figure out how to apply that knowledge as a pharmacist. Through the Ohio Pharmacists Association, I gave a CE presentation at their annual convention in 2017. Afterward, I had tons of pharmacists coming up to me and saying, "We're super interested in this." or "We'd love to learn more. Where can we learn more and stay connected?"

And that is how Functional Medicine Pharmacists started out: as just a Facebook group with maybe 30 of us in it. We were just trying to stay connected and talk about functional medicine and how we were using it. From there, it continued to grow as more and more pharmacists discovered functional medicine, many of them through their own personal health journeys or through patients who were asking about it.

Four years after I originally launched the Facebook group, we have over 2,600 pharmacists in it. Last year during the pandemic, I officially launched The Functional Medicine Pharmacist Alliance as a business. For three years, my work of building that community was not monetized at all. Hindsight really is 2020 because looking back;

I realize what holds so many people back is taking that first step—taking that first initial action.

For me, that was a big piece of it. I thought, "Oh, I don't need to make this into a business" or "People aren't going to pay money to join another pharmacy organization." People have so many complaints about them as is; they don't want to pay more dues or go through membership steps. I had all of these limiting beliefs about why I couldn't start a pharmacy organization. I think, in many ways, the pandemic really put that fear behind me. Suddenly it became clear how needed it was.

For so many pharmacists, what holds them back is not knowing how they should take action to fulfill their dreams. For me, that was it; I saw this group had the potential to grow. I realized that if I am limiting myself, I am also limiting other pharmacists from being able to discover functional medicine. When you think about scaling, that is what ends up being a big motivator. You realize the impact and reach you can have, is only going to happen when you start taking those steps to actually expand the dream. With that comes the entrepreneurial piece of it.

It is often said, "no margin, no mission" When you charge someone for something, you make that resource into a gift; it becomes something valuable. You're sharing your insights, and people want and need that. I clearly identified an area of need and interest, and it was something I was passionate about.

Functional Medicine: Disrupting the "Pill for an Ill" Model

For pharmacists getting into functional medicine, one question that always comes up is how these things can coexist. And when I first started this journey and was actually trying to figure out how I could make this work as a retail pharmacist, I was still working at Walmart, and I would have lots of patients come up to me and say, "I don't want to be taking medicine."

I really used that as my jumping-off point. The pill for an ill model doesn't truly serve patients. Patients rarely ever come up and say, "I'm so happy to be coming to the pharmacy and picking up my medication today." We experience that every day as pharmacists. We know our patients are struggling with the pill burden, so deprescribing is a really powerful tool to be used in pharmacies today. That is the first step I recommend to pharmacists who say, "How can I get involved in functional medicine?" Although most pharmacists are not ready to take the leap and become an entrepreneur and try to build a private practice, whether it's a brick-and-mortar practice or online, it all starts with mindset.

You can talk to your patients about how the pill for an ill model is not going to help them get better. There is so much more to their health that they haven't been told. Thyroid Disease is a really common example. So many patients think that they are just going to have to keep taking thyroid medication forever. It's not that we are saying drugs are bad or that you shouldn't use them. Modern medicine is truly a miracle and is life-sustaining for so many different conditions. But there is also so much power in food as medicine and in lifestyle as medicine. As pharmacists, we are perfectly equipped to be able to take those little moments and instill that hope into our patients.

Ask patients, "Has your doctor ever talked to you about lifestyle changes?" or "might there be other causes for your conditions?" Whether it's diabetes, heart disease, or thyroid, all of these different health troubles have lifestyle components. Using a functional medicine approach simply means getting to the root cause of that particular patient's condition. The next step is how you dig into that. If you have a patient who understands and doesn't want to simply rely on a pill anymore, then they have that buy-in to create a therapeutic partnership with their pharmacist and physician. How can you all work together to unravel the story of that patient's illness? That is really what the functional medicine approach is.

A lot of people will ask, "Do I have to get certified in some way?" "Do I have to go through training?" Or even "Do I have to change my career altogether?" The answer is no. Really, functional medicine is just a lens or process that you can apply to your pharmacy practice. When you are looking at really assessing the patient and identifying what is going on there, the next step is to develop a treatment plan instead of simply dispensing a pill. It is taking that clinical knowledge and putting the puzzle pieces together to be able to create a plan for your patient. I find that really exciting.

For many pharmacists, you're looking at adding all of these additional revenue streams; clinical services PGX testing; all of these can serve as a piece of the puzzle for patients who aren't getting better from a single pill. Testing is another area; more and more, we see tests becoming open to consumers themselves. We may think that we are limited as pharmacists in that arena, but that is changing. Knowledge is power. Whenever we can understand what is actually happening inside the human body through testing, we get a better picture of what the patient needs.

You can partner with a physician to create a collaborative practice and order labs, or you can actually sign up directly with certain companies and order labs for patients as well. These are all pieces of the puzzle; it's just a matter of making yourself aware of them and incorporating them into your practice.

Another element where I see a lot of pharmacists struggle is that they feel overwhelmed as they are going through this process of change management themselves. They're realizing, "Okay, I have this new way I can practice, but how do I actually take action?" How can you get past the feeling of being overwhelmed? That's really why I believe in the Functional Medicine Pharmacist Alliance, to help you plug in and connect with pharmacists who are facing the same challenges are also starting their journey in using functional medicine and can help you along the way. Whether it is connecting with people in your individual state or people in your particular pharmacy practice setting, there are a multitude of different ways you can utilize this resource.

I mentioned earlier; my background is in retail, so oftentimes, that is what I will speak to. But, we also have pharmacists who practice in physician's offices through collaborative practices. We have pharmacists practicing online through virtual practices. We have pharmacists who have independent pharmacies and have a brick-and-mortar establishment. Even within hospitals, there are ways to apply a functional medicine approach. There are so many different ways; it's just a matter of choosing what really lights you up. What do you get excited about?

Another thing I have noticed is that when pharmacists do start to feel overwhelmed, it is because the field is so general. Dr. Hyman refers to it as "super generalist." You really do need to have a knowledge of how everything is interconnected. And sometimes, that can feel overwhelming. But, I also think most pharmacists will have a few smaller areas that they are particularly passionate about. For some people, it might be metabolic health, hormones, or environmental illness. There are many different areas, and you can take that passion and hone it.

When you do that, you're actually identifying your own target market, your ideal clients, or patients. From there, it's just a matter of taking that next step and putting yourself out there. Actually saying, "Yes, I'm going to do this." Again, that can be really scary, but we all have this amazing knowledge, and it's just a matter of putting it into application. There are so many patients out there who are searching for this knowledge and this information, who are searching for someone like you to help them along their journey.

That was what I really wanted to establish in my business; a community so everyone can benefit because there is so much you can learn from others. How can we learn from one another? How can we build each other up and find that connection so we can advance the profession as a whole? There are so many different entrepreneurial models out there that are going to shake up our profession. How we see healthcare as a whole does need to undergo a transformation.

That is a big passion of mine: how we can change the medical model itself and begin to integrate these different lifestyle practices into the mainstream. It is part of my mission, integrating pharmacy and functional medicine, knowing that even within the functional medicine world, pharmacists are highly underrepresented. The first few conferences I went to for functional medicine, I was the only pharmacist in the room. There were all types of practitioners there; doctors, nurses, nurse practitioners, PAs, acupuncturists, chiropractors, nutritionists, and all these different professions. We were all coming together with the same goal of transforming healthcare because we knew that the model was sick. It's perpetuating a baseline level of functioning, and it's not actually helping people achieve the true outcomes of optimal health.

We need pharmacists to be able to be part of this movement because we have accessibility, and we have touchpoints with patients much more frequently than many other healthcare providers. We also are at this really unique turning point in our own profession, so if we can all come together and combine these different momentums, I believe that it has the power to really transform and change our profession as well.

That is a big part of why and how we can transform our own profession and set ourselves up as experts of medication, but also as functional medicine experts.

Advice for Aspiring Entrepreneurs

Obviously, I am a little bit biased, but the Functional Medicine Pharmacists Alliance was really created for the purpose of giving aspiring entrepreneurs and established entrepreneurs a landing page of where to start their journey with functional medicine. In our membership, we have two different options. One is our regular membership, where you get access to our members-only website. We're constantly adding new information. I have about 12 hours' worth of free video content on the website, along with previous lectures I have given on functional medicine. There are also links to free training through some of the different organizations that we've partnered with.

We also have a membership option with the Institute for Functional Medicine. It actually took creating FMPhA to get functional medicine pioneers to pay attention and realize that they need to bring pharmacists into the fold. They now realize that they need pharmacists as part of their functional medicine teams. Members can also get a 20% discount on their foundational training program called AFMCP, which is Applying Functional Medicine in Clinical Practice. That is actually the biggest discount you will find anywhere, and they are offering it, especially for our group. If you want to take the leap and get into a clinical learning path, AFMCP is what I would recommend. AFMCP was one of the first courses I took as part of my master's program, and it really gave me a solid overview and allowed me to access that clinical knowledge.

One of the biggest barriers we see is getting patients to engage in these conversations in a retail setting, where time with the patient is so limited. One thing we have done is partnered with another organization, which is Functional Medicine CE, run by Melody Hartzler, a fellow pharmacist. We did a training specifically on this topic last summer, and FMPhA members get a 20% discount on those trainings as well. These are fantastic resources to use.

Really what it comes down to, though, is opening up that dialogue and understanding the patient's desire to change. One question I like to ask is, "What is your understanding of how your food, sleep, and lifestyle can impact your health?" I use these open-ended questions and motivational styles of interviewing to get the patient to open up. From there, you can give them little bits of advice. I like to say, "When you come back next month, let's talk about how you can change your sleep patterns or reduce your stress levels to help make you feel better." It starts with taking baby steps along the way.

I also have a free downloadable resource at www.fmpha.org/newsletter, which contains a checklist of six tools you can use to help patients take charge of their health using functional medicine in your pharmacy setting. Whether you're new to functional medicine or you've been practicing for years, this checklist will give you tools to enhance your practice and help your patients. My hope is that every pharmacist can discover functional medicine and the impact that it can have on them both personally and professionally. Functional medicine is truly the future of medicine, and the future is here now.

CONTRIBUTOR CONNECTION

Lauren Castle, PharmD, MS

www.fmpha.org

www.linkedin.com/in/drlaurencastle/

JERRICA DODD

Biography

Dr. Jerrica Dodd is a pharmacist, entrepreneur, coach, and leader. She has been a pharmacist for 24 years and is the Founder and CEO of Your Pharmacy Advocate, LLC©, with a mission of providing pharmacist advocate care for patients seeking better health results. Dr. Dodd has spoken on many stages across the country; she is a coach to women in pharmacy to build businesses and is the Executive Editor of *PharmaSis™ Magazine: Celebrating Women in Pharmacy*. Dr. Dodd gets joy from traveling, reading, cooking, and attending cultural events. Dr. Dodd loves encouraging people to be their best and to get the most out of every opportunity that life presents. Her favorite scripture is Luke 12:48… "to whom much is given, much is required," and Dr. Dodd endeavors to live life giving back from the abundant ways in which she has been blessed.

Entrepreneurial Journey

I could never have imagined that over three years ago, my life would totally change. I have always had a plan. I was going to go into consulting, and I had a three-year plan, and I had hired somebody to make it happen. We had laid it all out perfectly so that when it was time to embark on that journey, everything would have already been prepared. But life doesn't always go as we plan. Anyone over the age of 22 knows this to be true.

I am only 25 (humor), but my life didn't go according to plan, and I ended up having to make a very hard decision to leave my job because of health challenges. Usually, when I talk about this, I say my health called me and said, "Hey, this isn't going to work anymore." I had to make a decision in about 30 days because I was falling asleep while driving, and I don't have narcolepsy, so I knew something was wrong. I knew that if I kept trying to function in that way, I was going to have an accident and end up killing myself or someone else. I knew I had to stop, even though I didn't know what the answer was.

Those were not the greatest circumstances, but looking back, I cannot believe what has happened in the last three years of my career compared to the previous 20. I would never have imagined it. And oftentimes, when we approach our careers as pharmacists, we are very risk-averse. We have to know what is going to happen from the beginning to the end. But when your back is against the wall, when something happens, and you have to make a quick decision, you don't get to figure out all of the calculations. You don't get to measure the doses; you just have to move with it. This is probably the greatest lesson I have learned in a very long time.

The reason for this is that I don't think anything else would have made me move. I was trying to plan it all out. I was trying to make sure I had dotted all my I's and crossed all my T's, and everything was absolutely perfect. But in truth, all that planning was me being scared. I felt that I couldn't do anything unless everything was perfect because I was afraid.

Methods to Monetize Your Knowledge

I've been trained in functional medicine, and I have a cash-based wellness business. I take care of patients whose wake-up in the morning problems are a result of their chronic illnesses. Their doctor said, "If you don't do something, you're going to be on insulin."

They come to me and are like, "Hey, can you help me?" These are generally the patients I love seeing because they are also motivated to take charge of their health. In my opinion, our healthcare system does not motivate patients to be in charge of their health. I take care of patients. I also coach women pharmacists as they build their businesses. A lot of times, this coaching ends up being a hybrid of career-life coaching. I really believe that until you put yourself at the center of your brand and at the center of your business, you're not going to succeed. Pharmacists are very good at leading with what they do rather than who they are.

I believe that if you lead with who you are, the people that are meant to work with you and the people you are meant to serve will show up every time. The third part of my business is the magazine I founded. It is to provide an audience as well as a tool for women pharmacists to market themselves. Most women pharmacists have never truly looked at themselves as the CEO of their business. But there is something that happens when you open the page of a magazine and see yourself. It allows you to see yourself as a leader, and so you can use that to market yourself and your business. It also allows these women to tap into my network and market themselves there as well. These are three ways I monetize my knowledge and my skills.

Your Dreams are Urgent: Why Now is the Time for Pharmacists to MOVE!!

Oftentimes as pharmacists, we tend to color between the lines. We don't stray. We don't do anything different. We follow the status quo. And if we do put one foot outside the line, we often worry about what other people think. If you're reading this book, it is likely because you feel a little bit lost. You may not know what to do because your heart is calling you to do something different. But it's not spelled out and becomes a battle between the head and the heart. But the truth is we are all brilliant because we're pharmacists. Each of us has a special place in this profession. These roles may not all look alike, but they are all necessary.

I remember meeting Lauren Castle before she monetized her business, and I am so excited for her. She is one of my favorite pharmacists. I remember Kimber Boothe before she transitioned to her business full-time; I remember her telling me, "I'm going to do it on this date." She actually sent me a message one day and said, "You know what? I did it!" I was like, "Go, girl!"

I met Sue Paul at a conference in Atlanta. As far as I know, we were the only two pharmacists there. But sometimes, you have got to step outside of your comfort zone and do your thing, even if it means being by yourself.

I didn't know then what I do now. But what I would offer you is that you also have to dream. I know it's a crazy word, and we are all analytical pharmacists; we prize analytical thinking. And that works when you are trying not to give someone the wrong dose, but in your life, you have to dream. I know that is a weird statement. You were just reading about functional medicine, and now I am talking about dreaming. But the truth is you cannot fix anyone else's life until you fix your own. You need to dream because if you're not dreaming, what are you doing?

Now you have to promise you won't judge me, but when I was younger, years ago, I wanted to marry Michael Jackson. I wanted to marry Michael Jackson and be a veterinarian so I could help him care for his animals. And you know what? At least I had a dream. This was in middle school, and when I got older, I decided I wanted to be a high school English teacher. I wanted to have my students read novels and diagram sentences. And then, I went on to pharmacy school, and I stopped dreaming. It was a great education, but I stopped dreaming. Somebody said, "Come on in, sit down, let me teach you what I can about being a pharmacist," and I stopped dreaming.

I got out of school, and I finished my residency at The Ohio State, and I was like, "What next?" Well, now I have to get a job. I got that job and once again thought, "What next?" I got another job and another, and here I am, 20 years later, and I had completely stopped dreaming. It took the incident with my health to wake me up and think about, "What do I really want to do next?". Even though I didn't have a blueprint for my unexpected exit, I didn't have it all planned out the way I wanted to; I still had to jump.

I did a video not too long ago where I talked about jumping and that I've been jumping since I was 26 years old, but now I've jumped even higher and further. Yes, I take care of patients too, and it is wonderful. But I promise you've got to get yourself together. I have an acronym for DREAM. D is for Dare. You have to dare to dream. Why were you placed here on this earth? Were you placed here to be a pharmacist? Is that your path? If so, that's excellent, but why are you here? What is your purpose? Sometimes people are afraid to dream; they don't want to tell anybody because they think, "Oh my God, can I really do that?" "What will people say?"

We think of success as credentials. When I talk to pharmacists, they have this credential and that credential and this certification. But in truth, nobody cares. Real success has so much less to do with credentials than you would ever imagine. When you really talk to someone, they put their PharmDs over on the shelf and speak to you human to human. That's not where my success lies; it doesn't have to do with credentials. The R is for Real success. Real.

The next letter in DREAM is E. The E is for Everyone. And I know I am biased, but I truly believe that everyone needs a pharmacist. I'll say it again. Everyone needs a pharmacist. There are so many ways that pharmacists can serve, whether it looks like pharmacy or not. Everyone needs a pharmacist. Understand that there is a place for you and what you're meant to do in this world, whether you do it with a license or not. Everyone needs a pharmacist.

My next letter in DREAM is A, and I say that you would be Amazed at what women pharmacists can create. I have been so amazed over the last three-plus years. And men, I don't mean to leave you out; however, I mostly work with women pharmacists. But male or female, you would be amazed at what a pharmacist can do. If you figure out what your dreams are and then build them.

There are many people that are scared; there are many people that don't know how to do it. But so many pharmacists do stuff like this every day. I want to create a platform to help other pharmacists share their stories. It's not about me. You would be amazed at what a pharmacist can create. I'm already booking features for 2022. Build your dream. Go create it. If you look at the professional world around you and you see a gap, ask yourself, "Can I fill that gap?" "Can I solve that problem?" Don't worry about whether anybody else has solved it before. Don't worry about whether anyone will buy it or not. Because I promise you, they will.

The last letter is M, and it refers to Massive Imperfect Action. That refers to the way I moved in the last three years. I took massive imperfect action. But if I had sat around and tried to keep figuring it out, I never would have accomplished what I have in the last three years of being a full-time entrepreneur. I had to take massive imperfect action.

If you ever watch me when I post on social media, if you read what I post, I promise there are going to be spelling errors from when I first began posting. I promise you there are going to be errors, but you need to get it out. Now I just go back, and I update it. I misspelled things. I typed people's names wrong. And none of it was intentional, but I can go back and fix it. We're going to go with it—massive imperfect action.

If you think long, you'll think wrong. If you sit and you try to figure it out, and you're like, "Well, I don't know..." No. Massive Imperfect Action. Go build what you want. And if you don't know what to do, one of my colleagues says, "confusion is a strategy." If you don't know how, then go find someone who does know how who you can say, "Hey, I need to build this, this, and this," and pay them for their services because you want to be paid for yours.

Take massive imperfect action, go back, and correct it later. The other acronym I want to give is MOVE. When I talk to people, I say, "I believe that there's a bell curve that is happening in our profession. And there are some people who are going to be on the front side of that curve. And they are going to be your movers and shakers, your innovators, disruptors, your entrepreneurs. In the middle are going to be ordinary people. These are the people who will end up paying those at the front of the bell curve. And you will have people at the back of the bell curve, and these are the people who are going to dig their heels in. They are going to remember the good old days of pharmacy and what it used to be like. And the truth is they are not going to leave unless somebody kicks them out, but they're not going to be accomplishing much either. They are not going to be innovating."

Don't worry about the middle or back; you want to make sure you are running at the front of the bell curve. There is so much more that can be done. Every single person has a place. I see this as an opportunity to build whatever it is that you want for your career. When I look at the acronym MOVE, there are certain things I had to do as I transitioned to being an entrepreneur.

I had to M: Make myself a priority. This is difficult because we are used to caring for everyone else, but I had to make myself a priority even when it wasn't always easy. There are going to be people who get upset because you are no longer making them your top priority, and they are no longer reaping the benefits. There are going to be people who are unsure about you because you're changing. But you have to make yourself a priority, even when it is not always easy. You cannot pour from an empty cup. You need your cup to be overflowing so you can pour into others.

O stands for Out there. Oftentimes when I talk to pharmacists, they will say, "Well, let me just look and see what is out there."

I say, "That's great. Look and see what is out there. But you don't necessarily have a prototype to build your dream. It may never have been done before. There may not be someone out there whose example you can follow." There was no functional medicine pharmacist organization before Lauren Castle built hers. She had to build it with no instructions, no prototype, no example. I'm sure she learned from looking at other organizations, but not everything is going to translate perfectly. What I'm saying is you also have to follow your purpose; only your specific purpose can help you build your dreams.

To build what is in your heart, you need to network, to connect. And if someone has done it before, that isn't a cause to worry. There will be people who do it after you too, I promise. It's flattery. Don't worry about what has or has not been built before. Follow your purpose.

V is for Valuing yourself; if you value yourself, others will value you in turn. Oftentimes we look for external validation. But you need to get that validation from yourself first, and then people are going to want you. But if you don't value yourself first, it becomes iffy. Value yourself first, and others will follow.

The last letter is E; Explore what is possible. Many times as humans, we make a lot of judgments. When someone suggests, "Well. What about if you try that?" or, "What if you try it this way?"

Our immediate response is to think, "No, that will never work" You have to explore what is possible. Ask yourself, "Is it possible? Maybe we should try it." DREAM and MOVE are the core ideas of how I follow my career. If you are still in the same place three, six, nine months, a year from now, you're not dreaming, and you're not moving.

Advice for Aspiring Entrepreneurs

I talk about dreams a lot, and I know that makes me a little unconventional. But I really want people to know that their dreams are urgent. And so, if I can leave you with anything, it is that we have seen our world change drastically in the last two years. And even though we have this semblance of going back to normal, it is still going to be different. I promise to you that the pharmacist who is creative will win, not the one who does things according to the status quo. The world is changing, and even though we don't know quite what things are going to look like as times move forward, you can be sure that the pharmacist that is the most creative is going to win.

CONTRIBUTOR
CONNECTION

**Jerrica Dodd,
PharmD**

www.drjerricadodd.com

www.linkedin.com/in/drjdodd

SHANNON EUBANKS

Biography

Shannon Eubanks has spent 20+ years in health and wellness innovation. She is known for progressive thinking and execution in the areas of corporate strategy, product development, operations, strategic partnerships, program management, and customer experience. She has serendipitously leveraged doctorate education and clinical experience to become a strategic advisor for the digital health industry and tech-enabled clinical service delivery. She has a proven track record of scaling operations and leading innovative product development from concept to successful commercialization.

Entrepreneurial Journey

I am generally known as an innovation strategy consultant, but it has taken me a long time to get to where I am today. I have been doing this for over 20 years, and I have learned a lot of lessons. I don't like the word failure at all. I think of those experiences as lessons; it's learning. But it has been a wild ride.

I am PharmD trained; I did a residency, I put in my time, and I have been around a while. But that's to my benefit. I'm starting to understand the healthcare system more holistically as I have gotten further along in my career. I was first introduced to innovative practices in pharmacy when I was at my first job out of my residency. I went to Vanderbilt University Medical Center in Nashville, Tennessee. This is where I am still based today, not at Vanderbilt but at Nashville. At the time, there was a big project going on. Vanderbilt was in the process of digitizing all of its paper charts. They wanted to make the very first electronic health record at their large medical center.

For readers who are old enough to remember, there used to be these handwritten charts, and we would tear off copies. Infectious diseases got green copies, and internal medicine got pink. We had to take these and transfer them into an electronic health record. And truth be told, not many pharmacists were interested, especially twenty-something years ago. But I saw the value of being a part of that project. I was ready to take it on. I wasn't paid as much as my fellow pharmacists at Vanderbilt. At that time, leadership knew this was an important project, but they didn't fund it the way they would today. It was a sacrifice I had to make.

That was the first time I worked with software developers, and I didn't really know what that was back in the day. We didn't call it a startup venture even though it was. That wasn't a term we used back then. Essentially, there was a startup company that joined forces with Vanderbilt medical center, and Vanderbilt supplied the clinicians. We needed someone to build this technology, and I got to see the whole process firsthand.

That was a real game-changer for the rest of my career. I keep going back to that. I sometimes think about how if I had never had that experience, I don't know what my career journey would have been like. I'm very grateful for it. Eventually, I became the program director in organ transplants at Vanderbilt. I got experience in clinical practice, but I was lured into the pharmaceutical industry because I was involved with clinical trials at Vanderbilt.

At the time, it felt like a risk, going into Pharma. A lot of people still think of this term as "the dark side of pharmaceuticals." I disagree with that. I think we should get that out of our heads. There really is no dark side at all. They have intelligent people who make drugs and test them. It's not a bunch of salespeople running around. That's not what the reality is. I was not in charge of selling. I was on the research and development side. With that experience, I spent five years in Pharma. I gathered research and development skills, business skills, marketing skills. And at the time, I didn't realize how much I was gaining.

Well, after I had been working there for a while, I got a call one day, and it was someone who had worked with me in my early days at the Vanderbilt startup joint venture. They said, "Hey, there is this company, and they want to do this pharmacy MTM." It was one of the very first MTM providers; they've since been bought out. But at the time, we were working off of card tables, and I was willing to take on the challenge.

Not very long into the new job, I realized, "Hey. I've done this before. I know how software development works!" And the rest is history. I got to experience that company in its very early days. We built everything from scratch, and I've done that process several times over throughout my career. I've got to have that practice and get better as I go.

I have been a solid founding team member for five startups, and I'm on my fifth one right now. That is my latest kind of project baby. We are in the process of building that company. The goal is to give independent pharmacy owners a leg up in the market. We want them to be able to compete with these big players.

I love to build and create things, so working with startups is really a good fit for me. But the world of startups is not for the faint of heart. You really need to know what you are getting into. They are very high risk. You have to be able to handle those risks. You have to understand what your level of risk adversity is. What are you willing to tolerate? That is a big thing, especially for clinicians and pharmacists. Historically we are very conservative when it comes to risk. It is something to keep in mind. I had to break out of my shell very early on to operate in those spaces.

But I was very wooed by the innovation. It is kind of like a shiny penny. That love of technology gave me something to work towards, but it's not all glamorous. I've done everything from taking out the trash and ordering coffee to meeting with venture capitalists, to showing up and giving presentations at huge meetings, to meeting with customers. You really have to be able to roll up your sleeves and make it happen. And if that isn't the life you want, if that doesn't match your personality, a startup may not be the place for you. It may be more of a sole proprietorship or a consulting business.

I have also done consulting throughout my career. It gets easier as you get more experienced because people will know to come to you. But developing that kind of reputation takes time. You have to be patient. If you're early in your career, you have to put a lot of hard work in.

For me, there was never a big jump ahead; I never fast-forwarded into the thick of it. And then, one day, you look up and realize how far you have come.

Methods to Monetize Your Knowledge

Let's say you've read the Lean Startup Method, you have put your business idea through rigorous experimentation, the product has grown, and it looks awesome. How do you get started? This is where people get stuck. I see this again and again. This is often the moment where I will step in and do some consulting. If you have gotten this far and now you're stuck, that is my sweet spot; that is where I can help you.

When testing and validating a business idea, you should think about your idea through the lens of three things: Desirability, Viability, and Feasibility. Desirability is simply how much do people want this product. Can you create a sustainable business model for this product? Viability is can it work successfully, do you have the operational capabilities for this product to work? Feasibility is whether or not infrastructure is required. How feasible is this idea? Can we even do it? Sometimes when thinking about feasibility, we run into regulations. There are laws all over the place that can really limit feasibility, especially in health care. We have to work within what is feasible.

Once you have worked through and found a solution to these three things, you are ready for the business model canvas. This is very important. If you look it up online, you can find templates and educational content. The business model canvas gives you the structure of a business plan without spending unnecessary valuable time. Early on in your business, you don't have time to waste. The canvas business model supports the big three: Desirability, Viability, and Feasibility.

There are nine elements in the canvas business model that represent key business drivers. The first is the customer segment; you have to know who your customer is. Now you can have more than one customer segment, you can have different types of customers, but you need to identify them.

The next thing to figure out is what is the value proposition for each customer segment. You need to figure out the channels through which your product will arrive in the hands of customers. How are customers going to find you? What are customers going to expect from you? The key to being successful in this step is thinking about it from the customer's perspective.

Next, you are going to want to look at key activities and key resources. This falls in the feasibility section. So, for example, to find your key activities, you would ask, what uniquely strategic things does your business do to deliver its value proposition? What sets you apart from your competitors in the market? What unique assets does your business need in order to compete? What resources do you need in order to fulfill those unique assets?

Next, you will want to think about key partners. Who are you going to partner with? Who is going to handle the elements of the business that you don't want to spend time on? Think about outsourcing, hiring a team; this also applies to external vendors. These are the things you don't want to be wasting your time on. These are the things that somebody else can do for you.

Now within the viability section is the money. Of course, you need to be thinking about revenue streams. How are you getting paid? How is that going to happen? And what is the cost structure of the business? What is it going to cost to make this business a viable success? These are things you need to be thinking about, and these are the things I provide coaching on to help people who are stuck.

Bringing Innovation to Market

Much of what I want to discuss today is through the vantage point of building software as a product. When I say product, it could be a physical product; it could be software; it could be your consulting services. Whatever it is that you're trying to sell.

Before we get into that, however, I'd like to establish some common terms. Firstly, what is a startup? When I say startup, I mean a human institution designed to create a new product or service under conditions of extreme uncertainty. I think the latter part of that is very important to understand. I've had new hires who didn't realize the extreme uncertainty that is present in working for a startup. Perhaps I didn't make that explicitly clear or vet them well enough. Now, when I hire, I make sure we have a conversation about what their tolerance level for risk is because it has to be high. What we're doing could be amazing, or it could fail. I take pride and enjoyment in the rollercoaster, but it's not for everyone. You have to be ready for the challenge.

But I also believe that is a skill that you can learn as you go. It doesn't mean you wake up every morning and are always ready to go. Sometimes you have to dip your toe in. That's what I did earlier in my career. I dipped my toe in.

As I mentioned, the product can be physical, digital, or service. Another important term is MVP. A lot of people think of sports, Most Valuable Player, but it means something different in startup life. In the startup world, MVP means your minimum viable product. What that means is features of your original product that are usable, that function. Some people say if you're not embarrassed by your MVP, you're not doing it right.

That should let you know right away that what you start out with is not going to be perfect. And you shouldn't wait until it's perfect because by then, everyone will have passed you by, and you will have missed your opportunity. It's a bit of a race and pivot. You have to go as fast as you can, and often while changing course or changing strategy. In building a new product or service, you have to be able to pivot. You can't be so staunch on one idea that you develop blinders. You have to be willing to pivot and change course if need be.

Otherwise, you are going to be irrelevant. Unfortunately, there is no way around that. Another term we use often is Runway. This refers to if a startup is going to lift off or not. It can also refer to how much money you have in the bank. How many months ahead can you pay your bills? Generally speaking, in healthcare tech, digital tech, and really any other startup, you would want to have a runway for about a year to 18 months.

Of course, it doesn't always work out that way. I've worked for start-ups that have been run into the ground to pretty much zero. That is why startups are such a rollercoaster, because before you hit the ground, you are at the top, and everything is awesome. Having a solid runway is really important from a finance perspective.

I don't like failure as a word, and I think, especially in this field, it is a prerequisite to learning. You're not going to learn unless you fall down in the mud a few times. And it can be embarrassing, but you have to leave your ego at the door. I would advise everyone to take some time to learn about their own ego. Recognize the signs of your ego emerging and learn how to leave it at the door.

I often reference the quote that you should "fail fast." You want to be moving. If you're going to fail, you want to fail fast. And in truth, I don't think you can get to success unless you have failed. I'm a pretty high-energy person, and so my energy level matches the pace that we typically have to move as a startup.

There are three main stages to building a startup. The first is the idea stage. I know everyone reading this book has ideas they want to fulfill. I have notebooks filled with ideas. Ideas are a dime a dozen; everybody has them, and yet you still need them to get started. They are still a necessary step. But you have to understand that if you have a killer idea, and somebody else does it first, that on its own isn't a cause to give up on your idea. It's the execution that really makes an idea great, which leads me to the next stage.

The next stage is validation. This is the stage where I spent a lot of my career. Most time is spent in the validation stage, getting your idea validated. Validation is a messy stage. It's unpredictable. Especially for pharmacists who are very used to structure, this stage is not going to be structured. It's not going to be perfect. Once your idea is validated, you're off to the races. You find a market that fits your product. Then you can start building your MVP, and this is your growth stage.

Another thing to be familiar with is the Lean Startup Method by Eric Ries. It's very important. If you want to start a business, if you want to build any kind of product or service, this method is really helpful. The book looks at old-school business plans and asserts, "These are going to die before they ever see the customer. They take too long." The thesis of the book is that too much time and resources are wasted on lengthy business plans. New businesses need to be nimble and fast. How do you do that? The book guides you through it. I highly recommend it.

It also talks about how entrepreneurs are everywhere. In truth, entrepreneurship is really management. Many people have an idea and think, "I'm an entrepreneur now!" But entrepreneurship is really the part in the middle. It's the validation stage. How are you going to manage this process? How do you handle the messy middle? That's what entrepreneurship is. It's the least artistic part of the process. It's where you test the idea, gather data, and analyze it. But you have to validate your learning before you can move on to the next stage of your business. You can't just step out the door and build your idea. You will lose a lot of time and money doing that.

There is an iterative loop The Lean Startup Method discusses. The process is the Build-Measure-Learn loop. Idea, Build, Measure, Learn. This is the way you have to get your mind thinking to develop a quality product or service. It helps eliminate wasted time and resources by teaching you to develop your product iteratively and incrementally. That way, each time you go through the loop, you get a little bit better. Your product gets a little bit better; your business gets a little bit stronger.

Let's say you have this idea in your mind; there are some key questions you need to ask yourself. First, what kind of startup is it? Are you a lawnmower business, a car business, are you building rocket ships? How much risk is going to be involved with this idea you have? What amount of resources are you going to need? In business, typically, the more resources you need, the higher the risk. Building rockets is riskier than building lawnmowers.

I started out my career in the lawnmower section. I moved on to race cars and rockets over the years, and that's proved to be my sweet spot. Over the years, I have learned I'm good at getting high-risk projects off the ground. But also, the longer I've worked with startups, the more tolerant I've become of risk, so it can be something that develops over time.

When you think about product innovation, the first place your mind should go is experimentation. That's what innovation means. You cannot have innovation without experimentation. This is why you need to train your brain to think in continuous cycles. If you want your product to get better, experimentation has to be continuous. You have to put that idea through the loop over and over again. You have your idea; now you have to build it and measure the results. Put it out on the market briefly. Just dip your toe in the water and see what the results are. You learn from that and do it again and again.

What is so interesting about the lean startup method is that it is essentially the scientific method. I'm sure most people reading this book know what that is. We're clinicians. We had to learn this early on in Chemistry 101. Inherently, we already have the skills and mindset to do this kind of rigorous testing because that's how we have been trained. In many ways, it is a benefit. As pharmacists, we have that level of thinking and can apply it to what we are trying to build.

Here is another way of thinking about it, your business idea is your hypothesis. And you're dreaming of your ideal customer and the problem they have, which you can solve. Now you need to design your experiment and test it. One thing the Lean Startup Method says is to get out of the building. This is huge. You don't need to be sitting in your office thinking about what your customers want and need. Why would you do that when you can get out of your office and ask them?

Talk to your potential customers. Get good at asking questions and be thoughtful in your approach. Come up with your questions before going to a customer discussion and be very intentional about what you want to ask. Ask more than one person so you can see how different people answer the same questions. Analyze what you gather from talking to your potential customers and make conclusions from that data.

From there, you can either accept your hypothesis, revise it, or reject it. Keep experimenting and keep revising and working to make the idea better and better. And over time, you look back at your MVP, your minimal viable product. And the MVP from round 1 should be embarrassing. You should be able to see clearly how far you have come and how much better the idea has gotten.

Advice for Aspiring Entrepreneurs

I thought early in my career that I would find success in every move I made. That was a mistake. I've had ups and downs. But once you get that mindset out of your head, you realize that stepping down, stepping sideways, is what is going to lead you to success over time. And you look back and realize you are still progressing. Even in moments that felt like a failure at the time, you were still progressing.

Shannon Eubanks, PharmD

CONTRIBUTOR CONNECTION

www.rxthat.com

www.linkedin.com/in/nashville/

TODD EURY

Biography

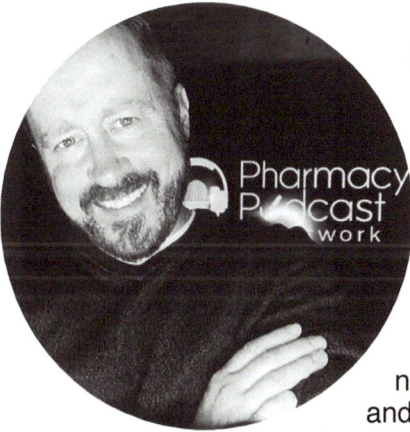

Todd Eury has been transforming the use of audio to improve education, professional development, and new business creation through the use of podcasting. He's studying new quality standards and content development with the provider in mind to support evidence-based information in the form of audio. He is the founder and publisher of the first podcast network dedicated to the business and profession of pharmacy, which was launched in March 2009: The Pharmacy Podcast Network© (PPN). There are now over 120,000 listeners and 3-and-a-half million downloads. It is the most popular podcast about the pharmacy industry. He hails from the great state of Pennsylvania.

Entrepreneurial Journey

A few years back, I told my wife that I wanted to leave New Season. As the Director of Strategy, I was making a little over $140,000 a year. I told her, "I'm going to jump off that cliff. I'm going to take over the pharmacy podcast as my primary income."

She said, "No, you're not. You're absolutely not doing that."

I did it anyway. It was very scary. There was a lot of prayer and a lot of counsel from fellow podcasters and people in the network, people who I trusted. My income completely collapsed. As an entrepreneur, that is something you have to be prepared for. Financially, there is an enormous difference between being an entrepreneur and having a nice salary to keep you going. But even when I originally started the podcast in 2009, I knew I had to really commit if I wanted to grow it into a business. My friend Darshan Kulkarni told me, "You cannot serve two masters. If you really want to build your business, if you want to keep it as a side hustle, there is nothing wrong with that, but you can't have both."

I know a lot of pharmacists who are real estate investors, and they flip houses on the side. There are pharmacists who do writing on the side and podcast creation on the side. But if you really want to create your business, at some point, you need to make a decision where your income can withstand it and make that jump. At some point, you have to put yourself 100% into your business.

And when I say to make that jump, just because something is a risk doesn't mean you have to do it recklessly. You must have a plan in place. You have to map out all the steps it takes to allow you to become a fully supported entrepreneur. You also have to believe in yourself and know that what you are going after is valuable enough that others will pay for it. You have to believe in your own impact.

My hope is that I influence other people. I hope I influence pharmacists and pharmacist technicians, and non-pharmacists who are in the business of content creation. My belief is in creating value in everything that you do. And I think that's an easy thing to accomplish in the world of pharmacy because it's in the data. The data reveals the impact of what a pharmacist does. I don't do my job solely for the love of podcasts; it's always been about serving pharmacists and helping them be more successful and profitable in what they do.

When it comes to income, my wife says we haven't recovered financially yet. There are still some bills that need to be caught up. But in terms of making the business financially successful, I would say that happened in November 2020. In October 2020, I hired an audio technician to take over our audio production; it was a good sign that I was able to pay them and still pay for everything else. The total income of the podcast has eclipsed my income from my previous job, but I don't pay myself all that, obviously. My personal income hasn't gotten back to that level. But the business is pulling in nearly twice the amount from when I jumped off the cliff, and we will be over that in the next year. We'll probably triple it, thank the Lord.

Methods to Monetize Your Knowledge

We've done a lot of things to set the stage so that we can supplement audio in the form of insights from pharmacists. Much of what we have done to lay that groundwork has been on social media. I started using social media as part of my business in 2008 and then really started to accelerate how that would help the publication itself. Twitter, Instagram, Facebook, and LinkedIn are the four main channels for engaging with our clients and with business professionals. But with as much that is happening on these social media channels, there are other platforms that are really starting to gain attention. There are consumer platforms and B2B platforms, and there are distinct differences between those two.

Power of the Pharmacy Podcast Network

I got my start in the pharmacy industry in 2004 as a nerdy technologist that sold pharmacy management systems to institutional pharmacies. Those long-term pharmacy care providers needed to have the right data in order to help change medication regimens and to prescribe and focus on the health issues that seniors were going through. I watched the data come in and out of our system. First, it was a sequel-based system, which was an open database. I noticed that over a period of time, the medication management plans were put into place by the consultant pharmacist. I saw results taking place within sixty, ninety, a hundred and twenty days and transforming the way people were feeling health-wise. We are talking about psychotropics and cardiac meds and lowering blood pressure and hypertension.

I didn't know anything about pharmacy at that time; I came from telecom and asked our head programmer, "Why don't we have more consultant pharmacists out there? People who can curb costs and make medication work as intended."

Now he wasn't a pharmacist either. He was like, "I don't know. Let me get back to programming and doing my job."

Fast forward to 2009; I was consulting with a big pharmacy management system about implementation and increasing the value of what they were doing. I was speaking to some brilliant pharmacists every week and writing everything down as fast as I could. And I asked David Coury, a pharmacist in Dublin, Ohio, who was working with Cardinal Health, if I could record our conversations.

He said, "Sure."

I said, "You were about to tell me about the API from your packaging system to your pharmacy system and how you're impacting patients." This was the very beginning of adherence packaging back in 2009. I recorded the conversation and, with his permission, sent these huge files and emails to other pharmacists so they could listen to this conversation.

My cousin actually made fun of me when he heard I was doing this. We were at a family gathering, and he said, "Why aren't you podcasting?"

I'm like, "I don't even know what podcasting is. I've never listened to a podcast in my life."

Long story short, I did a horrible job putting together the very first industry podcast, called *The Pharmacy Podcast Show*. And it was me interviewing technologists, all terrible audio quality because I didn't know how to record, and I certainly didn't know how to pass it through the internet network. But it became a passion project. And in 2012, I had a network of pharmacists that I was interviewing on a recurring basis. The one and only Tony Guerra, who is a pharmacist in Iowa and teaches pharmacy technicians, was my first host. And to this day, he is still in my network.

I have realized that the power in the show lies in the network, not the podcast itself. Even though I use it as a social media platform, it's the network of these people that I am truly passionate about. My mission is to amplify their voices and give them a way to share what they believe in and everything they know from an evidence-based approach.

These pharmacists know that what they are doing in healthcare is literally changing lives, and I want the world to be able to know it too. The excitement I get is not in hosting a podcast necessarily, but in supporting people like Dr. Kimber Boothe. It has really come full circle that I had this tiny idea to release something nobody but my mom and brother listened to in 2009, to today where we are the number one podcast on planet earth for the pharmacy profession. We are in the top 1% of the 2.3 million podcasts that exist all over the world. It is not lost on me that I have the means to amplify these voices and help strengthen this community. I had more and more pharmacists reach out to be on the network. And I saw an opportunity to help empower pharmacists and help elevate the voices in different facets of healthcare, pharmacy services, care technologist, and so on.

I see the difference these pharmacists are making in the acceleration of data and using that data to literally drive down high blood pressure. If I can take the world of audio and supplement the education that our pharmacy students receive, I am going to do it. If I can take people like Ken Sternfeld, RPh, who believe in changing how the role of the pharmacists impacts the role of the primary care provider, I'm going to do it. If I can take people that understand the impact of specialty medications, long-term care, compounding pharmacy and embed those ideas into an audio format, I am going to do it. The fact that my podcast supplements reading material and journal articles and changes the way consumers think about pharmacy makes me feel fulfilled.

I get so excited to help amplify the voices of pharmacists. I feel like my job, what I get to do every day, is simply bringing together champions. It makes me feel like I can't work fast enough or hard enough to continue to accelerate growth. It is truly an honor to get to be part of a book with so many amazing people in the industry. I can't partner with people who don't have a fire in their chest for an idea they have. You can't win over other people, whether they are pharmacists, physicians, clients, consumers, or patients if you are not passionate. I feel that God has truly blessed me with the people that have been a part of my network. People who really believe in pharmacy, who believe in serving their patients. Pharmacists are the hub of healthcare, and they believe in their patient's outcomes. They believe in their patient's health; I have seen this firsthand.

I am excited to share with you that podcasting is exploding. 56% of American consumers engage with podcasts; this is from PodcastInsights.com. 56%. There are over 2.3 million podcasts out there. As of April 2021, there were over 48 million podcast episodes in existence, and only a third of the podcasts that are being published are actually being maintained. It is hard work. Just because you have a microphone and internet connection and you can jump on Spotify and Apple Podcasts doesn't mean it isn't hard work. That is just the beginning. One of my favorite quotes is from Yoda in *Star Wars: Episode V - The Empire Strikes Back*. Yoda says to Luke, "Do or do not. There is no try." That is literally what I tell people when they ask me if they should start a podcast. Either do it or don't, but there's no just trying.

You either do a podcast, or you don't do a podcast. And that doesn't mean that you have to be perfect. Goodness gracious, I can't tell you how horrible my early episodes sound to me. I had a full-time job and was trying to build an audio blog on the side. I didn't have the time to make it really high quality back then.

Let's talk about the site. The site is an opportunity to take your passion for something and pull out what is inside of you. That's just what I did with the audio blog that I created in 2009, as I worked my full-time job in pharmacy technology to provide for my family.

Eventually, I became the Director of Strategy for one of our nation's largest medication-assisted treatment centers; it's called New Season. I was teaming up with pharmacists who were working on addiction. But I also met so many people that I wanted to talk to but didn't have the time. I would find a pharmacist who was a specialist for that specific disease or condition. It could be something like health equity, racism, sexual harassment. Something that was happening in our industry that was either affecting us as a community and as a family, or worse, was affecting our patients, clients, and communities. I would take the time to speak with them outside of a work capacity, and with their permission, I would record those conversations and market them as hard and well as I could.

I began to find sponsors that believed in what we were doing and believed in the collective voice of pharmacists. I approached them and said, "How would you like to represent these people?" I've been in sales and marketing and marketing for 27 years now, and it has never been so easy for me to develop a business for this network. Once they listened to several of our episodes, they were in. Now organizations like IBM Watson Health, Omnicell, RxSafe, and Cardinal Health are sponsors of the PPN. We're working to create a lot of content specifically for the different facets of their business. We also work to support community pharmacies and use our platform to promote local pharmacies.

It finally reached a level where we couldn't keep doing it all by ourselves. That's why developing that Pharmacy Podcast Network was so important. It gave us a collective voice. It provided us with a support system that allowed us to maintain the very thing we had worked to create. Now, when you're jogging or driving, whatever you are doing, you can consume valuable information just by listening. You have a resource.

The power of this network lies in the pharmacists and pharmacists technicians. They are the ones who are able to reach out to students, consumers, and patients and say, "Not only do you have an opportunity to listen to pharmacists who are pushing the envelope, but pharmacists who are creating a whole new role of what the pharmacist can do to impact health care, to impact the community. This information that is being shared on our podcast is going to change everything. It is going to change the way that you study pharmacology, or cardiovascular disease, or diabetes."

My role in all this is to take the art of audio and use it to supplement the information that pharmacists are giving me. I can take that audio and those conversations and use it as a means of public relations, use it as a way to show sincerity from the pharmacist to the consumer. There is something about audio that is different from reading. If you read someone's blog, you can listen to their voice through reading them, and you can pick apart their personality through their writing. Reading is an incredibly powerful way of taking in information.

But if you listen to someone's story, being told in their own voice, you hear their passion, cadence, and inflection. There is something intimate about that when it comes to conveying a message to the listener, to the patient, the provider, the nurse practitioner, even the fellow pharmacist. You get the chance to truly express what you believe in and how you want to make healthcare better.

Advice for Aspiring Entrepreneurs

Which social media platforms you are driven towards depends on what you do as a pharmacist, as an entrepreneur. I will say, though, don't ever just put audio out there. Audio will supplement everything. It can supplement 100% of what you do; your lessons, your consultancy, your engagement. If you're a pharmacist and have a podcast, why would you try and build it alone if there's a network dedicated to amplifying your voice and mission? Just like pharmacists who are members of the APhA, there's power in a network. Remember to help others and help stand together to accomplish a common goal. I would also recommend participating in other people's blogs and podcasts. It's an amazing way of getting your vision and your thoughts out there. It's what I have proven time and time again by amplifying the voices of pharmacists. I truly want to help pharmacists in any way I possibly can, whether it is something I can do myself or something that can be accomplished by connecting people to the Pharmacy Podcast's network. Because as I said before, it's not about the podcast; it's about the pharmacists that are changing healthcare.

CONTRIBUTOR CONNECTION

Todd Eury
🌐 www.pharmacypodcast.com
🔗 www.linkedin.com/in/toddeury/

LISA FAAST

Biography

Dr. Lisa Faast is an experienced innovator, business executive, and leader in the independent pharmacy industry. With over 20 years of experience as a pharmacy owner, consultant, compounder, and businesswoman, she can bring a unique perspective to the industry's problems. Her passion is helping independent pharmacy owners thrive by diversifying and growing their revenue streams. She is currently CEO of DiversifyRx©, a consulting and education company, in addition to being a wife and mom of four.

Entrepreneurial Journey

My hobby has always been starting businesses. I think it's somewhere in my DNA because my brother has it too. I have never been afraid of starting something new, which underlies what all entrepreneurs have, this mindset of not being fearful if things go wrong. Often, I'll ask myself, "What is the worst that can happen?" If I can live with whatever that is, I say, "Let's go for it."

I started my first pharmacy in my mid-twenties. And again, I asked myself, "What is the worst that can happen? Well, if we go bankrupt, I'll go back to working in my corporate job." I realized I could live with that.

After pharmacy school, my entrepreneurial journey began with a used car dealership with my brother. I graduated from pharmacy school in 2001. In 1998 I interned for Rite Aid and then went to work at Kmart after graduation. One of my best friends had a pharmacy, and he was having some medical issues, so I began looking into taking over his pharmacy. I created a business plan, and I worked with the Small Business Administration (SBA). Finally, I got a call from the SBA that said, "Hey, you're approved." I called my friend, and he had sold the pharmacy to Rite Aid the day before. I was left with nothing to do. I had created all of these dreams about how I would help patients and pour my heart and soul into them. I decided to go ahead and open my own.

My pharmacy entrepreneurial journey began opening my own in California in 2005. Since then, my husband and I have owned several additional businesses; paintball, gun painting, youth sports, solar, pharmacy, marketing, and movie making. I certainly have run the gamut of different types of companies. Over time, we racked up many lessons learned from these businesses.

I really appreciate looking back on how much I learned from my elders, not necessarily in age but in business experience. I hope that some of the insights I can give will help others along their journey. It is helpful to have insights from someone who has been there, done it, and is still doing it.

I've always said, I don't know why but God has given me the talent to help pharmacy owners. I can see order where everybody sees chaos. I can see a path. And it got to a point in my career where frankly, I was tired of making everybody else millions of dollars. My oldest child is entering high school this year. He's going to go to college in four years. I began looking at the bigger picture of what I want to be in life and the impact I want to have.

For those who have the entrepreneurial bug, it can feel a little like you don't know what you want to be when you grow up. Working with pharmacy owners, I realized that I have unique skills and needed to put them to good use. The previous year, I left my long-term employment of 8 years and took on what I thought was a dream job. In February of 2021, I was fired from the dream job, as we were going in different directions. In February, I was left thinking, "What am I going to do now?" I looked at many different positions, and finally, I just looked at my husband one day and had that "Ah-Ha!" moment. I realized that I was never happier than when I was helping pharmacy owners. Nothing gives me more joy. From that point forward, I dove all in on DiversifyRx.

Having self-awareness of what truly made me happy is the key. Because I know if I'm happy, my husband is happier, my kids are happier, and life is generally a little bit better. After making that decision, everyone I spoke to for the next few days said, "Wow. You seem so much more joyful, much more cheerful." It was really a moment where the universe aligned, and things just fell into place. I just had to figure out how to monetize this leap of faith, and for that, I was going to lean into my vast experience.

Methods to Monetize Your Knowledge

When it comes to monetizing your knowledge, I think passion comes first. I am on a mission to help save every independent pharmacy out there that wants to remain open and be profitable and thrive. I would do that even if I didn't get paid. But of course, there are bills to pay, so yes, you need to monetize that knowledge.

I would say DiversifyRx is different from other consulting businesses. At least I am running it differently as an entrepreneur. I mean that instead of doing a typical high-touch one-on-one model, I rely on technology to distribute my information and knowledge to the masses. Because the truth is if I want to save independent pharmacies, I can't do it one at a time. There just isn't enough Lisa to go around. It is helpful for entrepreneurs to understand that they don't always have to go after the big-ticket sale. While that is a common strategy, you may suffer from imposter syndrome or think you are not worth it. And it's okay to struggle with that. Starting small can help you overcome that mindset. You may also be surprised by how much money people are willing to offer you. I don't usually go for higher dollar coaching arrangements, but I've had more and more pharmacies asking to work with me on that basis because I have built trust with them.

There isn't only one right way to monetize your knowledge. My most important lesson, though, is that you have to ask for money and have a way for people to pay you easily. Even if it is a simple Stripe account where you can put in a custom amount, have some type of system in place through which people can pay you for your services.

There is no such thing as the top expert out there. There are always going to be people who know more than you. That does not mean your knowledge isn't valuable and worth paying for. And there are simple ways to start. You don't need a website from the get-go; you don't need a logo. Don't let these basic items hold you back from getting started helping others.

Another reflection I'd like to share is that the impact that you are trying to achieve is limited if you only do it one-on-one. While phone calls can provide a ton of value, you will be limited, and therefore you may be limiting your earning potential. Think about how you can leverage YouTube or podcasting. The Pharmacy Podcast Network can help you get started quickly. Other monetizable digital assets such as e-courses and eBooks are effective as well.

7 Lessons from a Serial Entrepreneur

I admit I am a serial entrepreneur. I also love helping others become entrepreneurs in and out of the pharmacy industry. It is fun seeing them succeed. And so, through both being an entrepreneur and helping others become successful entrepreneurs, I have accumulated several lessons.

Lesson One
Lesson number one gets to the heart of entrepreneurial failure. It is the number one problem for pharmacy owners and a significant stressor for all entrepreneurs. This lesson is about cash flow. You have to understand that cash flow is like oxygen to your business. You can be highly profitable, but you will have to close your doors if you run out of cash. And the reason for this is that many times when you're starting your first business, you don't fully understand the concept of accounts receivables. You don't understand that not everybody will pay their bills on time, or maybe even pay them at all.

Often when starting your own business, you forget to budget for yourself. You say, "Oh, I'm not going to take a salary." Even if you don't take a salary, you still have expenses. There are going to be start-up expenses. People overestimate revenue, how much they will collect, and underestimate their costs. So, cash flow becomes a big problem because of the wrong assumptions.

I recommend everyone starting a business to make sure you have an excellent understanding of cash flow. Take some courses, speak with an accountant, really take the time to understand the principles of cash flow because that will be the key to your business, and nothing is going to hold you back more than that. When I owned my first pharmacy, I almost grew myself out of business. The reason for that was that there was a stranglehold on cash flow. For pharmacies, in particular, you buy all your drugs upfront, and you bill the insurance. You get paid from the insurance 30, 45, 60 days later. It creates this effect where if you have a significant boost in business, there is a lot more money going out than coming in. Even solopreneurs can end up in that situation. If you get too busy too quickly, you can get ahead of yourself. Cash flow is uber critical to success, not only for the immediate but also for the long term.

Lesson Two

You must have a business plan. I talk to many pharmacists who want to break out and consult or get into PGx, and they think they don't need a business plan. I even know pharmacy owners with multimillion-dollar businesses who do not have a business plan. There is a misunderstanding in the pharmacy world. Many think a business plan is just something to show the bank. If they don't get a loan, they don't create a business plan.

That is absolutely not the case; the business plan is for you. It is the most critical work you can do in your business. After all, the research you do, the marketing plans, the financial predictions, and all of that effort will pay back in dividends and multiples because you put in the effort. The business plan is for you, the owner of the business. It's not for the bank. Even if you're not getting a loan, I highly recommend creating a business plan. Include market research, competitor analysis, SWOT analysis, financials, all of those things. That way, you are indeed the king of your castle when it comes to your business. And if you ever do need a line of credit or a loan, you already have that taken care of. Don't bypass that step.

Even if you have already started your business, you can still do one now. It's not one and done; you should be continually updating it as your business matures or your business changes. I love Business Plan Pro, now known as Live Plan online. You can use any software or method that works for you. Do not skip having a business plan.

Lesson Three

You have a new best friend forever (BFF), and it's called marketing. You need to love marketing. I say this because I have become an enormous marketing nerd since being an entrepreneur. I think it's super fun, but mainly because I have realized how critical it is to my business. The biggest problem new companies face is a lack of traffic and awareness. Traffic is just a fancy word for people coming to your website or your physical building. You have to become a savvy marketer. I had a tremendous fortune many years ago to spend time with Tom Feltenstein, who passed away recently. He was the guerilla marketing guru. Guerilla marketing is essentially grassroots marketing, a very low-cost type of marketing that is often more effective than just paying for an ad somewhere.

As an entrepreneur, take the time to dive into marketing. Join marketing Facebook groups, talk to people there, read some books. There are fantastic resources out there. And even though I have been a marketing nerd for many years, I still buy new marketing books, read them, and listen to them as I drive my kids to school. Marketing is now your new BFF. You have to tell your current BFF to step aside and just dive into marketing. Learn to love it because it will be critical to your success.

Lesson Four
One of the great benefits of starting a business is becoming an entity that you can tap into for tax benefits. Tax benefits become a whole new ball game once you create your own business. Now that you have your own business, the person who was doing your taxes before, when you were a W2 pharmacist or a hospital employee, should not be your accountant in the future. This recommendation is because a whole new section of the IRS code is now open to you that they may not be familiar with. Don't be ashamed or too afraid to take advantage of those tax benefits. They are there for a reason. Understanding how to leverage them to the maximum benefit will be beneficial. You will get to expense certain things you would not be able to as an individual employee.

There are certain things you can write off and depreciate; there's a Research & Development (R&D) tax credit, for example. You have to learn and be open to a whole new lingo. Take the time to understand them; just because you won't be the one filing your taxes doesn't mean you shouldn't educate yourself. You can follow a blog or two about accounting and business taxes. If you're in pharmacy, there are some great pharmacy-specific tax advisors out there, like Rx Advisors. Tap into people who know your niche market, especially if you're a solopreneur. Again, you want to work with a bookkeeper and accountant who work specifically with entrepreneurs.

When you dive into your new benefits, taxes become fun, at the very least more interesting as a business owner. Definitely take advantage of all of those benefits. And if you haven't taken advantage of them, maybe you kept doing your taxes the usual way after starting your business. You can now go back up to three years and have an account re-look at those taxes. You may be able to update them with something that you were unaware of before. You don't even have to wait until you have an LLC to do this. If you make some side income from speaking jobs or consulting, you can still take advantage of that on your taxes. You can do different things with your retirement savings once you own a business or pass some tax-free dollars onto your kids by having them work for your company. There are a lot of really cool things that can be done once you become an entrepreneur. It really does become a whole new ball game, and you owe it to yourself to familiarize yourself with those benefits.

Lesson Five
Work-life balance is a myth. I don't believe in it. It doesn't exist. I think the way we approach this is all in our heads, and when you become an entrepreneur, you are living to work and working to live. It's not a nine to five, Monday through Friday job anymore. Your job becomes deeply intertwined with your life. I opened my pharmacy when I was pregnant with my first child. I've been a mom and an entrepreneur for 14 years. There's no such thing as a work-life balance. I say this is a myth because once you start your business, there is no separation between being an entrepreneur and an individual. The lines are blurred, and it gets all mixed.

My 11-year-old plays water polo. The National Junior Olympics are coming up, and qualifiers were down in Houston for a couple of days. While we were there, I had my laptop. I was checking my email and completing tasks. When he is in the pool, my eyes are all on him, but when he's not in the pool, I'm back to work, I'm taking a phone call.

I had a Facebook memory pop up a few days ago. The photo was from years ago. It was my husband and me at the beach; we only had three kids at the time. We're at the beach with our kids, and we both have our wireless earpieces on. He and I took turns taking calls and talking to clients, but we were at the beach with our kids. We need to get the idea that there is a separation between work and life out of our heads.

It allows you to set better expectations for yourself and enjoy the life you are building for yourself. My kids know that we work all the time, any day of the week, because it is for their future. We have very frank and open conversations with them about that. It is imperative you understand that there is no more nine to five. You might be working at midnight or playing at midnight, and either is likely to happen on any given day.

Lesson Six
You are not alone. I made this mistake when I was opening my first pharmacy. I didn't know anybody who had owned a pharmacy. I didn't have a mentor; I didn't have any experience. I didn't even know any of the other pharmacy owners in the town I was opening in. I really did feel like I was on an island, and it caused much stress. Of course, now, many years later, there is Facebook. There are groups of people who are pharmacists and entrepreneurs.

I learned it is not a sign of weakness to ask for help. I still struggle with that to this day. For some reason, I think that if I ask for help, it means I am not good enough. It takes time to overcome this mental blockade. But if you ask for help early on, you will avoid potholes that otherwise will cost you time and money and stress. Learn from those ahead of you and pay it forward by helping those behind you. It creates a never-ending stream of support.

Get a tribe, whether locally, through a summit or a Facebook group with people from all over the country. Do something where you can lean on each other because that will be a big help when the dark times come and when the awesome times come. You want to have people you can share your successes with. Having a place to celebrate your success is just as important as having someone to lean on when things are hard. Lesson number six is that just because you are a solopreneur doesn't mean you have to do it alone.

Lesson Seven
Last but not least is to enjoy the ride as an entrepreneur. This one has actually been the hardest for me in the past. It's in our blood as entrepreneurs to always look ahead. We are always looking to see what comes next or which problems need fixing. We always see what's not perfect. It's easy to get caught up in the day-to-day, putting out fires and meeting the daily goals. You can forget to enjoy it and have fun. You fail to turn around and see how far you have come. One of the best lessons that I learned from a business coach is acknowledging how far I've come, physically taking that moment, mentally looking back, and enjoying where I am now. Yes, it's great to have goals, and it's great to always be striving for more. But you also need to stop and smell the roses, as they say. Enjoy the ride. It is fun.

Now that I'm in my early forties, I'm much better at it than I was in my mid-twenties. It is definitely something that you can learn. But as much as you're grinding, don't forget to enjoy it. Don't forget to have fun. Don't forget to take a break now and then. I love being an entrepreneur. I love having control of my destiny. I genuinely believe that you will relieve stress and be a whole lot more successful if you can smile along the way. These are my seven lessons.

Advice for Aspiring Entrepreneurs

Be aware of what your state allows for your scope of practice. Some states are much broader than others. Also, know that your state board doesn't regulate some opportunities that seem clinical.

Many health, life, and functional wellness coaching fall into this realm.

There are tons of opportunities now for pharmacists and pharmacy owners. A few of my favorites are pharmacogenetic testing, women's health, men's health, functional testing, and professional supplements. Many pharmacy owners don't have the bandwidth to do all of these programs. They know it is beneficial to their patients and the pharmacy's bottom line. Independent clinical pharmacists can approach pharmacy owners to bring these programs to the pharmacies. Pharmacies have the traffic the pharmacist needs. The pharmacist has the time that the pharmacy owners don't. It's a win-win-win situation. The patient, pharmacist, and pharmacy owner all benefit by working together.

Lastly, don't wait to outsource. By delegating tasks, you will free up your time to grow your business even faster. Typically, you will want to farm out admin tasks. A great one is your bookkeeping. There are fantastic virtual assistants that can be a big boost to your business. I have developed a strong outsourcing muscle now. I love having somebody to help with the heavy lifting. It frees up my time to do what I love, helping pharmacy owners increase their profitability.

Lisa Faast, PharmD

CONTRIBUTOR CONNECTION

🌐 www.diversifyrx.com

in www.linkedin.com/in/drlisafaast/

CHRISTINA FONTANA

Biography

Dr. Christina Fontana is a pharmacist, four-time author, rapid transformation coach, and hypnotherapist. She blends subconscious programming, hypnotherapy, quantum physics, spirituality, and intuitive coaching to help visionary women get unstuck so they can own their brilliance out in the world. She is the creator of the Monetize Your Magic Program that helps female entrepreneurs accelerate to their next level of income and impact. Dr. Christina's gift is that she can intuitively tune into the blocks keeping someone stuck and help them rapidly shift to experience more freedom, abundance, and joy. For the last nine years, Dr. Christina has been providing uplifting, transformational content through her YouTube videos, articles, books, and retreats.

Entrepreneurial Journey

I'm not going to be talking about medication or pharmacogenomics or anything of the sort today. I am a full-time entrepreneur, and I help women release blocks to amplify their income and impact. My work is relevant as I help pharmacists, and my journey started in pharmacy, but I don't do anything in patient care. My dad, uncle, aunt, and sister are all pharmacists. Naturally, I would be the one to write.

My journey was not very easy in the beginning. In my fifth year of pharmacy school, I was going out on rotations. My dad had a pharmacy, and I was working in his store while going out on rotations. I began to get this gut feeling that I no longer wanted to work as a traditional pharmacist anymore. I'm sure if you are reading this book, you can relate to that feeling. You reach a fork in the road. A feeling crosses your heart, and you realize there is another path. It could come with risk, but it is going to be so rewarding on the other side. You have a choice: you could stay in the traditional role, the path of staying safe and being comfortable. I could have stayed on that path and taken over my father's pharmacy, but I knew in my heart that something was calling me to a different purpose.

I subsequently got kicked out of my house because my strong Italian dad really thought I was betraying the family. It was very dramatic; I was kicked out of the house and fired from my job. I was homeless. A lot of people on this journey fear homelessness. I've been there. I've been homeless with no job and about to graduate pharmacy school, needing to figure out where I am going to live. I was at my rock bottom while also having anxiety and an eating disorder.

The reason I tell this story is because I want people to see that there is a transformation that happens. When you're stretching yourself, whether you're starting a business or something else, there is going to be an identity shift.

At that crossroads, I was at my rock bottom, but I still took the leap. It was scary to take action. Imagine not having a palace to live in, having an eating disorder, and waking up every night to binge on unhealthy food. I was smoking cigarettes. I was really unhealthy. And at the root of that was a vicious cycle, and this is what I help people with now. I had a lot of really old programming from my childhood that told me I was not worthy enough, I was unlovable, that I was too sensitive. Much of the work I do now is with women, teaching them how to own these gifts. I work with empaths, and I teach them how to own their sensitivity.

Methods to Monetize Your Knowledge

I have a video that I created on YouTube; it's called "10 Ways to Monetize Your Magic in Your Soul Aligned Business." In the video, I go through 10 different ways you can begin monetizing. For me personally, I have done every single one of those things. I have a YouTube channel, and I run in-person retreats. I have an Elevate membership where you can come in and receive this transformative work in which I give training, meditation, workbooks, affirmations, and support. I have a Monetize Your Magic e-course. There are many different ways I monetize my knowledge in order to help people.

When we operate in a place of stress, we can really only see what is directly in front of us. You're in survival mode. But if you expand your perspective, when you open your vision, that is when you can identify your gifts and begin to monetize them.

Releasing Blocks to Amplify Your Impact

Many women are highly sensitive but also highly intuitive. You can use these gifts in your career to create a soul-aligned business that really fulfills you. My advice is to always follow your intuition. That is what I did. It was scary as hell for me to make this choice that I knew was going to be risky. I had probably $10,000 in my bank account. I didn't have any support; my family had left me. I was living out of my car for two weeks. And I say that because we all have fear. And we also all have opportunities.

You have that intuition within you to tap into and ask, "What is it that I really want for my life?" And you can choose; you can choose to stretch yourself out of your comfort zone. Yes, it is going to be scary. Yes, you may fall on your face. But that is why you need support. You need people who are going to encourage you along the way. In addition to that, it is also about your belief system. I was helped by a woman through rewiring that subconscious blueprint of how you see yourself. Do you see yourself as, "Oh, I am just a pharmacist; I don't really have an impact." Or are you like, "I'm here. I'm commanding the room. This is what I have to give. This is what I have to offer." I do a lot of embodiment work and belief work with my pharmacists.

We are all here with soul gifts. We are born with gifts. You have experiences that you have learned from. Maybe you have gone through experiences like mine. Maybe you have had relationship issues. Maybe you have gone through a loss. Whatever it is, you can use those experiences to monetize your magic and create a soul-aligned business that serves other people. My mission is to empower pharmacists to create a business out of anything.

I have helped pharmacists to create a self-love coaching business, a fitness business, nutrition, herbalism, functional medicine, the list goes on. I have helped so many pharmacists create soul-aligned businesses, and with that comes transformative work. This is the inner work that I talk about; subconscious beliefs, who you are, how you see your self-image, how you show up in the world energetically, what needs to be released in order to shine? I am going to talk about that a lot today. We have these self-sabotage blocks that keep us stuck. They keep us in these lower frequencies that don't allow us to stretch and expand, to impact the patients and people that we want to.

Some of the biggest blocks I've seen are procrastination, overthinking, being caught in people-pleasing, fear of failure, perfectionism. I can relate to these too, and I have overcome them. I have been a complete nerd over the last decade and studied programming energy work. I have spent multiple six-figures on how to help people shift rapidly, in addition to honing my own intuitive gifts so people can come to me. I can sit with you for all of five minutes and tell you, "This is what is happening." I can help you rapidly shift so you can reach more people. This is ultimately what I want for pharmacists, to be able to expand your energy so that you're not hiding; you're not sitting over there thinking, "Who am I to do this?" You're not succumbing to imposter syndrome or feeling like you have to control every little thing in your business. I have helped so many people with many of these different blocks.

There is a study called *Power vs. Force* by David Hawkins. I highly recommend looking at that book. It talks about how when you move up to the level of love and connection to your heart, that is where you have more power. That is where you can impact more lives. It has been proven in different studies that when you connect to your heart, you radiate. I think for entrepreneurs, but especially pharmacists, we operate in a masculine mind because we've been conditioned to be perfect, to control everything. And that's part of the lower frequency of force, power versus force. That behavior is an ingrained pattern, and you can let go of that control. You can dive into these old beliefs and release them. Then you are able to amplify your income and impact. I went from making less than $10,000 a year to tripling my pharmacist income because of this transformative work.

This is my work and how it has impacted thousands of people. This is the work that is truly going to impact the world. If you want to achieve your desired impact, you have to be doing the inner work. Let's say, for example, that one of your blocks is overthinking. You're constantly overthinking instead of taking action. As a result, you end up just sitting behind your computer in fear. That is a fear frequency. If you're constantly thinking, "I'm not good enough," and most of humanity believes this at their core, then you will be held back. You will be anchored to your old timeline and your old identity.

In order to show up for yourself differently, you need to think differently. You need to be thinking new thoughts feeling differently about yourself, and only through doing that can you embody the confident leader that has a thriving business. I talk to so many pharmacists who say, "I don't want to do retail anymore. I want to go from retail to being a full-time entrepreneur." But what they don't realize is that making that change isn't just a career shift. It requires a shift in your identity. This work is paramount.

When I was first starting my business, I did a pharmacy residency. I went through integrative nutrition, and I completed all of these certifications. But I was so stubborn that I would not hire a coach. It took me seven years to hire a coach. In 2019, I hired two coaches who helped me move the needle in my business and help me with this transformative work. Now, this is the work I do to help women accelerate their path and amplify their income and impact. Because that is what we are all wanting, isn't it? No matter what you do, we all need to be able to pay the bills, and we all need to feel like we have an impact.

The core tenets of my coaching practice are helping women shift their beliefs, their embodiment, their self-image, and that in turn impacts how they show up in the world. One thing I recommend is taking the time to connect with yourself every single day. This can be as simple as putting your hands over your heart, and the Heart Math Institute has done research on this. When you put your hands over your heart, you increase the electromagnetic frequency around your body. It allows you to connect more with yourself and to reach more people, doing this through an intention setting practice like meditation. I have a bunch of guided meditations on my YouTube channel. Making this practice a habit will allow you to overcome your blocks and shift your mindset.

Advice for Aspiring Entrepreneurs

I was working in a retail corporate setting, and I was working back-to-back 12-hour days. I was miserable. I was burnt out. At the time, I was doing more health coaching, but that wasn't really my zone of genius. My zone of genius is transformation work and helping people rapidly shift. I quit my job, and I hired a coach. It was a big leap of faith, but I knew it was what I needed to do. I knew that if I didn't do it, then I was never going to do it. Thankfully it worked out, and I haven't gone back.

Sometimes you need to fully burn those boats; you need to make a clean break, or else you don't truly think of yourself as an entrepreneur. You have to force a shift in mindset and say, "Okay. I'm an entrepreneur now. My money is coming from my entrepreneur business." And until you have that certainty, it is difficult to grow your business.

Don't be afraid to hire coaches. I have hired multiple coaches at different points in my life, depending on what I am prioritizing. But having that paid expert has been paramount to my growth and development. Hiring coaches allows you to get a return on the investment in yourself. I've invested over $260,000 in myself over the course of ten years. And I'm still learning. Another thing it helped me to realize and to own is that I'm not a jack of all trades. I can't do it all, so I am going to focus specifically on my zone of genius and get really good at that particular area.

As I said earlier, we all have soul gifts. You have experiences throughout your life that give you a unique talent and a unique perspective. You have schooling and certifications; you are a pharmacist. How do you weave these together to create a soul-aligned offer you can bring to your clients? How do you market in a heart-centered way? These are the kinds of training I provide. I cover all of that; how to succeed on enrollment calls, how to market, how to nurture your audience. If you have never started a business, everything you need is covered in my training.

The biggest thing I can give you as a takeaway is if you are feeling that inkling, that intuition that is calling you to entrepreneurship, you have found this book for a reason. That intuition has led you here. Lean into it, trust yourself. A lot of us don't trust our intuition because we're operating in the masculine mind, we overthink things, and we worry. But what if you tapped into how you feel? Trusting my instinct is truly how I came to be where I am now.

I could have stayed in fear and continued to work for my dad. It would have been safe. But I didn't. I took the courageous step. I encourage you to do the same. Find people who support you; find people who can mentor you in whatever capacity you need. And trust yourself because you are here for a reason. That is the best advice I can give.

Christina Fontana, PharmD, CHC, CHT

CONTRIBUTOR CONNECTION

🌐 www.pharmacistcoach.com

in www.linkedin.com/in/dr-christina-fontana-pharmd-chc-cht-56367355/

MICHELLE FRITSCH

Biography

Michelle Fritsch is a Board Certified Geriatric Clinical Pharmacist with a passion for healthy aging and education. She is a specialist in medication use for people over the age of 60 and a founder of Retirement Wellness Strategies LLC, which supports a transition to health, retirement, and beyond. During COVID, she added a subscription-based version with partner Ellen Platt. This is Propel Comprehensive Wellness LLC. Her purpose is to inspire transitioning leaders to transform the world. She works with a broad definition of health: physical, mental, emotional, spiritual, and social. She is also co-founder with Sue Paul and Anna Garrett of Medipreneurs.

Entrepreneurial Journey

I'd like to share how I got to this point in my career because Retirement Wellness Strategies would not have been born if it weren't for all of the things that came before it. I want to talk about finding holes as you go through life. You might notice areas where there is a need that is being unmet, and you may have a passion for that particular issue. Of course, there are more aspects to this that I will discuss later, but I'm sure people can relate to this idea of finding holes that need to be filled.

My word for 2021 is undeterred. When I look back at this crazy, adventurous journey that has been my life and career, undeterred has really been my word for a long time. Another is gratitude, grabbing the golden nuggets at each step along your path. I used to think that I had gotten all of these amazing opportunities because I was simply in the right place at the right time. And that was a huge part of it, but I've also had colleagues who were in those same places at the same time and didn't get joy out of it. They focused on the negatives and were put off by the work because it was so difficult.

I'm on the older end of the contributors to this book. I think in telling you about my background, I can shed some light on how the pharmacy system was built into what it is today. When I got my PharmD, it was separate from the BS. My class was tiny, so we got to know our faculty really well. And when I started to teach myself, my classes were tiny, so I got to know my students very well.

I come from a town of 500 in rural Indiana, going to pharmacy school was an adventurous decision for me. I took two opportunities to work with the Public Health Service (PHS) as a COSTEP, and this was their Commissioned Officer's Student Training and Experience Program. One of those was in the Washington, D.C./Southern Maryland area. I got to draft the first recruitment brochure for pharmacists for the PHS. This really meant that I got to know everything. I got to know the surgeon general. I got to go to meetings at the state department and other really incredible opportunities. That introduced me to a lot of very powerful people.

The next summer, I went to Kayenta, Arizona, which is about six hours away from the nearest cities. At the time, it was the most remote they had ever sent a student, and they really just wanted to see if I would survive. I loved everything about it. This was right when the Public Health Service's three prime questions that enhanced patient care were being launched. I got to be there in the beginning and work with the people who developed it. I really incorporated those ideas into my philosophy about patient care.

I then did a residency in primary care in Madison, Wisconsin, with a guy who had been doing primary care since the 1970s. He is one of the fathers of clinical pharmacy, getting out there and being a provider. He gave us a unique type of training. We were working with a geriatric facility that truly enhanced interprofessional care and with some of the people that have written so much of the literature that has defined what it means to work as a healthcare team. It was amazing to be trained in primary care in that way, as a team member, right from the start.

I then got to practice at the Veterans Affairs Medical Center (VA) in Leavenworth, Kansas. There, I learned how to take care of those men. And so, because my residency was with the VA, and my first practice was with the VA, most of my experience was in caring for men. I then got pregnant, but it was long before the Family Medical Leave Act. I was at an American Association of Colleges of Pharmacy (AACP) meeting; this was a pharmacy professor's meeting where they had a women faculty special interest group. Women were such a small subunit of academia. There were hardly any women. I asked a woman, "How do I negotiate for maternity benefits? I have no idea."

She was A woman from New York who had just gotten tenured. She took me aside and explained the process. And I will never forget, she flipped over her business card and wrote her home phone number on the back. She didn't know me. She said, "2 AM, breastfeeding, whenever you have a question, give me a call." I thought that was so powerful.

Eventually, the university where I was working had increased research demands, as the VA was reconfiguring in a way that would decrease my patient and research base. My husband and I made a big life decision and moved to North Carolina.

I became the geriatric resource for a group of internal medicine physicians. We signed on the dotted line in March and arrived in August. It turned out those doctors had a fight and completely disbanded. The administration of the hospital said, "We need a geriatric resource and a clinician for the whole community." But some of the physicians really fought it; it was an uphill battle. Thankfully it all worked out beautifully in the end. It was also at that time when North Carolina reframed its Pharmacy Practice act. At the time, it was thought to be way out there. North Carolina is still a leader, but that was huge in 2000, 2001.

One of the physicians from the State Medical Association was in my facility and not a fan of pharmacists. And so, we had to turn him around in order for the State Pharmacy Practice Act to pass. I said undeterred was my word; I would sit with this poor man at every meeting. I would join him in the lunchroom uninvited; I would stand outside his office. I bugged the heck out of him. And it worked!

We also had a state legislator from my district who was not a big fan of pharmacy. He had some health issues and had to walk really slow. I would go to the state capitol and catch him between meetings and lobby for the pharmacy industry because I knew he couldn't run away from me. The end result was that a lot of people were doing many different things for pharmacy. North Carolina was able to enhance its pharmacy practice act.

I loved practicing at that community hospital; I designed a program for senior adults who were underinsured. This was before Medicare, so they did not have prescription insurance. Even if a doctor made a diagnosis and prescribed something, patients couldn't necessarily get those meds. We went through a process of using the pharmaceutical company Patient Assistance Programs to acquire millions of dollars of medications. We were able to help senior adults, and I loved it. I never anticipated that I would leave that practice. To this day, I still consult with that group.

The woman who flipped over her business card and gave me her home phone number became the founding Dean at a pharmacy school up in Maryland, and she gave me a call. I told her, "Oh, I don't do cities." And she said, "Just get up here."

My family moved to Maryland, and we lived there for twelve years. My kids loved it there. They learned to walk and talk in North Carolina, but they had their education through high school in Maryland. Starting that pharmacy school was amazing. A lot of that was getting to know the administrators, the independent pharmacy entities, the chain pharmacies, all of the hospitals and clinics around Baltimore so we could place faculty and students. It was pretty awesome.

And then it just got to the point where the school was accredited. My energy can sometimes put people off. When the school became status quo, and my mindset was still go, go, go, I just wasn't a good fit anymore. I left and jumped into the entrepreneurial life. I had been planning to do that, but I took the leap more quickly than I originally planned and started a company called Meds MASH.

MASH stands for "Mature Adults Safe at Home." I wanted to work at the very early end of geriatrics and help people come up with a plan to stay healthy and stay out of nursing homes for as long as possible. I wanted to help people live those years of their life fully. Well, the boomers said, "Oh no. That's not me. Don't call me a mature adult. Don't use geriatric or aging or any of those other words." They thought those words were offensive.

It took two years and literally asking hundreds of people, "What word can I use?" and that's where retirement came from. Even if people aren't planning on retiring, they were willing to talk about that word and not feel like they are being discriminated against treated in an ageist way.

When I was early on in my entrepreneurial journey, someone who I had collaborated with at the pharmacy school became the Pharmacy Director at the Federally Qualified Health Center (FQHC) in downtown

Baltimore. For a girl who said that she wasn't going to do cities, I kept doing cities. I was in the FQHC in the heart of Baltimore. I got to be right smack in the middle of one of our biggest transgender hubs in the mid-Atlantic region and got to know so many people and hear their stories. Baltimore has a huge HIV population and a lot of people with syphilis and gonorrhea. We had a huge infectious disease epidemic and a huge opioid crisis.

With FQHC colleagues, my family, and friends, I ended up under 83, the highway to Baltimore, teaching the homeless to use Narcan. I grew to love providing care in the heart of the city.

Again, I was just blessed with many amazing experiences along the way. Through my career, I saw all of these men that were my bosses and other leaders who were bigger than life. And I saw as they retired too many became these little shells of themselves. Some only survived for 18 months or two years after retirement, even though they seemed healthy going into it. I saw them in hospital beds and clinics as I was providing patient care. And I thought, "This is preventable."

I talked to them after they had heart attacks or major falls, or they had depression and attempted to commit suicide, and I began to realize not only what was happening but how preventable it was. That became what is now my major focus and passion. I work with people one-on-one.

Methods to Monetize Your Knowledge

When I started my business, I really had executives in mind as my ideal clients. And so, throughout the process of running my business, I have developed 16 tools that can help someone to build a retirement plan. And again, this is a very one-on-one, personal process. This makes it an out-of-pocket expense that not everyone can afford. It is a little less per person if they want to do it as a couple. Propel Comprehensive Wellness provides the opportunity for a more affordable, scalable, subscription-based format.

One of the ways I get the word out is by partnering with people who have clients in the same age range. I have a number of financial planners and lawyers as partners. I frequently speak with their clients in webinars. In some cases, they pay for all or part of their clients to work with me so they, as a financial planner or lawyer, can provide a more comprehensive service to their clients. That has been a big learning curve for me.

Another thing I learned after doing this for a while was that I realized it was not just executives struggling with retirement. Since 2020 there have been horrible statistics of many kinds; suicide and overdose rates going up. And the retirement community has been hit especially hard, especially men over 50 years old. This was a driving reason I partnered with a colleague who is an aging life care manager. We created Propel Comprehensive Wellness during COVID. We designed this product with the hope of getting it into the hands of a lot more people and making it really easy for them to understand. I dream of a day when insurance pays for such a thing, but we are not quite there yet.

I don't think people should be afraid of designing their products in a higher price range because there are people who are willing to pay for them. Then, we are trying to develop this other option for people who may need these services but aren't able to afford them as well.

It is also worth mentioning that I began my business at the world's worst time. I had three kids, all getting ready to go to college. The business doesn't begin when you start something new. It doesn't necessarily generate a lot of income right off the bat. There are other ways to compensate. I am a big proponent for keeping your job and starting the other stuff on the side, and over time gradually decreasing your job and increasing your business. But you have to do it in a way that makes sense for you and for your family. I'm a professor at heart, so I continue to teach, and that brings in some revenue. Since I no longer teach pharmacists, I teach doctors of physical therapy, physician assistants, and other groups. I also still consult with some of the practices I have developed in the past to help sustain them.

When it comes to consulting, I have found that there are a lot of innovators outside of medicine who need the input of a scientific doctorate or people at the pharmacy level. If you have made it through pharmacy school, you are automatically incredibly smart; there are a number of people out there with ideas who need your input. Make yourself known as an innovator with the knowledge base people are seeking. That will allow them to come to you and partner with you. They can use your knowledge to help enhance whatever it is they are doing. That has definitely been a fun part of entrepreneurship for me.

Filling Holes in Transition— Retirement Wellness

As I got started my transition to focus on Retirement Wellness, I had a chance to meet someone who had been trained with the National Science Foundation. I learned the process of starting a business. It is an interview process to identify people that are your ideal clients; you interview them and ask specific questions. It really helps you frame what it is you want to do and put it in the vernacular that makes sense to your clients. That was an essential part of framing and starting my business. One day I was talking to a CEO in Baltimore, and he was being very gracious. It was probably my third or fourth interview with him. He had an entire succession plan; he knew who would take over his business when he retired. The guy he had in mind was a former NFL player. During one visit, the successor says, "Michelle, come here. Let's talk about this." That led to potential applications of the process for retired elite athletes who often see rapid health decline at the end of their athletic careers. To help create options, having been trained in the value of interprofessional care, I pulled together these experts from across the country who had either worked in sports medicine or were dieticians, physical therapists, epigenetic physicians, etc. as well as a team of people who had either been athletes themselves or had specifically worked with professional athletes. We have developed a plan for when this athletic organization is ready, quite the process. But I am grateful for each and every step and opportunity I have gone through and all the people that have been there.

Advice for Aspiring Entrepreneurs

My biggest piece of advice for aspiring entrepreneurs is to maintain the relationships you develop over time and to have gratitude. Grab the golden nuggets at each step, even when the steps are difficult, and use those to build your next steps. Part of claiming those nuggets along the path is in forming these relationships. I still know my professors; I still know my administrators. I got to know them all well when I worked for them, and so they can't escape me now.

CONTRIBUTOR
CONNECTION

**Michelle Fritsch,
PharmD, BCGP**

www.retirewellness.com
www.propelyourwellness.com

www.linkedin.com/in/michellefritsch/

TONY GUERRA

Biography

Tony Guerra is a part-time entrepreneur with various talents. Originally from the Baltimore/Washington corridor, he has combined creative writing work with his knowledge of pharmacology and career to author many audiobooks. His book, *Memorizing Pharmacology: A Relaxed Approach*, is a guide to help students more easily learn drug names. He has also authored *Good Night Pharmacology: 350 Brand and Generic Drug Names with Classifications* and published *Pharmacotherapy: Improving Medical Education Through Clinical Pharmacy Pearls, Case Studies, and Common Sense*. Those are just three of the 30 books he has written or produced in four major categories of pharmacology, pharmacotherapy, career residency, entrepreneurship, and professional school admissions and interviews. He has taught college pharmacology and chemistry for over 11 years and lives in Ankeny, Iowa, with his wife Mindy and their triplet daughters: Brielle, Rianne, and Teagan.

Entrepreneurial Journey

Thinking back on my entrepreneurial journey, the frustration that aspiring entrepreneurs seem to have is that they want a step-by-step process. They want to know what to do first, second, third, etc. But they end up being frustrated because all people can say is, "One, it wasn't what I planned. Two, it's different for everybody." All I can do is share how it worked out for me and go from there.

I was teaching pharmacology classes as an adjunct professor. I wasn't making much, only like $4,000 a class for an entire semester. And one day, a student approached me and said, "You know, I wish I had a pre-book so that I could study before the class started and begin learning drug names." It turned out when my students were listening to my lectures, a lot of the drug names I was mentioning were complete blanks for them. They didn't understand what those words meant.

I said, "Okay, let me see what I can do."

Around this same time, I had another student email me saying, "Can you record yourself saying the names of the top 200 drugs? I am a new student, and I don't even know how to pronounce them yet."

I realized there was something here; there was a need for a rudimentary listing of drugs. I put together a book and some mnemonics so my students could better understand popular medicines. It worked very well within my skill set because I was an English undergrad. My parents had been a little skeptical about that. I combined my pharmacy knowledge with my English background and put together a book.

I have always felt, and I think many people do, that they have a book inside them. I always really wanted to write a book, and I just never had the time. The nice thing with mnemonics and the top 200 drugs was I could go one at a time. I would think, "I'll just do one mnemonic today, and that is it." Some days I would do one; some days, I would do three. Some days I would do ten. Finally, I did all 200 by breaking the book project down into tiny pieces.

I wrote the book for my students, and they were like, "This is great!" I made very little money off it, but it was of great value to my students. A publisher contacted me about recording an audio reading of the book. So, I recorded myself reading. I even tried to hire a speech acting coach so that I would sound good. It turns out no matter what I did, I still sounded terrible. I could pronounce the drug names, but it wasn't something you would want to listen to for seven hours.

Finally, I hired a guy to read the book. Initially, I was worried because he was from Scotland, he used to work for the BBC. But he had a soothing voice. And when I thought about what my students wanted, it made perfect sense. They want something to reduce their anxiety. Why not give them the material they need in a calming way?

That is why I ended up calling the book "A Relaxed Approach" because it was like ASMR for pharmacology. I just wanted my students to listen and learn and hopefully calm down a little. It was a bet. I think every entrepreneur takes a big gamble. In my case, the bet was $400 per finished hour, which worked out to about $3,000 for a seven-hour book. So, I put $3,000 down on a book that wasn't selling print and eBooks editions, but it turns out, a quarter-of-a-million dollars in audiobook sales later, it was a good bet. That is total, not just that audiobook but the others I have made. But without that first book, I never would have gone down the path of becoming an entrepreneur. Funny, people buy the print and eBook after the audiobook.

That was how it all started, and since then, I have used the books as opportunities to solve problems that I have seen arise. I wrote another book on Unicorn Jobs because I noticed that students were not getting as much exposure to non-required rotations as they should have. Accreditation Council for Pharmacy Education (ACPE) requires four rotations, which means if you are doing six-week rotations, four of your blocks include ambulatory care, critical care, internal med, and community. That leaves you only two or three opportunities to look at non-required rotations.

I began thinking, can we put a couple of hundred people together that are potentially working in other areas? And I found that pharmacists are doing well in financial services, real estate, and other very niche entrepreneurial jobs. That is one book I made that I would recommend to you all. I think it can help you find your path through listening to the experiences of others. It allows you to explore and say, "Oh yeah, I could see myself doing that."

A nod about this chapter and financial freedom: I am writing on a Friday, and I don't have work. I work Monday through Thursday at my community college. I don't work nights and weekends. I got to coach my daughters in soccer until they were ten. And now I can afford to send them to expensive soccer camps, gymnastics, and cross country while still having time to attend their meets and go to their games. I know many families can't say that. So, for me, that is a real win. My wife and I had a recent opportunity to get $35,000 in bonuses each if we took retail jobs with a two-year commitment, and we both said no because we can prioritize our quality of life. So, my goal for this chapter is to show you how you can get to the point where you can turn down opportunities that might pay a lot of money but result in a lower quality of life.

I started as a pharmacist in 1997. I went out to Arizona and began working in retail. I was making quite a lot of money for a young kid. I came back to Baltimore, and I had something wrong with my knee. It ultimately ended up being my iliotibial band. What was happening was the band in my knee was so tight from standing for twelve hours a day that it was pulling my knee in the wrong place. So, I started doing stretching and physical therapy. Thankfully everything ended up resolved, but it still really scared me. That fear ended up pushing me to get my real estate license.

I thought, "Okay, let me give this a try." And in the first year, I sold a house or two and made $4,000. I took some real estate coaching and went on to make $40,000. By the time I left, I had sold ten million dollars in houses in a single year and earned $255,000 in commissions. That was the first time I realized that I didn't need to dread my job. I had always thought of a job as something you had to do, and the more money you make doing something you don't like, the better you are. But becoming a real estate agent made me realize that a job can be cool. You can do something you enjoy for the most part. I had never felt like that before, like I was a master of my destiny.

Methods to Monetize Your Knowledge

In addition to the books, another way I monetize my knowledge is through Teachable. Teachable is a platform where you can build online courses and things of that nature. Many people are in that space; it's not easy to enter.

Part of my desire for that was my dad being an immigrant. He could not get a degree because he was working and had kids that he needed to provide for, but I saw firsthand how he struggled because of it. I am sure he could have gotten one, but we were the reason he didn't. The language barrier was also a real issue. So, I find that when people are getting jobs and need to submit any piece of writing, whether it's a letter of intent for residency anything you need to submit before you meet the people in the room, it can become a real barrier.

What happens is whoever is responsible for hiring will think, "This person is great, I would love to meet them," but the candidate will struggle to write that letter because they are not entirely fluent in English. So, if you do not have access to the audio part of the application, and only the written, that becomes a natural barrier. Pharmacy schools are now accepting almost 90% of applicants, which means there will be students coming in who are struggling with the language. That means that by the time they get to graduation, only 25%

of a graduating class of pharmacy students will get a residency as opposed to 95% of medical students. There is this huge barrier.

So, I began thinking; there are writers and coaches whose whole business is CVs. They are excellent at making CVs. I can do that for letters of intent and cover letters. Let me try to help people with this. So, I have an entire course I charge $95 for, but I will also help polish a letter of intent and create templates so they can do it themselves and have a unique application. It's not even that I need the money. I did it for free for one year, and the applicants did not have the emotional investment. But with a nominal charge, they are very invested. I started last season and had a couple of people sign up over the summer and into September and October. By December, I had made $15,000. I'm like, "Whoa. What happened?" I had not meant to sell these courses, but there was a need, and my courses were filling it.

There are so many people applying for residencies who don't understand the process. The penalty for messing up is very high. If you don't get into a residency in your first year, your chances of getting in the following year halve. Your chances of getting into a residency program are already only 64% if you get an interview, and if you try to get in the next year, they drop to 32%. This percentage varies depending on the school, but the stakes are still incredibly high. We found that the letter of intent, letters of recommendation, and CV/grades each count for about a third within the application process. So, you have to make sure your writing is strong. If you can write your way in, why not do that?

This extra income also allowed me to quit one of my adjunct teaching positions, a night-time job. I did not want to do it anymore but wanted to have that safety net before leaving. This job also allowed me to work from wherever. You'll find me working on an airplane, at my parents' house in Arizona, all of these incredible places where I am fixing letters of intent. It gives me the flexibility that many other people liken to a road to financial freedom.

Writing Your Way into Residency & Pharmacy Careers

There is one big mistake I see people make with their cover letter and letter of intent. It can be helpful to think about the process like a bodybuilding contest. The guys like Arnold Schwarzenegger pose and stand for judges. Their score comes from their physique and how they look. What I see repeatedly is people come with a cover letter that is essentially saying, "look at me, look at what I've done" It's effectively posing with all their muscles out, telling you about how great they are. But what is missing is the other half—why do you match this program?

This analogy not only applies to residency programs but university applications, job applications, everything. It is easy to tell when someone has barely read a job listing because they don't respond to any of the criteria listed in the posting. They don't say, "You listed the job as having these responsibilities; here is an example of when I used those same skills." Or, if you can't say that, you need to say, "Here is how I am working towards obtaining those skills to help me get better in my career."

So, the way I describe it is by saying you do not just have bodybuilding contests. You also need to sit down with the person, put your tie on, and get rid of the skimpy bathing suit. You need to sit down and explain why you want to be at this company. I see it repeatedly. That matching content is absent from so many of the letters I see.

I understand why. Many of the templates out there tell you to explain what you did in leadership, explain what you did clinically, or as service. The writer puts down their job experience, teaching experience, and research experience. They hit all these areas, but they don't answer the question, "Why here?" They never say, "This is why I want to be with you."

So, the most frequent thing I tell people is, "Why do you want to be at UNC?" For example, don't just say, "I want to go to UNC." You have to say why. It doesn't require a massive shift, you only must change a few sentences, and you will have answered that question. A helpful visual is to imagine 300 pieces of paper on the floor. There are only four spots available. You have to find your application out of those 300 pieces of paper. That needle in a haystack is precisely what the people reading residency applications are going through. But as soon as they see those keywords, they know an applicant knows the school, they understand the program. Do they see their program's acronyms, the words from their website, the areas they specialize in? That tells the admissions people that you are using their language. It's that simple, but that lets them know that you are one of them, and they need to interview you.

The most common mistake I see is continuing to talk about yourself. Think of it as a ten-minute conversation. Nobody wants a conversation with someone who only talks about themselves. You must talk about yourself and the other person. I ask people, "There are 4,000 positions you could apply for; why did you pick this one out of the 4,000?" And the answer is not what makes you so great, but what makes you an excellent fit for this institution.

I didn't speak English as a child. I didn't learn English until I was about six or seven. Yet, I went on to get an English degree, so my writing is pretty good. It's at a Ph.D. level. And I can see English from a different perspective because it is not the language I was born speaking.

I first became interested in Unicorn Jobs, specifically at APhA in Seattle. Hillary Blackburn, who is another contributor to this book, had invited a group of entrepreneurs to have coffee. She bought the coffee from Starbucks in one of those big boxes. It looks kind of like boxed wine, only it's coffee. And it was amazing, we all got together, and we realized that none of us had traditional jobs. We began wondering, do the people who come to these meetings not have traditional jobs? Or do they go into non-traditional jobs because they come to these meetings?

I think it's a combination of the two. There are people at these conferences who do not have traditional jobs, and people are seeking out the steps they can take to become entrepreneurs. The book about Unicorn Jobs came out of that. I was curious and began thinking, why not write about people who have these non-traditional jobs, and it just grew and became person after person.

I spoke to my friend Mike Lenz who does audiobooks full time. He was mayor of his town and had a compounding pharmacy as well. I talked to people with such flexible work-life balance who are doing the "impossible" to replace a pharmacist's salary with a completely different career.

Recently, on one of the *Your Financial Pharmacist Podcast* episodes, someone came on and talked about how they don't want to leave their job. They enjoy their side-hustle, but their job gives them enough time to spend with their special needs child. It allows them to have that extra time and money too. One of my daughter's medicines is $4,000 a month. You can have a job you enjoy that also takes care of your needs. These things are possible.

I have a podcast called *The Pharmacy Residency Podcast*. It is ultra-niche. It has had almost half a million downloads, not counting the YouTube views. Each episode gets another 300 or so views on my TonyPharmD YouTube channel, totaling about 1.2 million views or something like that. The channel itself has almost 35,000 subscribers and 12 million downloads.

So, you can find me at TonyPharmD on YouTube or *The Pharmacy Residency Podcast*. Either one is a great way to follow what I'm doing and get advice on getting where you want to go. My niche is helping those looking for residency help or wanting to succeed in residency, but in truth, I support anyone facing a writing obstacle.

Advice for Aspiring Entrepreneurs

All my side hustles come from meeting a need that somebody else has. It's like give, ask, receive. You give that person the solution, ask for their business, and then receive it. So, it may sound strange, but that is the way to become a successful entrepreneur, to dive into someone else's needs.

If you work to solve someone else's problem, you will be amazed at how it helps solve your problems.

CONTRIBUTOR
CONNECTION

Tony Guerra, PharmD

www.pharmacyresidencypodcast.com/

www.linkedin.com/in/tonypharmd/

NATE HEDRICK

Biography

Nate Hedrick is a full-time pharmacist by day, husband and father by evening and weekend, and real estate agent, investor, and blogger by late night and early morning. He has a passion for staying uncomfortable and is always on the lookout for a new challenge or a project. He found real estate investing in 2016 after his $300,000+ student loan debt led him to read *Rich Dad, Poor Dad*. This book opened his mind to the possibilities of financial freedom, and he has been obsessed ever since. After earning his real estate license in 2017, Nate founded Real Estate RPH© as a source for real estate education designed with pharmacists in mind. Since then, he has helped dozens of pharmacists around the country realize their dream of owning a home or starting their investing journey. Nate resides in Cleveland, Ohio, with his wife, Kristen, his two daughters, Molly and Lucy, and his rescue dog Lexi.

Entrepreneurial Journey

I started off as a clinical pharmacist through and through. I did residency, and I thought I would be a clinical pharmacist my entire career. I loved the pain management and palliative care space and worked in hospice for several years after residency. However, around the time my wife was pregnant with our first child, I read *Rich Dad, Poor Dad*. It had been on my bucket list of books, and I finally got around to paging through it while we were on our last vacation before the delivery. That book completely changed my mindset from one of being an employee forever to one of financial freedom. It became more and more apparent that financial freedom was something I wanted to pursue. I began simply by having conversations with people who had achieved financial independence or were in the process of doing so, and real estate started to really stick out as key to the process. One of those conversations was with my father-in-law, who had been a real estate developer for years.

He said, "If you like real estate, why don't you just become a real estate agent?"

And I said, "I can't do that. I already have a career. I'm already a pharmacist. I can't take on a second career."

And he said, "It's really easy. You get the license and hang your hat with a brokerage. You can find a flexible one where you don't have to go to the meetings. You can have both careers at the same time."

That concept was something I had never thought of before. About the time I should have been going to get my Board Certification, I completely shifted gears and got my real estate license, much to my wife's dismay at the time. And it turned out to be a great fit for me. I really fell in love with the idea of real estate, and I immediately wanted to get more involved.

I thought that as soon as I got my license, all of my friends, family, and coworkers would come to me and say, "Hey, I'm ready to buy a house. You're the real estate agent for me!" About six months went by, and I had no deals whatsoever. I couldn't figure out why. I didn't understand why business wasn't flocking to me. That made me take a step back and start thinking about what I wanted my niche to be. If you Google real estate agent Cleveland, Ohio, a thousand people come up. I started wondering how I could develop my own niche and build my customer base. And how can I do that while also being a pharmacist?

I realized that my network was right there in front of me. The pharmacy community is very small; I should start there because I know these people. I can talk to them and understand what they are going through. I began working with my first pharmacist client, an investor here in Cleveland. From there, I started Real Estate RPH in 2017, a website dedicated to helping pharmacists learn more about real estate, whether they are first-time homebuyers or purchasing their first investment property. From that core concept, I began to grow the business.

Methods to Monetize Your Knowledge

When I first launched the website, I had no idea how I was going to monetize it. It was more about sensing a need for a resource and wanting to be the one that created it. Now one of the unique things about being a real estate agent is that when you help someone sell or buy a house, you get paid on a commission basis. But what many people may not know is that if you give a client to someone else and that real estate agent helps them close that house, you get a portion of their commission as well. It's simply called a referral, and you usually get about 25-30% of what that agent would make for sending them a "ready-to-act" lead.

I quickly realized that there were pharmacists all over the country who needed my help. Being based in Cleveland, Ohio, meant there was only a small pocket of people that I could personally assist. From there, I began to build a referral business that I call the home buying concierge service. Pretty much all of the monetization done today is through that service.

What that looks like is if you are a pharmacist or someone you know is looking to buy or sell a home, you come to me, and we have a 30-minute one-on-one planning session to discuss that. We talk about your must-haves, budget, questions about the lending process, whatever I can do to get your feet off the ground. And then, I'll connect you with a real estate agent I have personally vetted in your local market. This is someone who is going to help you have an awesome home-buying experience. If I do my job right, that house closes, and I get 25% of the real estate agent's commission. For every four people I refer, it is equivalent to selling a house here in Cleveland. But again, it takes only a fraction of the work. That is the core monetization of what I do. I wasn't the first person to ever have this idea. Referral-based programs are out there. But they aren't designed in quite the same way mine is.

Combining Careers:
How Pharmacy & Real Estate
Meet with the Real Estate RPH

I started Real Estate RPH in 2017 while still maintaining my pharmacy career. I am a full-time pharmacist here in Cleveland. So, there are a number of things I have learned along the way that I think are really important. When you look at combining real estate and pharmacy, most people see two completely unrelated fields. What I see is an opportunity for combination.

There are three main points that I believe have allowed me to combine these two fields successfully. The first is this, don't be afraid to NOT be a pharmacist. We go through six years of school, eight years in some cases, a year or two of residency. And we get out with a six-figure salary and, a lot of times, six figures of student loan debt. My wife and I are both pharmacists, so we got out with a little over $300,000 in student loan debt. It was terrifying to even think about not being a pharmacist.

And again, I am still a practicing pharmacist today. But as soon as I set out to get my real estate license, I got all these questions from people. They would ask me, "Oh, you're quitting pharmacy?" "Are you going to be a real estate agent now?" "Why are you doing that?" But you don't have to be afraid of that conversation. I'm not even looking to leave pharmacy any time soon, but what I've done is create an opportunity to if that is something I choose.

As pharmacists, we get ingrained in that idea for so long, but you shouldn't be afraid of having that conversation with yourself. Your degree does not equal your identity. I can't tell you the number of people that reached out to me and said, "If you're doing real estate, you must be done with pharmacy," and that just wasn't the case. As human beings, none of us is only one thing. Just because you're a pharmacist does not mean you are a pharmacist 24/7. I'm also a dad; I'm also a real estate investor, I blog. There are all of these other things I am outside of my degree. Don't be afraid to take on something that is outside of your "path."

I have a friend who was a pharmacist for a few years and realized it was not a good fit for her and her family. She slowly transitioned out of pharmacy into insurance sales. It's scary, but it was the right decision for her. People look at her and ask, "Why would you quit pharmacy? You have spent all this time. You *have* to do that." But you don't. I promise you it is not going to ruin everything.

My second point is that you should look for conversations, not clients. When we start a business, it can be very easy to fall into this trap of thinking that you need to create business for yourself; you need to create opportunity. And so, when I started the concierge service, I was immediately worried about automation. I was afraid I was going to get all of these phone calls and people, and I wouldn't have the automation to handle it. I was so concerned with automation that I lost out on my first three or four clients. These people who I had connected with a real estate agent didn't close the house because I hadn't taken the time to make those conversations meaningful. I didn't nurture the relationship in order to actually create business because everything I was reading said, "You have to automate." Don't forget to actually work with your clients and form those great relationships because truly, that is so important.

The co-host for my *YFP Real Estate Investing Podcast*, David, I met through a conversation. We would never have met if I had not had that conversation. We were two pharmacists interested in real estate investing. That one conversation led to many more great conversations, and eventually to this partnership that has given way to a podcast. We have even done a couple of real estate investing deals together. But that initial conversation was just two individuals who shared something. Look for those conversations, don't look for clients. You will create business and clients by having meaningful conversations first.

Finally, I want to mention social media and specifically LinkedIn. I love LinkedIn and am very active there. But something I often hear from people who are not yet entrepreneurs but want to be is that they feel that their LinkedIn account belongs to their employer. There is this weird concept that because LinkedIn is a professional network, it's owned by your employer, and you can't have anything of your own there. You can't post anything that isn't associated with your employer in some regard. But that's not true at all. I have my employer listed on my LinkedIn page; you can see my company right at the top. But my banner and posts are all about real estate. Again, yes, I am a pharmacist, but I am also the founder of Real Estate RPH, I am a real estate investor, I am a realtor, I am a podcast host. Here are all of the things I do. LinkedIn is not owned by employer groups; I encourage people to look at it as their own platform because it is hard to grow your business if you feel like your identity is bound to your employer.

Advice for Aspiring Entrepreneurs

My advice for aspiring entrepreneurs is pretty simple, don't be afraid to follow your passion. Don't be afraid to do something other people think is weird. I think back to all the people who said, "Why are you doing real estate? That has nothing to do with pharmacy." But I have been able to turn it into a really successful business. And it is something that I'm passionate about. I stay up late working on real estate and my business, and people think it's nuts, but that is what I like doing. And if I had listened to everybody who said, "Well, you went to school for six years. You spent all that money on a pharmacy degree; you have to keep doing that." I'd be much worse for wear. Don't be afraid to be a little different. Stay uncomfortable.

CONTRIBUTOR CONNECTION

Nate Hedrick, PharmD

🌐 www.realestaterph.com

in www.linkedin.com/in/natehedrick/

BRITTANY HOFFMANN-EUBANKS

Biography

Dr. Brittany Hoffmann-Eubanks earned her Doctor of Pharmacy and Master of Business Administration degrees from Drake University College of Pharmacy & Health Sciences in 2012. After graduate school, she completed a Postgraduate-Year-1 Community Pharmacy Residency, where she earned her teaching and learning certificate, dedicated herself to patient-centered care, and learned the business of pharmacy. During her residency, Brittany discovered her passion for education and desire to be an entrepreneur. Brittany is the Founder and CEO of Banner Medical LLC. Her work at Banner Medical integrates her passion for writing with her medical background as a pharmacist. Brittany is an expert content developer for both healthcare providers and consumers. She has also created two online medical writing courses entitled Medical Writing Jumpstart and Medical Writing Mastery, which help pharmacists start their medical writing careers. Brittany also enjoys giving back to the profession of pharmacy and currently serves on the Board of Directors for the Illinois Pharmacists Association. In 2018, Brittany was awarded the Edmond P. Barcus Distinguished Young Pharmacist Award for her service to the Illinois Pharmacists Association. Brittany loves to travel with her husband and family in her free time and play with her two dogs.

Entrepreneurial Journey

When I started Banner Medical in 2015, I never imagined that I would have this platform or be amongst such great company. I started my career in community pharmacy as a pharmacy student and, like many others, went on to do a residency after pharmacy school since I really wanted to immerse myself in patient care before jumping into being a pharmacist full time. And that was very enlightening for me. People often ask me how I got into writing and pharmacy because the two don't necessarily seem to go together. But I had the great fortune of having a librarian for a grandmother, who instilled in me very early on the importance of being able to communicate.

As a child, I wrote creatively, and over time that evolved into technical and medical writing, which I do now. That led to doing some research in pharmacy school, and afterward, during my residency, was when the light bulb went on for me. I realized I had the opportunity to help the pharmacists in the company I worked for. I had gotten some positive feedback on a particular CE that I had written, and that really got the wheels turning. I began thinking, "Hmm, I wonder if this is something that is actually needed? How does the process work? We all love free CE, and we need it to be able to renew our license, but what actually goes into the process of creating that, and who does it?" Those were the questions I was asking myself.

That was what planted the seed, but for the next few years, I continued just working in practice, getting my feet wet after residency and becoming comfortable. And it reached a point where I began to wish that I was able to do more. I wanted to have more opportunities. I graduated in 2012, and during that post-2008/2009 time period, there were very few jobs. My class didn't have many jobs when we graduated, so being able to begin my residency was very fortunate. But even afterward, things were still very saturated with few opportunities. Therefore, when I talk about my start as an entrepreneur, I tell people that it happened by accident.

I wasn't looking to be an entrepreneur as much as I was looking for more opportunities to help people. As a result, I took a leap of faith. I went to LinkedIn of all places and started with my network. I reached out to a former colleague I had worked with who was then running a major national publication. I said, "Hey. This is what I am interested in; we have worked together in the past. How do you create this content because I would love to be involved?" At some point, you just have to take the risk and put yourself out there because what is the worst that could happen? They could say, "Hey, thank you for reaching out, but this is not how we do this." And that's it.

To my great fortune and excitement, they said that they were looking for more practice-based writers and that they would love to work with me. And that started my very first project, which launched my company, Banner Medical. It was a really exciting opportunity. One thing led to another, I got some great feedback, and I was able to keep building my business into what it is now. I began as a freelance medical writer, picking up projects on the side to make some extra money and pay off my student loans. But what ended up happening was that the caliber and quality of the work were so high we started getting more repeat clients, what I call core clients. We no longer had to hustle for every single project that was out there and grew rapidly.

As a result of this growth, I transitioned into a CEO role where I help pharmacists leverage their backgrounds and create revenue streams. This was an exciting transition for me personally. I never envisioned it, but it was gratifying to be able to help other pharmacists perfect their skillset or go out and create their business. I love working with the team I have at Banner. But I think part of why I never imagined this could be my career is that I didn't understand just how valuable my skillet was at the time. However, our clients are very appreciative of the work that we do, and this has been personally gratifying and validating. Our pharmacists on the Banner Medical team have also shared great feedback, and I love creating a positive environment where they can thrive and leverage their backgrounds in medical writing.

Even though we're not participating in direct patient care, we are contributing in a different way. I know what we do directly affects how clinicians, other healthcare providers, and pharmacists make decisions about patients. Whether it is their care or the coordination of care, ultimately, the outcomes for those patients are impacted by my business. It has been an exciting opportunity and something that I am looking forward to continually growing and expanding.

As I said before, at some point, you have to stop being afraid and just take a leap of faith. I'm hoping I will be able to run my business full-time within the next year.

Methods to Monetize Your Knowledge

When it comes to monetizing your knowledge, I think it is really important to be able to focus on your zone of genius. For example, I started with continuing medical education before I branched out to other areas of medical writing. Today, we have three main areas that we provide medical writing services for. The first area is continuing medical education. We have a variety of products that we offer in this space. For example, we may create training information, supplemental education pieces for journals, slide decks, and more. However, our bread and butter are educational needs assessments. Needs Assessments are essentially justification documents for why a company should award grant monies for CE programs. As healthcare providers, we are required to complete continuing education to renew our licenses. You may get access to a free CE at no cost, but it still costs money to create those products for you and other healthcare providers.

The second area is the blog consumer health space. Here we write content directly for companies for them to distribute to their audience, or we might work directly with a healthcare group. It really depends on what kind of content the clients are looking for. The third area is academic and scientific writing. Academic and scientific writing is a lot more technical, but it is something that I personally really enjoy. We will help companies or individuals that need assistance publishing their manuscripts in a journal, textbooks, test questions, and more.

More recently, we had the opportunity this past year to help student pharmacists, too. This has been really meaningful for me to be able to give back to the profession through the creation of a quick review guide for the North American Pharmacist Licensure Examination (NAPLEX). It is nice to know that our work will directly benefit student pharmacists.

Finally, I have created two medical writing courses (Medical Writing Jumpstart and Medical Writing Mastery) that were created specifically for pharmacists to help them get started in medical writing. Pharmacists have the capacity to do so many amazing things, and it is an honor now to help pharmacists go beyond the traditional boxes and leverage their backgrounds in new meaningful ways. I now help pharmacists turn their writing into paychecks! We have had some really great success stories, and I cannot wait to see what the future pharmacists who utilize my courses do as medical communicators!

The Power of Medical Writing

Many people don't realize how integral pharmacists are to the health care process when it comes to education. We are all very familiar with counseling and the importance of having those discussions with our patients. But we often don't consider the deeper level of education, that is, how do we learn, how do we better understand the various disease states and educational components that are essential to help patients. This is a crucial foundation and only one area of medical writing. Medical writing is such a broad field. I often share the statistic that it is a $3 billion industry. This makes me excited because it means there is ample room for other pharmacists who are interested in carving out their own space, especially when you consider that everyone has their own particular zone of genius.

For example, if you are a pharmacist that has a greater understanding of medicinal cannabis, your knowledge is highly valuable because we need more educational materials on this topic! Or, if you are an oncology pharmacist, your knowledge base will certainly be an asset because the oncology field changes on a daily basis, sometimes multiple times a day. It also is incumbent on us as pharmacists to stay up to date and be able to understand all of the different guidelines of the areas that we practice in.

As busy professionals, staying up to date can be very difficult! Therefore, medical writers can help ease this burden on healthcare providers. It becomes our job to create meaningful education to assist our healthcare providers in taking care of their patients. I think we all have heard of a story where a medical mistake was made. It is the third leading cause of death in the United States; it is a major concern. For example, after a recent ultrasound I had, I overheard another ultrasound tech talking with a doctor, saying that they had mislabeled something on an ultrasound they conducted. Thankfully the doctor reviewing the ultrasound caught the error, but if left unchecked, it could have negatively impacted the patient's care. While this was a case of human error, every day, patient safety and outcomes are impacted by knowledge gaps. Therefore, medical writers have an integral role in helping to bridge these knowledge gaps, communication of best practices, and evidence-based medicine. It is also essential that medical writers are able to communicate in ways that are understandable and meaningful.

I will often tell people anyone can regurgitate a package insert, data from a particular article, or whatever resource you are using. But medical writing *is* storytelling. It doesn't have to be boring. We want to engage our healthcare providers and consumers, so they feel empowered to invest in themselves and their knowledge. Therefore, it is essential that medical writers always keep the audience and end-goal of the medical writing product in mind. For example, are we intending the reader to walk away with surface-level knowledge? Is it a deep dive so that a meaningful change can be made in someone's practice or personal life? Or are we educating about potential treatments coming down the pipeline for a particular disease state? Will this future drug therapy change the scope of practice for a certain disease? As you can see, there are a lot of variables that factor into learning and education beyond cursory knowledge. I think this attention to detail is the root of what we do well at Banner; and why our clients keep coming back to us for repeat work. They know that we have a fierce focus on quality and balance, but we also care deeply about the end result regardless of who the intended audience is.

I've taught many pharmacists about the various medical writing opportunities out there. Talk about a gig economy is common in medical writing, which is very true, but there is a skill to keeping clients coming back to you. Repeat clients are essential to growing and scaling your business; that is something I teach in my medical writing courses. The great news is that there are so many ways pharmacists can get involved in the medical writing field. For example, if you desire to be a medical writer, you could either work for a medical writing communications company full time, or you could freelance and pick up individual projects on a contractor basis, which was what I did when I first started writing. Plus, freelancing is great if you are only interested in a side hustle for some extra money. The beauty of the gig economy is that you can take on as much or as little work as you want. You just have to decide what you are interested in and what your personal goals are (i.e., working full-time or on a freelance basis).

There are sites out there like Upwork and Doximity where you can search for jobs. However, I'll caution anyone who is interested in being a medical writer since these sites frequently do not pay an appropriate amount for the work being requested. Not too long ago, I saw a listing requesting 15,000 words for $400. To give you a sense of scale, 1,000 words is about two pages, roughly 30 pages of writing for $400. That is a huge undertaking for very little money. Oftentimes you will see thousands upon thousands of people competing for jobs on sites like this which allows for these bottom-of-the-barrel rates. But in general, the GIG economy is made up of contractors looking for individual opportunities and clients who want to hire them. You just have to find the right clients for your business.

I have also seen a lot of pharmacists using sites like these to work for free. And I understand it is mostly those who are unsure of how to get started and are just trying to get their feet wet. But if you're going to work for free, it should have a very specific purpose to support that choice. Working without pay should not be something you do on a regular basis, and that does not serve your bigger purpose and goals.

Your services are valuable, and we shouldn't devalue ourselves as entrepreneurs and pharmacists with doctoral degrees. In short, you have to make sure you are being paid what you are worth and refuse to settle for anything less.

Refusing to settle for less and how to ensure you are paid what you are worth is another key area I work through with the pharmacists who take my course! We focus a lot on negotiating prices, finding the right clients for you, and what to do when you have difficult clients.

There are also very specific challenges we face as entrepreneurs and freelancers. For instance, how do you build a writing portfolio if the companies you freelance for won't allow you to share the work? Banner Medical is no exception to this common concern. The nature of my business is that we do a lot of proprietary work, a good portion of which we are unable to share. An easy way to bypass this issue is through the creation of case studies. Case studies are a way to legally share what the project was, your role in the project, and what the outcome was. This way, you can share examples with your prospective clients and highlight your skill sets without breaking any intellectual property agreements you might have with the previous client.

Prospective pharmacist medical writers may also want to consider creating a speculation (spec) article. A spec article is written on a topic that you have identified fitting well with the target audience of the prospective client you are going after for business. This approach would require you to research the company or publication you are interested in working for, but you can create content ahead of time and ensure it is a representation of your *best* work. My mantra is, "the first draft is the last draft." In this way, you are working to create your final draft the first time where no to minimal editing is required. Then you can take the spec article and go out and market yourself.

Marketing yourself is a whole other conversation, but I encourage the pharmacists I work with to have an elevator pitch ready. Having an elevator speech was something I had to do in the early days of Banner because very few people in pharmacy were familiar with what medical writing was or what I was trying to do. There were a lot of conversations I had with pharmacists and family members that consisted of, "What is medical writing?" "What do you mean?" when I told them what I was doing in my free time. But this is how you leverage yourself; it is how you show what your value is and distinguish yourself from all the other writers out there.

Advice for Aspiring Entrepreneurs

There is a quote that I absolutely love and that really resonated with me when I first began my journey. Because there was a moment of real fear, I didn't know if I was either going to continue taking projects as they came up and scale back or grow Banner into what it is today, which is a multi-six-figure company. This quote by Robin Sharma really helped me, and I think it is something we can all benefit from.

"Your excuses are nothing more than the lies your fears have sold you."

And I share this because it is the number one thing I see holding other pharmacists back. The fear of shame and not being able to succeed. The fear of not being able to do everything as it relates to their family, their careers, their financial freedom, and security. My biggest piece of advice is just to start. We often see the highlight reels of all the influencers and people out there doing amazing things, and you think, "Oh, I wish I could do that." And yes, you may have three kids and a full-time job, but it doesn't have to be huge. You can start small and work up to the big things. This is exactly what I did. I started small and worked up to where I am today, and you can too!

Brittany Hoffmann-Eubanks, PharmD, MBA

CONTRIBUTOR
•••
CONNECTION

🌐 www.bannermedicalwriting.com

in www.linkedin.com/in/brittany-hoffmann-eubanks/

CORY JENKS

Biography

Dr. Cory Jenks earned his PharmD from the University of South Carolina in 2011 and completed a PGY1 residency at the Southern Arizona VA Healthcare System in 2012. His past pharmacy experience has included time as a retail pharmacist, outpatient clinical pharmacist, and inpatient clinical pharmacist. Currently, he practices as an Ambulatory Care Clinical Pharmacy Specialist, where he applies his passion for lifestyle interventions in the management of chronic disease. Cory is also an accomplished improv comedian, having started on his comedy journey in 2013. Since then, Cory has coached, taught, and performed improv for thousands of people. Today, Cory travels the country teaching other healthcare professionals how to apply the valuable skills of improv comedy to create a more adaptable, empathetic, and humanizing healthcare experience. He released his first book, Permission to Care: Building a Healthcare Culture that Thrives in Chaos, in 2022. When not working or performing improv, Cory enjoys raising chickens, playing racquetball, basketball, and golf, exploring the science of disease management through lifestyle, and is currently earning his Master's Degree in "Dad Jokes" with the help of his kids.

Entrepreneurial Journey

I've always loved comedy, and when I attended the University of South Carolina, they had an improv group I went to see, and it completely blew me away! "Naturally," I did not pursue improv because I was in school to be a pharmacist and thought that's where my focus needed to be. Once I got out of school, I began practicing got my PGY1 and a couple of board certifications under my belt, but something was missing. I was still struggling to make connections with patients.

My now-wife-then-girlfriend asked me what I wanted for my 26th birthday, guitar lessons or an improv class. Well, my guitar is still gathering dust in the corner, so you can probably guess which gift I chose. So, I began taking improv classes and moved on to performing. After some on-stage experience, I began teaching and coaching improv comedy as well. I realized that the skills I was learning as an improv comedian: listening, communicating, empathizing, being in the moment, and making adjustments were making me a better pharmacist. Suddenly I was able to respond to the unknown and connect with my patients quickly and easily in a way that I had never been able to before.

Now our reality in healthcare is we don't get enough time with our patients regardless of our practice settings. In an improv scene, I have to make a quick connection with my scene partner while also engaging an audience of strangers. With a patient, we have to connect in a short period of time and make them care about what medicine they're taking or how they can manage their particular condition. I made that connection; improv is helping me be a better pharmacist.

I live in Tucson and like it here. It's not exactly the comedy hub of the world, but we have our improv theater I can perform at. Another factor is I have kids and a wife that kinda like it here, so it's not like I can just move to New York or Chicago to pursue being a professional comedian. I needed to figure out another way to pursue improv because this has become a really valuable skill set. And I realized there is a great need in the world of pharmacy and healthcare to help us better empathize with our patients and to adapt and provide a humanizing healthcare experience.

Methods to Monetize Your Knowledge

I have been doing improv for a number of years now have focused on being a professional speaker and trainer applying improv to healthcare. I do keynote addresses, workshops, and seminars. I may have picked the middle of a pandemic to become a professional speaker, but thankfully, if improv teaches you one thing, it is to adapt. That is how I monetize my knowledge.

My book, *Permission to Care: Building a Healthcare Culture that Thrives in Chaos* was released in February 2022. I see this as an opportunity for an additional revenue stream but also to help attract me to other speaking engagements. Speaking and working with others is really where the magic really happens. That's the moment where I see the light bulbs go off with the healthcare professionals I work with. They'll say, "I'm not funny. I can't do this." And then, all of a sudden, there is a mindset shift. And it's not just, "Oh wow, I can improv." It's a realization that all of the other things you thought you could not do, you can. It isn't just a comedy skill but a life philosophy that I try to embody.

Find Your Identity, Create Your Path

Thinking back to when I began pharmacy school, I was so determined. I was a pharmacy student and an intramural athlete. I played a little baseball in high school, but I wasn't good enough to continue into college. I was incredibly focused because my entire identity was wrapped up in being a pharmacy student. I spent all my time in the library. I was part of pharmacy organizations. I didn't go to concerts or parties (or join improv groups!), and I honestly didn't have as much fun as I could have.

I was set to graduate in 2011. And two months before graduation, I was on rotation with our Assistant Dean. His name was Dr. Wayne Buff, and he was the first guy I met when I visited the University of South Carolina back in the summer of 2004. He inspired me to move across the country and get stuck with out-of-state tuition just to go to this school. And he says, "I have some advice for you."

I'm like, "All right, finally. After four years of pharmacy school, two years of pre-pharm, I am going to get the advice that is going to make me a superstar pharmacist."

And Dr. Buff told me to find a hobby.

Now I was thinking, "What! No, I'm graduating next month. I need to know what is the *real* secret to being a great pharmacist. It can't just be "find a hobby" And I didn't follow his advice because, for a long time, I was all wrapped up in being a pharmacist. It went right over my head. I didn't have time to find a hobby because I was too busy trying to be a pharmacist.

Finally, I graduated. I was in a great mood. I'm cocky. I was ready to take on the world. I was going to help patients and save the world. I came back home to Tucson because as much as I loved being across the country, I missed my parents. After I finished my residency, I was kind of like a Johnny Cash song, "I've Been Everywhere," of Pharmacy. I wasn't quite sure where I wanted to be yet. I did all kinds of different jobs to figure out what my pharmacist path would be. Out of residency, I became a support pharmacist. Within a couple of months, I was an ambulatory care clinical pharmacy specialist. I was doing scope of practice, managing diabetes hypertension. I was working as a per diem community pharmacist, and I was a pharmacist, but I had begun to get some new identities too. I got engaged and became a fiancé. I had also started doing this improv comedy thing.

Yes, finally, I had the time to take those improv classes, and I really liked them! I was frustrated by being a new practitioner. I was not connecting to my patients, I was feeling behind all the time, and I wasn't sure if ambulatory care was what I really wanted to do. Then I switched to being an inpatient pharmacist. My pharmacist identity changed. Then I got married and was a husband. I started teaching improv for local theatre classes and had an identity as an improv instructor. I also started presenting CE at our state association and realized I really liked presenting in front of others.

I'm one of those weird pharmacists that enjoy getting in front of people, which also works well as an improv comedian. I quickly realized being an inpatient pharmacist wasn't for me. It didn't take me long to realize I actually liked ambulatory care. I think there were some underlying issues that improv helped me discover, mainly that I liked connecting with patients rather than working overnights.

Fast forward to 2018, I went back and became an ambulatory care support pharmacist. I started working per diem at a community health center. At this point, I had so many identities: I was a pharmacist, I was a husband, I became a dad for the first time, I directed a comedy school in Tucson. I got the experience of running a school and developing a curriculum, dealing with complaints and registration, and things of that nature. I actually started helping to teach a course at the College of Pharmacy. We teach here in Arizona, where we incorporate improv into the curriculum. The course predates me; I do not get to take credit for it. But I got to share my clinical expertise in comedy with students, which was incredible!

I also started to expand my world beyond just being a pharmacist and an improviser. I was reading and listening to podcasts. I started a podcast for about a year and got really into nutrition. I was presenting on integrating nutrition with Pharmacy. Yet another identity/thing I am passionate about is minimizing medications. I am interested in learning about how we can incorporate nutrition into how we manage diabetes. All of these identities were taking shape as I went back to being a support pharmacist. After some time, I arrived at where I am now as an ambulatory care clinical pharmacy specialist.

My non-pharmacist identities continued to blossom as I booked my first paid gig in 2019 by accident. I did an improv CE at our state association. Someone came up to me afterward and said, "Hey, I think you would be a great fit for presenting to my sales team. Can you do that?"

And I said, "Sure can!" All of a sudden, I had stumbled upon another identity: paid speaker.

I thought 2020 was going to be my year. My projects and identities were continuing to grow; I was going to go out and give more talks, participate in videos, get testimonials. And then COVID happened. Initially, my thought was, "Well, not exactly a great year to become a professional speaker." But I was able to accept the reality and adjust. I was supposed to do a TEDx talk that year, but it was canceled due to COVID. I shifted; we have to adjust what we do with life.

As pharmacists, our job is perfection. But being an entrepreneur isn't being perfect. It is focusing on progress, realizing our mistakes, and learning from them. This is also a key tenet of improv; there is no script. Often if we make a mistake, we have to see it less as a mistake and more as an opportunity. I think that is where applying the improv mindset is really valuable.

Improvisers are the ones who accept reality and thrive even in really challenging moments. I accepted the limitations of 2020. I accepted that I couldn't go places to speak. I did Zoom webinars; I was able to adapt my identities of diet and lifestyle into presentations and apply them to my day job. Through all of that, I developed a greater appreciation for being a pharmacist and being able to love what I do.

Everyone reading this book has had a bad day as a pharmacist. You have probably had several bad days. I have worked at this since leaving high school. I knew I wanted to be a pharmacist. For seven, eight years, everything I did was toward the end goal of being a pharmacist. You put everything you have into this thing that you love, and it does not always love you back. And it sucks. If you don't have another thing you can focus on, it will drag you down.

When you're a pharmacy student, that's your entire life. If you fail a test or have a bad day in rotation, it is devastating. But when you are having a bad day at the Pharmacy, and you are able to go home and make a silly joke to your son, go feed your chickens, or go out on an improv stage, it provides other outlets. You are able to forget about the other identities for a little while.

What I will say to those seeking to be entrepreneurs is don't discount your other identities. They are not just a form of self-care, but they can also be helpful when applied to your career. Being a pharmacist is important, but it is not everything. Curiosity is not rewarded in healthcare. Who remembers the person in pharmacy school who asked all the questions? The attitude was "stop asking questions unless it is going to be on the test." Stop being curious. But when you follow your curiosity, you find what you care about. Find a hobby and apply what you can to Pharmacy. I teach improv to pharmacy students, pharmacists, nurses, and physicians. It's really fun. I love when people are skeptical, and then I get them to have fun.

If you can adapt to the unexpected and thrive, you'll be so much better for it. Because as pharmacists, we love control. But we don't have control over much, if anything. Learning to roll with those waves and having the ability to embrace whatever happens will serve you so much better. And that is a skill improv teaches you. You're going to have much more success when you let go of that paralyzing perfectionism. Yes, perfectionism is good when checking prescriptions. But when it comes to a new venture or business, it's not going to be perfect. But it is from these opportunities that you learn and grow. If your plans don't work out, that's ok. Accept, regroup, and take those lessons on to the next thing.

Try new things. Pharmacists are bred to be perfect, but if we continue to be disappointed in our imperfections, we are going to be wildly disappointed by life. But you can use those mistakes to narrow down what you really want to do. I am not going to build a business doing oncology; it's just not something that I am passionate enough about to devote my extra time to. Find what interests *you* and build from there. Do you remember being in pharmacy school and having to do a project on a drug or disease state? Those projects were awful unless you picked something that already interested you. Start with your interests. I was already doing improv; I'm good at it, and I proceeded from there.

What I'm trying to say is to cultivate your passions deeply. And if you're not feeling it, if you're burned out, try something else. It's not an easy formula to follow, but it is simple. Try something new and follow your interests. Your identities will develop from there.

I'm so appreciative for the opportunity to join these heavyweights of Pharmacy as a contributor to this book.

Advice for Aspiring Entrepreneurs

My favorite improv tool is saying yes. An Improv scene dies when somebody in a scene says no. But I use yes in real life too. At work, if there's a disagreement with a patient, oftentimes, our instinct is to fight back and say, "No. I'm the pharmacist. I'm right." But what I try to do is agree with them and turn the argument against the larger system. So, for example, I had a patient with a bunch of prior authorizations come through another facility. I needed to get all of this information to process. He was pretty upset; he was like, "This is ridiculous. Why do I have to do all this?"

Now the pharmacist's brain says, "It's not ridiculous. We need this information so we can serve you safely and appropriately." But I said, "Yes. This is ridiculous. I wish we didn't have to go through all of these steps to get the medicine you need. And I want to get you everything you need, so if you can just give me the information, we'll make this as quick and painless as possible so we can both move on with our day." When the instinct to fight or have a disagreement emerges, instead, I say yes, and I agree so we can get on the same page and move beyond it.

My advice to anyone looking to begin their entrepreneurial journey is to believe that you can do it. Just start. Say yes and just go. Pharmacists are analytical; we like to think things through and have a plan. But to use an improv analogy, scenes are better when you listen and respond. We don't have time to wait; we don't have time to sit and think of the funniest line. That is how you miss all of the information that is being given around you. My best advice is to go and listen to the feedback you get on your journey. Like improv, entrepreneurship is about listening and responding. But that means you have to react; you have to go. You have to keep pushing forward. But you should listen too, gather feedback and take that information to heart as you adjust and find your way.

CONTRIBUTOR
CONNECTION

Cory Jenks, PharmD

🌐 www.coryjenks.com

🔗 www.linkedin.com/in/cory-jenks-3ba17314/

ASHLEE KLEVENS HAYES

Biography

Ashlee Klevens Hayes is the founder and executive career coach of RX Ashlee©. Dr. Hayes began her career in hospital pharmacy administration at a large academic medical center before pivoting to a nontraditional role in a healthcare tech startup company. That transition opened her eyes to many unique opportunities that were available within the industry. After many years her peers and colleagues connected with her to discuss transitioning to non-clinical roles. She realized there was an opportunity to be had in providing mentorship, coaching, and helping others in their career development. At RX Ashlee, she has provided career coaching at the University of Southern California. She has been published in Thrive Business and has traveled all over the world, giving keynote presentations. She runs online communities focused on career development. She facilitates women's mastermind programs and coaches interview prep clients on a one-on-one basis. She currently lives in Orange County, California, with her husband, daughter, and two rescue dogs.

Entrepreneurial Journey

I had no plans on being an entrepreneur; it was not in my ideal roadmap. I went to pharmacy school and got my master's in healthcare administration. I did a PGY1, PGY2 with a health system administration background. I was very much on the road to being a CEO or chief pharmacy officer at a large academic medical center. But as we all know, life happens. If you're married or have a partner, things change, and you have to be flexible.

My husband and I moved all over the country. Because of my husband's career, we have moved 15 times in the last ten years. I had to take a step back and ask myself, what did success mean to me in my career? I got the opportunity from my academic medical experience, being in operations, to switch to consulting for a medical device startup company. And I found it super fun. I was there for two years. The company eventually sold to a large pharma organization, and my position was displaced.

That was incredibly difficult because I had a three-month-old baby, I was the primary breadwinner for my family. It was quite literally one of the worst days of my life. When my manager called, she was in tears; she felt terrible. It was a whole mess.

I had never thought in a million years that I would be unemployed. I was thinking, "What the heck do I do next?" We were in the middle of moving from Kentucky back to California for my husband's job. And it was at that moment that I took a step back and reflected on what was most important to me in my career and what type of impact I wanted to have on the profession.

I began interviewing for jobs, but I had to turn a lot of them down because I had just had a baby. I turned down 35 six-figure jobs. At the same time, I was seeing my friends, family, and colleagues struggling to land jobs simply because they didn't know how to articulate their key stakeholders. One morning, I was out at breakfast with my friend. And over coffee, she says, "Ashlee, why don't you just start teaching people how to interview?"

I was like, "But I'm a pharmacist. That doesn't make sense. I went to pharmacy school; why would I do that?"

She's like, "I don't know. You're just good at it."

I started. I began posting on LinkedIn; fast forward to four years later, and I am working full time as an entrepreneur. As I said, this was not in my pipeline. This was not something I woke up thinking I was going to be doing, but it became my career. I think this is happening to a lot of people these days; there are people who aren't getting jobs and facing challenges and are turning to entrepreneurship.

Methods to Monetize Your Knowledge

My main form of monetization is interview prep. Every single day I have clients who enroll in my one-on-one interview prep programs. I now have over 250 clients, with over 4,500 students in my online courses. I monetize my knowledge by teaching high-level professionals how to stand out and really communicate their values in an interview. I also teach networking skills how to talk about yourself when meeting people. Helping develop your elevator pitch. Most people find that sort of thing uncomfortable, so I give my clients the tools and the roadmap to effectively talk about themselves.

I have my women's mastermind groups, I do speaking engagements, and I just wrote a book. I also offer online courses. There is a whole subdivision when it comes to monetizing my knowledge. I ran a Career by Design course for two years, which I just closed in December. It is now an evergreen course, so it lives on my website, and people can just enroll in it whenever. But what I do every single day is meet with clients in order to help them prep for interviews.

When it comes to how I was able to do this, I simply followed my strengths. I stopped making it so challenging for myself and found that it works. Now I have helped over 250 clients negotiate over $1 million in salary. I know strategy, I'm good at it, this is what I teach now. If coaching one-on-one is something you resonate with, you should spend your time there. You can even turn it into group coaching. I also have clients that I have been geocoaching one-on-one for several years now, which is another component of my business.

I have been in multiple different small business groups, and I think everyone has a different understanding of what mastermind is. But for me, how I have run my programs over the last four years, mastermind means gathering like-minded professional women who want to have the tools to advance their careers. What the women's mastermind group entails is meeting once a month for a judgment-free zone, where these women can have a confidential space to bounce ideas off one another. I currently have about 40 women enrolled. And each month, we have two women take the hot seat. They each get 15 minutes to coach one-on-one with me, and then we open it up to the group for feedback and ideas. Alongside that, there is a closed community for daily support and accountability.

I don't run Facebook groups; I run off a platform called Circle. It is a fairly new platform. I was part of the beta group, and so far, it has been good. I got off Facebook about a year ago, I have found a lot of people shifting away from Facebook. And I wanted to make the investment in my mastermind group and use Circle.

Finding Your Voice & Owning Your Value

Before I began my business, I was a pharmacist working in operations until I transitioned into consulting. But I am also a mom and a wife, and just like many of you, I juggle a lot of different roles. But the mission for my business, RX Ashlee, is to really teach professionals how to communicate their value to key stakeholders, employers, and clients.

I got very tired of seeing overqualified candidates not land the jobs or get the clients they deserve simply because they didn't have the tools to communicate their value. That's really what it was. I got so tired of seeing it that it kept me up at night. I decided to do something about it.

One of the most common things I hear from clients is, "I hate talking about myself." People want help building up their confidence. They don't know how to answer the "tell me about yourself" question. That is what it really comes down to, A difficulty when it comes to talking about yourself. We are in a unique landscape right now. We are evolving from a traditional marketplace.

I am a third-generation pharmacist. When my grandfather went to pharmacy school, when my dad went to pharmacy school, they graduated debt-free, already having pension plans. My dad bought a Porsche and had no student loans. He was living in a completely different economy than the one we are in right now. The current generation isn't evolving into the traditional marketplace; there is no road map for anyone of any profession anymore. Certainly not pharmacists or healthcare providers. I think what gets us tripped up is we know that we're smart, educated, qualified people. But we don't know how to articulate that.

What I have seen, the two major areas that hold professionals, particularly pharmacists, back are strategic action and personal obstacles. I am mainly going to focus on strategic action because that is what I teach my clients. Personal substances would be something like imposed syndrome, getting in your own way, a lack of confidence. But strategic action is really where I support my clients the most.

The truth is people come to me with their heads down. They are embarrassed or even mortified. I have had people come to me in tears because they feel so much shame over not knowing how to communicate their value. What I tell them is, "Hey. Nobody taught us this." I have spent hundreds of hours, thousands of dollars on my education. I am very trained. I have a master's degree and a doctorate. I graduated with two bachelor's degrees. I am very educated, and still, nobody taught me, "Here is how to build confidence in talking about yourself so you can thrive in your career."

I really encourage people to drop the shame because there is nothing to be ashamed of. The odds are nobody has taught you how to talk about yourself. Nobody has given you the tools to show your value.

I want to go into a quick strategy for communicating effectively. The words entrepreneur and intrapreneur are going to come up. I want to clarify, when I say intrapreneur, I mean a W2, someone who works for someone else, whereas an entrepreneur is someone who works for themselves, an S-corp or 1099 tax form.

The reality is everyone, even parents, spouses, neighbors. Everyone needs the tools on how to effectively communicate their value. If you want to build lasting relationships and thrive in today's marketplace, you need to learn how to stand out.

Advice for Aspiring Entrepreneurs

One thing I teach all my clients is how to position yourself as an expert. This is incredibly important. The first thing you have to do is begin building your personal brand. What exactly is a personal brand? Your personal brand is the value that you as an individual bring to the table. It is what makes you different, your voice, goals, tone, style, aesthetic. All of that plays into your personal brand. Your brand is everything that people say about you when you're not in the room. And being a differentiator is a good thing. It is what makes you unique; it is why people come to you. Being the same as everyone else is not cool anymore.

I want to encourage you if you feel like you are different, if you feel like you don't quite fit in, if you don't know how to use your differentiators, that is okay. But know that is your secret sauce.

Step two, understand the benefits of being known as an expert. When you have the tools to stand out, amazing things happen. You can help more people; you can make a wider impact; you can stop trying to be liked by everyone and actually step into your strengths. I never in a million years thought my expertise would be in interview coaching. It's not something I dreamt up. But I'm good at it, and my clients see the success that they want. It has created a ripple effect in my business. It has become absolutely life-changing.

Instead of chasing after people, let them chase after you. Imagine applying to jobs without having to go through job boards, without hustling and networking through LinkedIn. I love LinkedIn, but sometimes it can be really challenging to be seen on these platforms. We all want higher career satisfaction and more money. I know you do, and it's okay that you do.

Number three is building awareness. You can't be known as the best-kept secret. You have to tell people who you are. I know it is awkward at first. But when I hosted my first event, it was terrible. I got really sick and thought, "I can't believe I'm doing this." But if I hadn't told people, If I hadn't shared myself with people, nobody would know. If social media isn't your favorite thing, that's okay. You don't have to post on LinkedIn or Instagram to build awareness. But you do have to tell people. When someone pops up on your network and they have a question you think you can solve, do it for them.

Visibility is credibility. When you're visible with your brand, with what you want to be known for, it innately builds your credibility.

Number four is kind of the hard one, and it has to do with comparing yourself to others. Everyone has different backgrounds. Everyone has different strengths. You need to focus on yourself and your zone of genius.

Some of the common brand awareness mistakes I see clients and past clients make is that their number one concern is how many likes, clicks, and subscribers they get. The most important tool you have at your disposal is building relationships. Especially if you are a service-based provider, another mistake I see is that many of us give up too easily. When things get hard, we're out. We think that we have to have it all figured out before we can move forward with building awareness of our expertise. That is not true.

Another very common mistake is not seeking feedback. Once you start building your brand awareness and your expertise, you start talking to people. Ask them questions, see what they say about you and how you can improve. Find out how you can continuously support and serve them.

Another thing I tell my clients is to tell people why they should trust you. This is probably one of the most uncomfortable parts of being an expert in positioning yourself. If someone were to ask me four years ago about myself and what I do, I would be very uncomfortable. I turned down 35 jobs in six months in a very competitive marketplace. I felt guilty. I typically wouldn't even say, "Yeah, I've worked with over 200 clients," or, "I have 4,500 students enrolled in my programs." That still feels uncomfortable for me. But the reality is a lot of people don't know me; in order to build my expertise, I have to share the things I am good at.

We have to get comfortable talking about the value that each of us provides in the marketplace. And the way that you can do that is by doing two things: reflecting on why you're doing it and practicing. Most people don't practice this skill, and so, of course, it continues to be uncomfortable and awkward.

My last piece of advice is to be crystal clear about what you really want. What does success mean to you? If anything was possible, what impact would you want to have on your profession, on your community, on your family? I come from a long lineage of pharmacists. And so this is important to me. What do you want to leave behind?

My dad passed away very suddenly when I was in pharmacy school, and he had such a big legacy. It was frustrating to me to even think about how I was supposed to step into his shoes. But I think the gift of owning your own brand and being an expert is you get to create that legacy for yourself. That is what I am going to leave you with, how to navigate the discomfort of building your brand and being an expert.

You have to curate your story. People need to know what you are doing. Get comfortable with being uncomfortable. Learn how to tune out the noise and stay focused, and I promise you will become much more confident in yourself and your abilities.

I want to leave you on this note: what you think, you become.

**Ashlee Klevens Hayes,
PharmD, MHA, CELDC**

CONTRIBUTOR
CONNECTION

www.rxashlee.com

www.linkedin.com/in/ashleeklevenshayes/

CHRISTINA MADISON

Biography

Christina Madison is the founder and CEO of the Public Health Pharmacist©, a public health consulting firm. She is a clinical pharmacist specializing in public health with a focus on infectious communicable diseases. Dr. Madison acted as the part-director for the Roseman University of Health Sciences COVID vaccine operations, logistics, distribution, and administration. As well as a point of contact for the state of Nevada COVID vaccines. She has personally facilitated the administration of over 10,000 doses of COVID vaccine in the southern Nevada community since January. As a past president of the Nevada Public Health Association, she has been asked to share her clinical public health and infectious disease expertise with local state and international media outlets.

Dr. Madison has been featured in over 150 on-air TV appearances related to the pandemic and public health. She has an intimate knowledge of the impact public health messaging has on policy and legislation. She is a trusted and valued healthcare professional with 14 years of experience as a pharmacy professional. She's currently an associate professor of pharmacy practice with Roseman University of Health Sciences College of Pharmacy. She maintains two active positions with the Huntridge Family Clinic, which focuses on the LGBTQ+ community and is one of the largest providers of HIV prevention and gender-affirming care in the state of Nevada, as well as Volunteers in Medicine of Southern Nevada, where she offers immunization and communicable disease care. Advocating for public health and the profession of pharmacy to improve the health and wellness of vulnerable populations and the underserved is her passion and mission.

Entrepreneurial Journey

As far as my entrepreneurial journey goes, it wasn't something I had thought I needed, but I had some amazing chance meetings. Part of this was through networking, the power of connecting with people and individuals. I was lucky enough to connect with a lot of wonderful people. I attended a number of summits and got to be in rooms with like-minded people. Those are really moments of affirmation when you realize this little thought you had in your head isn't actually crazy. It's a moment of acknowledgment. That was really the seed that was planted in my mind that said, "Hey, I can do this."

Now public policy isn't something that is considered "sexy," but due to the pandemic, it has propelled me into the public sphere. Unfortunately, public health wasn't managed very well, so it created a need for reliable expertise. The beauty of public health is that when it is done well, nobody knows we exist. Because there is clean air and water, disease outbreaks are able to be managed, and everyone is happy and none the wiser. I began this journey in November 2019, just in time for the pandemic.

My goal initially was to do public speaking, keynotes, and consulting. I was going to open a coaching business for individuals that wanted to do public health and pharmacy services like HIV prevention, contraception, access to Narcan, and harm reduction strategies like needle exchange and disaster preparedness vaccinations. That was my goal initially. I thought 2020 was going to be my year just like everybody else did. I thought I was going to get so many contracts. And I thought, "This is going to tell me if I can take the leap and do this full time and quit my job in academia."

And then everything started getting canceled. I started thinking, "Okay, maybe this isn't the time for me to do this." Through my job at the university, I was asked to go on the local television networks.

They said, "Hey. We have this new virus. Nobody knows much about it. Would you be able to come in and talk to us since we know you specialize in infectious disease?"

During my very first interview that day, the WHO came out and said that the virus, which up until that point didn't have a name, was novel Coronavirus. It was January 29th, and my first in-person interview. They had me come in, and the rest is history because I have been on my local television networks pretty much once or twice a week ever since. It has been an amazing ride.

It has made me realize that at the heart of everything is good storytelling. We as healthcare professionals need to do a better job of telling our story so that people know what we offer as pharmacists, that we are experts, and that we provide amazing patient care.

Methods to Monetize Your Knowledge

I have been able to do a couple of things to monetize my knowledge. I do direct-to-business consulting, I have helped several businesses develop their vaccine operations through COVID-19. I have also worked direct-to-providers, which is basically helping pharmacists and other healthcare professionals implement public health services into their practice. I have also done podcasting, and I've been a spokesperson for a mass company. I've had some sponsorships where I've been the spokesperson for a particular thing. And I have been a regular recurring guest on a sports radio show.

I've pretty much done it all. The big message here is that public health needs to be talked about. Another thing is representation; as a woman of color, I think it is so important that we have more representation in the media because when people look and sound like us, we are much more likely to take the message to heart.

Publicity & Storytelling for the Pharmfluencer—Why is It so Important?

I wanted to begin with this quote: "Stories give color and depth to otherwise bland material, and they allow people to connect with the message in a deeper, more meaningful way." This quote is by Peter Gerber, the CEO of MGM Mirage. And it really highlights the importance of being able to tell a story and why people find it easier to connect with you and potentially purchase from you because you have made that connection.

When we think about storytelling, what is it that we are really doing? It is a way for us to see our past and envision our future. It is also a way for us to convey a message. What is your message? What are you trying to tell the public? In some cases, we know when that goes really well. We're able to get people to do things en masse. But when we get it wrong, it gets really wrong, unfortunately, and people become very resistant to our messaging. This is what we are seeing now with our vaccine efforts. But ultimately, all it is is a way of describing a product or service.

I was told not long ago that I have a great online presence, but my audience was unsure of what I was actually selling. I think that is what it really comes down to. When we are able to tell our story, people know exactly what we do and what we are selling. There are some really great examples of this kind of branding and marketing. Think about the Nike swoosh. When you see that swoosh, you automatically know it is about sports, and it sells tennis shoes and apparel. Verses when you see other brands, it may not tell you right away what they do.

There is a whole business around choosing the right color, the correct font, all of these specific things that make the consumer feel a certain way. And ultimately, when we look at these stories, we realize how powerful they are in connecting and engaging with our audience.

When I talk about storytelling, the biggest thing I want you to know is that as healthcare providers, we need to tell better stories. We need to do a better job of telling people why we are here, what our why is, and what we can bring to the table. With that being said, I am going to talk a little bit about what I have done personally to get my story out there and make up for some of the deficiencies that I see, particularly in pharmacy.

It has to do with our lack of public relations (PR) and marketing and communication. That is not something we talk about in pharmacy school. But from a public health standpoint, it is important that the public can understand our messaging, that they want to do things based on knowing and trusting us. And that comes from telling better stories.

One of the ways we can tell stories is through podcasting. I have had the amazing opportunity to interview so many outstanding guests on my podcast. One of my guests was actually my entree into the Pharmacy Podcast Network. When I launched with them this year, my very first guest was Sandra Leal, and she is now the current president of the American Pharmacists Association (APHA).

I had the most amazing conversation with her. And it goes back to storytelling. She had so many different opportunities within her career because she was able to raise her hand and say, "Yes. I can. I can be here, and I can show up." Knowing you can do that in areas where pharmacists aren't necessarily thought of as being part of the conversation. I always say, "My place is at the table." That is where decisions are being made.

And as a woman of color, I am aware of the factor of representation and how important it is. I make a lot of contributions to minority health and correcting inequities in vulnerable populations. And again, I think it goes back to not only the story that is being told, but who is telling it. Things like podcasting are a great way to get your message out there.

As I have mentioned before, television appearance wasn't a skill I ever thought I needed. But when I showed up to that very first studio interview, I contacted a friend of mine who I knew was a media coach. She helped me a lot. I think having a bit of training before you go into doing media interviews is optimal because you want them to ask you to come back. One of the things they asked me when I sat down in the chair was, "Have you done this before?" I totally lied and said yes. Because sometimes you have to fake it until you make it. That air of knowledge and credibility goes a long way.

And sometimes there is a hesitancy to take a chance on somebody who is new to things. But you're not going to get the experience unless you get the opportunity. Sometimes you just have to say, "Yes." My girlfriend Janine Schneider coined that term "the messy yes." I love it. I think it is way better than saying no. It's because of this mentality that I have had some amazing opportunities.

One thing I have really enjoyed is actually getting to know some of the reporters and better understanding the motivation behind their storytelling. I have really dove into the journalistic aspects of it. Because again, they are just looking for stories. They are always looking for stories. It's just whatever is media-worthy at the time. And what you think is media-worthy may not be the angle they want to take. But when you develop a relationship with those reporters, it allows you to craft your story so that you can still get your talking points in while still helping them get their story as well.

I had a recent appearance with PBS, and it was great because I was sitting around the table with all of these people who are considered experts in the field of public health. There was the Dean of our college of medicine for the University of Nevada Las Vegas.

There was one of the leading biologists and fertility experts and an epidemiologist who also works at the College of Public Health with the University of Nevada Las Vegas (UNLV).

These people were sitting around the table with me, and they had all been asked to give their opinion throughout the pandemic. They all had been really outspoken in terms of providing accurate and factual information. The fact that we were all sitting around a table together really was a testament to modern medicine. We had made appearances together virtually, but none of us had met in person.

The fact that we were able to meet in person because of vaccination was just amazing. And we talked about vaccination hesitancy as part of the panel, but it was just one of those things where the reason we were all even there was because of the advocacy work we had all done and the power of modern medicine.

During the pandemic, media contribution was very difficult; I am not going to lie. Obviously, we figured out how to do interviews live through zoom, but it required coming up with creative ways to tell your story. I did an interview with Fox Five. They were doing social distancing in order for me to be able to give my talk, and that in addition to wearing a mask. Trying to do a good TV interview with a mask on was rough, but we did what we could. And I think it made a difference, getting out there and telling your story in front of the public.

The other part of this is sharing your expertise with the world, being able to do that in the public sphere. I did interviews in person; I did interviews through the phone; I did live streams; I did interviews in my house. All of these things helped me learn skills. It's something I've really invested in over the last few months in order to help me give better interviews, tell good stories, and be an expert in some of the more cosmetic things you wouldn't normally think of.

I invested in good lighting and good technology for my camera. I also started bringing around a media bag that had everything I needed in it. I got my own personal earpiece, so when I was doing events in person, I had everything I needed. I even started keeping separate clothing in my car at one point so that I had a media bag ready to go if I got asked to do an interview, I would be immediately available. This is important because the news cycle moves quickly. You typically only get an hour to two hours' notice when you get asked to do an interview of some kind.

This is an example I am especially proud of. One of the biggest press gaggles I was a part of was at a community center in a predominantly African-American neighborhood. And one of the things that came out of it is that I am actually a part of Getty Images now. If you are familiar with Getty Images, when you look up something like "vaccinations," these images come up, and they are of me. It's very heartwarming to see because it has been difficult to see all of the bad immunization techniques spread all over the television. It was a big deal for me, especially because now when people look up vaccinations, they will see Black and brown bodies accepting the vaccine. This was a big deal for me as part of my work of advocating for the underserved.

Spencer Hayworth, who is an NBA star who lives here in Las Vegas, contacted the University I work for because he knew we were giving out COVID vaccines. We arranged everything for him to come, and they specifically asked me to be the one to give him his vaccination. We had a news crew on hand, ready to capture the moment. And it was great for so many reasons. We were showing the public African-Americans getting the vaccine. And for him to use his celebrity status to tell his story and advocate for the vaccine was really wonderful.

I also had the opportunity to be in the press box with our NBA team, advocating for public health measures. And knowing there are so many of our professional athletes who are Black and brown, getting to talk with them about vaccination and why public health matters was really special. I was also on a panel that was part of Myth vs. Fact about COVID-19, and again there was just amazing representation there. There was the president of our local National Association for the Advancement of Colored People (NAACP) chapter, the Dean of our medical school, all these people who are considered experts. It was an amazing opportunity for me. As I said earlier, getting access to those opportunities really just requires someone to show up and say, "Hey, I can speak to this. Let me help be a spokesperson."

I was on a retainer for a mask manufacturer called Boomer Naturals; I was under contract with them for about six months. I did all of their media appearances with the masks. I actively posted on social media for them. I was on about three of their national television commercials. Again, it was a skill I learned. I had never read from a teleprompter before, but you show up, and you do what you need to do. I have recently been a spokesperson for Station Casinos (STN) Sports. I am a regular guest on their radio sports show and do some advertising for them. They're also part of the sportsbook in Las Vegas, so they do a lot of sports betting.

Again, it goes back to how to get back these kinds of events safely. Mask wearing, vaccinations, testing, all of these things combined, and things you would never have thought of being a part of the public health landscape. But public health goes on in all kinds of places, including professional sports.

I had the amazing opportunity to be part of our This Is Our Shot Campaign, which was a national campaign for minority health. I got to be part of a Facebook Live with experts from across the country. It's all about sharing your passion. When you lead with passion and love, nothing can go wrong.

I want to talk a little bit more about marketing and branding. All of these appearances are opportunities to talk about your brand. Obviously, the appearances I have had are related to what I do, the podcasts, and public health. But any appearance you do is an excellent opportunity to talk about your brand. It's all about what you are bringing to the table. We should all strive to inspire. And pharmacists should certainly be inspiring other pharmacists.

I'd like to leave you with a few takeaways. The first is that storytelling is powerful. Leading with your passion and showing your expertise is always a good idea. These are learned skills; it is okay not to master them immediately. But they will aid you in both your personal and professional brand.

The COVID-19 Pandemic has accelerated the need for pharmacists to get their expertise out there, expand pharmacy services, and really help the public. Pharmacists and public health providers can help increase community care as well as advance the profession. Working to inspire others is the best way to get the word out about why pharmacists rock!

If you are interested in learning more about what I do, you can find me at The Public Health Pharmacist.com.

Advice for Aspiring Entrepreneurs

I would say to aspiring entrepreneurs that you don't have to do everything yourself. Hire people, hire a coach or someone who has the expertise to help you. You can't do everything, but you can have a team. I really believe in that thought process of building a tribe. I think it is so important.

Another thing is to invest in yourself. Pharmacists really don't take the time to invest in themselves. Make sure you invest in yourself and in your dreams. Following your passion will allow you to do what you love.

CONTRIBUTOR CONNECTION

Christina Madison, PharmD, FCCP, AAHIVP

www.thepublichealthpharmacist.com

www.linkedin.com/in/drchristinamad isonthepublichealthpharmacist

CHRISTINE MANUKYAN

Biography

Dr. Christine Manukyan is a Functional Medicine Practitioner, two-time bestselling author, and top-ranked *STORRIE™ Podcast* host. Prior to becoming an entrepreneur, she spent 13 years in Corporate America as a Clinical Pharmacist with various leadership roles. After experiencing her own health transformation with Functional Medicine, losing 100+ lbs. and becoming a natural bodybuilding athlete and marathon runner, she found her true calling: empowering others to reach their health goals without pharmaceuticals and using a holistic lifestyle approach. Since then, Dr. Christine has helped more than 300 clients transform their health.

Dr. Christine is the founder and CEO of The STORRIE™ Institute, the world-leading accountability-based business incubator and Functional Medicine certification program for clinicians to launch and scale a profitable 6 to 7 figure Functional Medicine practice. She is on a mission to impact 1 million lives around the world with functional medicine.

She is a frequent speaker on holistic lifestyle choices, creating a virtual business, founder, and entrepreneur mindsets, and creating multiple income streams. She's spoken in front of audiences numbering 15,000+ and has been recognized globally for her entrepreneurial achievement and dedication. Her past publications and magazine features include *Forbes*, *Yahoo*, *Disruptors*, *Authority*, and *BRAINZ*.

Dr. Christine is leading the Functional Medicine Revolution and is passionate about mentoring burned-out medical professionals struggling to balance family, career, and their health to take control of their life and career and create a profitable Functional Medicine practice.

Dr. Christine believes that everyone deserves a second chance to rewrite their story and become the best version of themselves.

Entrepreneurial Journey

I call myself an accidental entrepreneur. Unlike a lot of people, I never woke up one day and decided I was going to be an entrepreneur. But what I do have in common with many entrepreneurs is that pivotal moment in life that made me think twice about my career. For me, that moment came six years ago when I was 35. I was in my doctor's office for my annual checkup. On the outside, I seemed like I was glowing; I had an incredible job and kids, everything I wanted. But on the inside, I was slowly dying because, at that time, I was trading health for my career, for letters behind my name. I was striving towards the glamor of leadership and success but at a great cost.

My doctor told me that I was going to have a heart attack in the next five years if I continued at the speed I was currently going. I decided enough was enough. I'm not going to become a statistic; I'm going to take control of my health. I began digging into holistic health. I wanted to know how I could actually change my life. And I didn't know it then, but I was starting my entrepreneurial journey. I began coaching people that were undergoing the same life transformation that I did. But I was still balancing a foot in each world, and I was beginning to wonder what more I could do.

My next pivotal moment was during the pandemic. My husband and I were both pharmacists in hospital leadership and could not work remotely. We were forced to choose between our careers and our family. We had no babysitter; it was brutal. I had to beg people to come to my house and watch my kids because I had to go to work. It was not fun. I stopped and asked myself, "What can I do now to follow my passion, my purpose in life? How can I take that leap of faith?"

There are many of us who really want to create something new but are stuck in these two different worlds. Do you stay home and take the pay cut, or do you go to a job you know isn't your calling and make money? That was what began my next chapter of life. I talk a lot about really trusting your gut, taking the chance, and becoming a full-time entrepreneur. I became a full-time entrepreneur a few days before my 40th birthday. I stepped into this functional medicine space, I had my own online practice, but also, at the same time, I was reaching out and helping my colleagues who are in the same position I was. I asked them, "How can I help you have something to do on the side?" "How can I help you develop an exit strategy to where this becomes your full-time business?"

In many ways, the Functional Business Academy was born out of conversations with other moms and other professionals experiencing burnout. People just like myself, and asking them, "What's going on in your life?" "What can I do to help you?"

And the idea came from them telling me, "You need to tell us what the heck you just did."

A lot of people in my network thought I was going through a midlife crisis. Who leaves their six-figure job during a global pandemic to step into an entrepreneurship space? It was not something people could understand, but it was something I was passionate about. Trust your gut and go for it. We are not born with all the skills, but you can surround yourself with people who are doing it and listen and implement.

Methods to Monetize Your Knowledge

When I launched my practice in May of 2020, I began with one-on-one private coaching about functional medicine. I had a number of clients who wanted to know how they could improve their health holistically. And that was a great stream of income. I have my e-courses as well. I have also done a number of speaking engagements; I wrote a book. It has been a rollercoaster ever since leaving corporate. I had a full-time job while essentially home-schooling my kids. It wasn't doable and certainly not scalable. In trying to better utilize my time, I started having group sessions. I worked to really introduce the concept of a tribe to my clients, creating an environment where people could show up for their health transformation. It's a combination of one-on-one private coaching and the academy, which is a group setting.

That was a big decision-making point for me as well. I invested a lot of time and money into figuring out what was the best model for my audience and for my soul. I didn't wake up and know the answers. I had to hire three different coaches to get me where I am today. And when you go through a coaching program for a few months, it's great. But nothing is more powerful than a longitudinal connection with your mentor, especially if you are starting your respective journeys together. My first business coach was a nurse practitioner and was also in the functional medicine space. We worked together for five months; I launched my practice and then was like, "Now what? How do I get my message out?"

I hired another coach to help me with visibility and credibility, being seen as an expert in this industry. Thanks to her, I was able to launch my podcast and put out my best-selling book. There were things that I had to constantly invest in. With my third coach, I invested in how I could scale my practice and business. When I looked into creating the academy, I was asking myself what my audience needs, but also what I need. It's exhausting being part of all of these mentorship groups at the same time. I wanted to bring everything into a one-stop-shop while also having my certification program. That part of it was crucial for my audience. I'm investing time and money into bringing my audience what they are looking for. I need to become an official certification program. When my clients graduate after 12 months, they become certified functional medicine specialists.

And this is indicative of the field changing very fast. It's not a requirement today to have this designation and certification, but it may be tomorrow. They may say, "Even though you're a doctor, you can't practice functional medicine without formal certification." Preparing for that and helping my students gain those qualifications if the time comes they do need it. My first graduating class will be in November of this year.

I encourage my students to prepare for the future but also to take risks. In creating this business, that was a huge risk on my end. I had no idea how it was going to look, how I was going to do it. There was nobody I could turn to and ask for advice. I just had to figure it out. This is real life, and I know it may sound scary, but let me tell you, when you're facing those challenging moments, you just have to push through them. And there is nothing more beautiful than overcoming those challenges and stepping into a new space.

I offer that coaching for 12 months because you need it. Trust me; you need it. You need it because your life is going to change.

Your Functional Medicine Legacy

Before I even begin talking about legacy, I want to actually paint the vision of what is possible. I was not given a recipe of what to do to become an entrepreneur, but I constantly surround myself with people who are doing it in their industry. They may not be in the pharmaceutical or functional medicine space, but that is good. That way, I can surround myself with people outside the pharmacy space and learn what everyone else is doing. That's why it's important to watch every other clinician and how they step into their zone of genius.

You can bring those same skills into your own space and start having those conversations with some of our leaders. We can work with the American Pharmacists Association (APHA) and the American Society of Health System Pharmacists (ASHP) to bring pharmacy entrepreneurship and functional medicine into the profession. Yes, it is nerve-wracking, but through having those conversations with pharmacy leaders, we can create more opportunities.

It's not sexy or exciting to hop on the podcast and interview the president of Patriot, but together we are dreaming and creating. And who knows, my Academy could turn into a fellowship for our pharmacy graduates. I have two students who are in my Academy, I gave them a scholarship, and now these ladies are launching their practice. They are writing a book with me as a coauthor. It is possible; you just have to know where your heart and desire align.

Functional Medicine Academy is a tool for someone who is trying to figure out what to do with their skills and knowledge. Step one of creating your own legacy is deciding that you are going to make a change. That change can be anything from simple steps to going full-on. Don't quit your job yet; decide if you really want to do this. Decide if having your own practice is something you are sure about. You have to protect yourself; you have to create your own LLC or corporation. Before you can be CEO of a company, you have to figure out what the company is named. What is it going to do? What services will you offer?

From there, you can use that question to narrow down your audience and identify; who am I going to help? A lot of people wonder if there is enough room in functional medicine for them. Yes. There is. It is a broad field. Focus on what you already know. When I launched my business, I was and still am very passionate about autoimmune diseases. My mom struggled with three different autoimmune diseases and was constantly in pain. I know I want to help women and men struggling with that. But again, I didn't know enough, and I wasn't going to wait until I had all that specific knowledge to launch my practice. I didn't only want to help one niche.

I started with my story. What do I know well? I know the power of nutrition. I know the power of detox and intermittent fasting to reduce stress. I know how to help you become a better version of yourself by looking for the root cause of your problems. That is where I started. But I am still accumulating knowledge on autoimmune disease treatment. I am between two different schools right now. I just finished SAFM and enrolled in Functional Medicine University because as I scale my practice, I am constantly learning.

It's really about understanding; what do you want to do now? What are you passionate about? What do you want to learn more about so you can start helping people? Don't make it too complicated.

I would highly advise anyone looking to go into functional medicine to create contracts with the functional medicine labs and supplement companies. Because again, our position is not only to educate about what supplements you should take, but our audience is looking to us to make a recommendation. They want us to actually say, "If you're looking for fish oil, here is an example. If you're vegan, here is an alternative." I also do not recommend anything that is over the counter. I do not shop from over-the-counter stuff. As a clinician and pharmacist, you have access to several companies' full scripts. You have access to all of these pharmaceutical-grade medical supplements.

Learn what supplements are out there. Look into what kind of functional medicine labs you can have contracts with. I worked really hard to create a relationship with companies, especially for our pharmacy students who don't have their license yet but are in my Academy. I worked my butt off to get a relationship with these companies so they could create their own lab accounts. Now my students are ordering their own stool tests for themselves while healing their own health. It's not hard. It's not complicated.

My most important piece of advice is that if you are creating something, you have to go public. You have to lunch and get your message out. If you're not telling people what you are doing, if you feel like your ego is stopping you from being on social media, from promoting yourself, you need to get out of your own way. How is anyone going to know what services you provide if you don't talk about it? Mindset is everything.

In the Academy, we spend so much time talking about mindset. Even for myself when I was starting my company. I was like, "What do I say? How do I launch?" But being in the right mindset works every time; being surrounded by other clinicians who are doing this makes it doable. This is the power of influence that you can have. If you don't talk about it, nobody is going to know what you have to offer. I tell all the ladies in my Academy, "Don't be selfish. You never know who wants to hear your story."

You never know who is praying to receive the answers you have. Don't be selfish. Open your mouth even when it is uncomfortable. And I know it is uncomfortable. I have interviewed many of the ladies in the Academy on my podcast. They talk about their journeys and how they are stepping into this space. But you have to start somewhere.

Advice for Aspiring Entrepreneurs

In regard to functional medicine being an all-cash business or bill insurance as well, that depends on what you choose to do. If you're like me and you are the owner and CEO of your company, you might choose a cash-based model. But there are other clinicians who like to bill insurance. Usually, those who are billing insurance have brick-and-mortar setups. It might be, you're a functional medicine practitioner and a pharmacist, but you're working at a wellness center, where the chiropractor is. You know acupuncture is done by a nurse practitioner, so it becomes more of a collaborative space. If you have the billing set up, go for it. I choose not to do that.

It's complicated. It's brutal. Every time I order a lab from the companies I have contracts with, they'll ask me, "Are we billing insurance?"

I'm like, "No. My client is better." I have to go through this and not deal with the receipt, and if it gets rejected, then it's just too complicated. However, a lot of the companies that I have contracts with, and I teach this, a lot of these companies will allow your clients to pay using their Flexible Spending Account (FSA) cards or are offering payment plans. One of the labs that I have a contract with, Genova Diagnostics, for stool testing. They offer a payment plan split into three payments. It becomes more affordable for your clients to pay. To answer that question, I choose to be in a cash-based service space. I can bill insurance, too, it is just too complicated, and I don't want to deal with that. And I don't want to have to tell a client who is ready to change their health, "Hold on, I'm waiting for reimbursement. I'm waiting for approval."

There is nothing more precious than time. I don't want to take time away from people who are ready to change their lives. Having to say, "Let's revisit this next month." Next month might be too late if they are ready to invest and work with you. You have a duty to tell them right now how to get to the next step.

If this is something that interests you, I am writing another book collectively with students in my academy, really sharing our stories, how we pivoted from traditional medicine to functional medicine, and how you can do the same. It should be coming out in the next couple of months.

I'd like to leave you with a quote because this period was such a huge pivotal moment for me. You find yourself on this path to discovery, and you really have to ask yourself, what are you willing to give up so you can make room for more greatness? The quote is, "The journey isn't about becoming anything. Maybe it is about unbecoming everything that isn't really you so you can be who you were meant to be in the first place."

My motto is that everyone deserves a second chance to rewrite their story, to become the best version of themselves. Get out there and make that decision to rewrite your story. It's never too late. It will be scary. I guarantee that it is going to be uncomfortable, but it's worth it.

CONTRIBUTOR
CONNECTION

Christine Manukyan,
PharmD, MS

www.drchristinemanukyan.com

www.linkedin.com/in/dr-christine-manukyan/

MEGAN MILNE

Biography

Dr. Megan Milne is a third-generation pharmacist who experienced a mysterious rash and nearly bled to death, starting a roller coaster medical journey. One day she was a normal, healthy, young mother of four children, and the next, she was forced to take Prednisone to save her life. This inspired her to become the Prednisone Pharmacist to overcome side effects and invent Nutranize Zone™, the first and only supplement for people on prednisone. She earned her Doctor of Pharmacy degree at the University of Utah College of Pharmacy and is a Board-Certified Ambulatory Care Pharmacist. Megan was given the Innovative Pharmacist of the Year award for her efforts in launching the Medication Therapy Management (MTM) program at a Fortune 200 healthcare company. She enjoys speaking professionally and has been invited to speak across the country throughout her career. Megan has the heart of a teacher, having been offered faculty teaching positions at both a medical school and a pharmacy school.

Entrepreneurial Journey

Oops—right before I needed it, I gave away my entrepreneurial guidebook. When I read *The 4-Hour Workweek* by Tim Ferriss, I thought it was meant for people in another stage of life than me, so

I gave it away! I couldn't see at the time that I could fit in and be an entrepreneur even though I'm a mother with five small children.

Next, I listened to Blair Thielemier's Elevate Pharmacy Summit in April 2018, and after, I talked to a fellow pharmacist mama about how we could each create a side hustle. I said to her, "I wish I believed in supplements because that would be the perfect side gig."

Imagine my surprise when the very next day, I had an epiphany. It was like a flash of inspiration meant just for me. I knew I had to create a dietary supplement specifically for people on prednisone.

It was exactly what I said I couldn't do. Yet from that moment on, I jumped in to find a deep evidence base for the vitamins and herbs in the supplement I patented. Having had to take prednisone for nine months and being in the midst of receiving chemo at the time, it seemed crazy—yet it was precisely what people on prednisone like me needed.

Once I created the formula, found the best manufacturer, and had my product tested by a third-party lab, my next step was learning how to sell it. I've spent the last several years getting what feels like an MBA in marketing from the online gurus.

Methods to Monetize Your Knowledge

Right now, I monetize my knowledge through my YouTube channel. I have enough followers and watch hours that YouTube pays me to create content. It's not very much; this is not a way to get rich as a pharmacist unless you go viral. But I do get paid that way. I am also planning on creating a course. I have it all planned out and know exactly what I am going to do; that is going to be awesome. But I have five kids, so right now, step one is to get my supplement out there. I want to have a funnel built so it can get out to the public, and I can focus on the next step, which is better monetizing my knowledge.

People are desperate for the information I have. They want me to tell them how not to gain weight while on Prednisone and how to feel better while on Prednisone. I could make a lot of money doing one-on-one counseling. But the truth is I can really only recommend doing one thing at a time. That one thing for me right now is my supplement. In 2022 I am hoping to do a course and help people understand that there is so much we don't know about Prednisone at this point. There are so many nutrients in your body that Prednisone depletes.

I included all of these nutrients in Nutranize Zone so that your body can be replenished.

How to Plan a Year's Worth of Content in Only One Afternoon

I have one main problem, and this huge problem was that there are so many regulations surrounding marketing a supplement. I really wanted to hide behind the supplement label I had created for myself. I wanted to have it stand alone; I wanted to be able to say, "Look. It has all these amazing ingredients. They're from the best manufacturers. They're pharmaceutical-grade ingredients. It's an amazing product. Look how pretty I have designed it. Just buy it." I thought that would be enough. But I realized you cannot actually say to the public in a product's marketing materials, "this cures the side effects of Prednisone."

You can't claim efficacy. You can't claim a product cures or prevents a specific side effect. There are restrictions against the kind of general health claims you can make. Thankfully, I discovered my product had a predecessor. There was someone I could take inspiration from. This was a product created by the Thyroid Pharmacist Isabella Wentz. What she does is she creates content about the thyroid, and she monetizes that knowledge through selling supplements to people with a legitimate need, people who are suffering from thyroid issues.

I saw what she did. I saw she had two separate websites, thyroid-pharmacist.com, and her supplement website. I saw what I had to do. But it took me a year to figure it all out. To figure out that I can't hide behind my brand. I didn't want to be a public person. I didn't want to have a YouTube channel with over a hundred videos and over a thousand subscribers, but it allowed me to monetize to make money off of YouTube. But I didn't want to have a website, a blog, or Instagram and post pictures of myself. I didn't want to do any of that stuff. I wanted to just build the product and hope that people would come. And that didn't happen.

The supplement I created has two capsules in the morning, which is the Nutranize Zone Morning, and two capsules at bedtime for the Nutranize Zone Bedtime. "Get back in the Zone of Prednisone" when you finally start feeling like yourself again because people who take prednisone constantly feel like they are strangers in their own bodies. They feel like nobody warned them that they were going to gain weight, they could get osteoporosis, they were going to experience insomnia. Many people who take prednisone feel completely betrayed.

It really feels like you are in someone else's body. You don't feel like you have the same personality. Everything is different when you take prednisone. When people take Nutranize Zone, they start to feel like themselves again. It's like pouring fertilizer on a yellow potted plant that you let go of, and it has gone yellow because there are not enough nutrients or water, and it is causing it to wilt. Giving Nutranize Zone to people on prednisone makes them turn green again. They feel invigorated. They get that vitality back that the prednisone was stealing from them.

What I want to share with you is how you can create your social media content because you can't expect other people will build it and that customers will just come. I have a Facebook page, a YouTube channel, and my blog. My goal is to optimize content for each channel. Each social media platform has a different strategy. Facebook wants you to go live and stream live videos. YouTube wants a constant stream of engaging content for people to consume. My website and blog I optimize for Google search so that I can have more people searching for my product. My product pops up when you search "side effects of prednisone" or "does prednisone cause hair loss?" That is something that is not on any side effect list, but it does. It is crazy; I have a whole blog post about prednisone causing hair loss.

To distribute this content, first, I went live on my Facebook page. I then downloaded that video and uploaded it to YouTube. I also had the video transcribed and used that as the text for the blog post on my website. I was able to take one video and turn it into all of this content. I use Instagram as well; I'll post a picture and use the comments to tell people to watch the video or read the blog post. That way, people who follow me on Instagram, in turn, Google me. No matter what channel my followers prefer, they can find the information. From there, they sign up for my email list, or they'll watch one of my live videos and ask questions in the chat.

Answer Burning Questions
A burning question a prednisone patient may have right now is, "Am I losing my hair because of prednisone?" A lot of people will start there, and once they learn helpful information, and they can know, and trust me, they feel like they can buy my product. Because they are reading my emails, watching my videos, and reading my blog posts. That is how I finally figured out how to sell my supplement online. This method can work with anything; it could work with cannabidiol (CBD) or skincare, any problem you need solving. You can use this exact same system to distribute your content.

What is MLM?

MLM stands for Multi-Level Marketing. I personally was super opposed to any form of multi-level marketing, which is what led to me creating my own company. But essentially, it is a big company that sells its products through influencers. I know a skincare pharmacist that works for Rodan + Fields and sells products for them. She will post content on Instagram and answer skincare questions, and then she'll say, "Hey. I have a great product that helps solve that problem." Multi-level marketing uses the people underneath them to sell their products. If you are at the top of the triangle pyramid, you can get people under you to sell the same product and get a cut of their sales, and they get a cut of the people under them. If you're at the very top of that pyramid, you make a lot of money.

There are a lot of pharmacists out there who make it work for them to do multi-level marketing. It's also one of the reasons I created an affiliate program for my product. That itself isn't multi-level marketing, but if you sell the product, you get a 50% cut of the sale.

Passionately Study Your Customer

The way I do this is; first, I studied who my audience was. You have to find out exactly who you are serving. I would go on Facebook support groups for prednisone; there are tens of thousands of people in these support groups. I would jump in the comments and help out. I would listen to what people were really saying, and then I would post on all of those channels.

In the online marketing world, the term "organic" refers to things you don't have to pay to reach on social media. Facebook, Instagram, YouTube are good examples; LinkedIn is probably the best right now for organic. But the organic reach you have gets less and less every day. The more time goes on, the more you have to pay whether to boost your posts or to advertise. It becomes less effective over time. The sooner you start using these platforms, the better. That way, over time, you can build your audience and develop your social media reach, hopefully without having to pay too much.

I've created memes, blog posts, and graphics. And at first, I would use all of these big words. I thought that I needed to show people I was an expert. But I found audiences didn't really connect with that. What I try to do now is take science and make it applicable to people's lives. I use language people can understand and not fancy science words. That's what I really learned in pharmacy school, how to counsel patients, How to explain this drug without using all these big words, to talk to patients using their language. It was the same exact principle.

I found a helpful tool; if you are looking to go into online marketing, I would start with Neil Patel. He is amazing, he knows everything, and it is all offered for free. He has all of these training programs, and you don't need to pay. I wish I had this back when I was starting because I had to pay for everything. He has a tool where you can type in a keyword; for example, I would use "prednisone side effects," and you can find every hit from Googling it. This shows you areas that are missing so that you can put your own individual spin on it, or if there is no good information, you can be the person to add that information.

Tools I Recommend for Planning Social Media
I would use this to plan a whole year's worth of social media content in one afternoon. I would go to Neil Patel, put in my keywords, and cater my content to fill in the gaps. From that information, I would create ideas for blog posts and topics to cover on Facebook Live. I would create all of these content ideas. I would use the website Trello to organize it all. I would search "prednisone side effects for women," "prednisone side effects for men," "prednisone side effects hair loss," and I would use Trello to put down all of these different terms and organize them, mark the dates I want to post that specific content, and it made it easy.

I should charge you for this information! These are all of my tips and tricks. This is how I create a year's worth of content in a single afternoon. And then later, I can check what content I have to post today. At that point, there is no planning involved. Everything is already there and scheduled. Scheduling it all out in advance is so helpful. I like to focus on one specific element every week. I have these deadlines set for myself, and I do what I said I would do.

The truth is, that is the hardest part of becoming a Pharmfluencer or entrepreneur, learning to be your own boss. You stay up late and get up early and do whatever it takes until you have that engine going. There have been a lot of late nights, a lot of early mornings to get this ball rolling.

Advice for Aspiring Entrepreneurs

I went straight from never selling anything to developing and selling my own product. To be completely honest, I would not recommend that. I recommend that aspiring entrepreneurs learn how to sell other people's products before they start their own. This is why I offer my affiliate program so that people can get experience from selling my product and maybe one day develop their own. It also is a good deal, you can turn a $4 prednisone prescription into a $45 profit, or if you don't have a brick-and-mortar store, you get a coupon code that is specific to you and make money off of your sales. I pay my affiliates $40 a month for every single person that subscribes to the product. If you get ten people, that's $400 per month!

That is my number one piece of advice, learn how to sell a product by marketing someone else's product, and then make your own product later when you know your market well enough.

CONTRIBUTOR
CONNECTION

**Megan Milne,
PharmD, BCACP**

🌐 www.www.prednisonepharmacist.com

in www.linkedin.com/in/megan
-jolley-milne-pharmd/

KIM NEWLOVE

Biography

Kim Newlove is a pharmacist, voice actor, podcast host, volunteer, wife, and mom of two. She earned her Bachelor of Science degree in Pharmacy from the University of Toledo in 2001. She had been an Ohio-licensed pharmacist for 20 years. In 2017 she founded The Pharmacist's Voice© and launched *The Pharmacist's Voice Podcast* in 2019. Her website is the-pharmacistsvoice.com. Finding the right voice for an audio project can be a challenge. There are thousands of voice actors to choose from. Kim brings her years of experience as a pharmacist to her audio and voiceover projects. Her delivery style is confident and trustworthy. *The Pharmacist's Voice Podcast* is available weekly on thepharmacistvoice.com and all major podcast players such as Apple Podcasts, Google, and Spotify. She alternates solo shows and interview shows. The solo shows share her journey from pharmacist to a voice actor. Her interview shows feature a variety of guests who use their voices to advocate for something, educate in some way, or entertain. Kim hopes her podcast inspires listeners to use their voices.

Entrepreneurial Journey

I did something that not a lot of pharmacists do. I did not go directly from being a pharmacist to becoming an entrepreneur; I was a stay-at-home mom in between. I left a job working at a behavioral health hospital, where I was a relief pharmacist for a friend of mine who I knew from volunteering at the University of Toledo. And I wasn't sure what to do next. I didn't really want to go back to school, and I had pretty time-consuming childcare needs. I have an 18-year-old son with autism; at the time I started my company, he was about 14 or 15.

I was trying to figure out how I could use my identity as a pharmacist and do something that I already knew since I had been an Ohio pharmacist for 16 years at the time. No matter what I'm doing, you can't take the pharmacist's identity away from me. I started thinking, what can I leverage? What do I already know how to do? And I looked at my son for inspiration. He is non-verbal; he uses a communication device called an Accent1000 and speaks in pictures. He'll touch a picture on the device, and it speaks the word. He likes it when I read to him, but he can't read, write, or speak. My husband and I read to him. It got me thinking, how can I use my voice?

I use my voice with my son, and he likes it, maybe somebody could pay me to do something like this. My first thought was serving other pharmacists through narrating continuing education journals. There are not many continuing education audio materials. We can listen to webinars and podcasts but taking a Pharmacist's Letter and turning it into a monthly conversational newsletter in audio format seemed like a completely new idea.

I pitched the idea, and nobody was interested. I don't know if the world just wasn't ready for it. I pivoted, as many entrepreneurs must do. I found a problem I thought I could get paid to solve, and that was providing pharmacy continuing education in audio format. I loved the idea of using my pharmacist identity and my voice. I pivoted in such a way that I could continue to get paid while also using my voice either in audio or writing. I had no idea what the voiceover industry was, but that is where I ended up.

Now I narrate audiobooks for women authors and provide medical narration as well as voiceovers for e-learning projects, explainer videos, and podcasts. This is my only job. I do not make six figures, but I will tell you that being an entrepreneur is not going from zero to six figures. I was a stay-at-home mom right before I started my business, and I really had nothing to lose. That's why I started off by saying that I am doing something not a lot of other people did. I went from being a stay-at-home mom to a voice actor.

It works out really well since I'm not available for traditional clinical practice because of childcare issues. Finding care for children with disabilities is hard to come by, especially since the pandemic began. There has been a real shortage. My parents are alive and well, but they can only handle him for a little bit. I needed a job I could do part-time and in the margins. By doing this, I can pick up work when I have time. I audition for jobs, and I direct-market to potential clients. I do something called proactive auditioning, which means auditioning for jobs that nobody is actually casting for.

It is similar to how the Pharmacist's Letter project was not casting voice talent, but I proposed the creation of the service anyway. They said no, which is fine. In the voiceover industry, you have to audition for a lot more than you get; that is a normal part of the work. You have to deal with rejection and work to slowly build your company.

When the pandemic started, I had just cut my demo on March 11, 2020. That was the moment when my career was supposed to take off, but I ended up homeschooling my kids. I'm not complaining about that; it is just a fact of life. Even though I wanted to do this work, a lot of the jobs available for voiceover newbies kind of went down the drain, they weren't hiring much anymore, and the projects that were hiring wanted folks with a lot more experience. It was not like I decided to be a voice actor, opened up my wallet, and all this money started falling in.

I work part-time because of my family situation. But I really value being a stay-at-home parent for my kids and a support person for my husband. We've been married for 20 years, and I'm very much in love with him and want to make him happy. I call myself a gap-filler. By working part-time, I can fill the gaps.

Methods to Monetize Your Knowledge

I am in the gig economy, so I go from job to job, and in total, I have counted five different streams of income. Firstly, I have audiobooks. I set my own rate and get paid to produce an audiobook in accordance with that rate. On top of that, I earn royalties through audible or amazon.com, wherever the audiobook is selling. I just got a royalty check not too long ago. And I'm not saying it's huge, but it's cool to have already done the work and still get paid continuously.

If I do a four-hour book, I get paid per finished hour, and once that book is done, I continue to get paid. I believe it is quarterly through Amazon. I get paid every time that book sells. I get about $2 per book. That's great because I constantly have money coming in through Amazon. And the more books I do, the more royalties I earn. I have found that as much as I enjoy producing audiobooks, I don't have as much time for it as I would like. It has started going on the back burner a little, as much as I love it and have had really good experiences with it.

It sounds selfish, but now that I'm running a business, I need shorter projects that pay more. That way, I can keep rolling through those and increase my income. These kinds of projects would be, for example, an explainer video. Depending on how complicated the material is, I can get paid $350 for 90 seconds of audio. The rate really depends on how much the author is willing to pay. I could get $100 per finished hour, which would be $400 for a four-hour book. Or I could get $400 per finished hour and make $1,600. It depends on who is paying me. I'm starting to think in terms of how many explainer videos I would have to do to equal a four-hour book paying $400 per finished hour. Well, roughly four videos with 90 seconds of audio each. That's a lot easier at this point; I can rip through that in a day, whereas it would take me a month to do a four-hour book. I just don't have the time.

It's a personal preference. And as selfish as it feels to say that, the amount of time I dedicate to a project depends on who is paying me and how much. You have to become a negotiation ninja in voiceover. I also have to think about the fact that the time I'm not spending doing an audiobook is time I could spend marketing myself. I could use that time to proactively audition for explainer videos, e-learning projects, medical, narration. If I spent time marketing myself rather than doing the audio for books, I could guarantee myself more voiceover projects in the future. You really miss out if you don't market yourself.

Another way I monetize my knowledge is through consulting. You know I just mentioned proactive auditioning. I have had to turn down five-figure consulting jobs because what ends up happening is that I donate my time in pursuit of the five-figure job. I donate my time so that I'll do good work, and they will want to hire me. But in the process of explaining what I do and what they need to give me, we discover they're not actually ready yet; they don't have a script or something. I have begun turning down these jobs because there have been multiple instances where I end up working for free only not to get the five-figure job because they are not ready. And if they don't have a script, we can't go anywhere because my price is based on words. I charge 15 cents per word for general e-learning and more for medical, up to 50 cents a word, depending on how tough the material is. Some of it is really time-consuming because there is a lot of prep work on my part, and I do that for free because it is rolled into the total price. You can say I get paid for consulting if they are in a place to move forward with the job.

I also have an online course; you can find it at kimnewlove.com, or you can find a link through The Pharmacist's Voice website in the store tab. The name of the course is Pronounce Drug Names Like a Pro. It is about how to pronounce drug names, both brand and generic, and I get paid for that. I charge $99 for each participant.

The Power of Having a Voice & Using It

I was inspired by my son with autism because he has no voice. He can talk through his communication device, but that's about the extent of it. However, I have a voice, and I'm very fortunate. Whether I am using my voice through print, audio, as a volunteer, as a wife, mom, pharmacist, or voice actor, my voice has power, and that is something nobody can take away from me.

My son helped me learn what it truly meant to have a voice. And I love to use my voice. I'm not saying that I'm in love with my voice, although I ended up in a career where I do have to listen to myself talk all day. I mean, I have learned to love the power of my voice and what it can accomplish.

To me, knowing the power of your voice means you have something to leverage. I appreciate that my career is one where I have the opportunity to share my voice and use my identity. It's something nobody can take away from me. I earned my pharmacist degree; I earned my license. I am a BS pharm, meaning I went and got my Bachelor of Science degree in pharmacy. I don't have a PharmD, but I have a five-year bachelor's from 2001 at the University of Toledo. I never went back and got my PharmD, I have no initials after my name except for RPH, and yet I was able to become an entrepreneur.

I want to encourage any pharmacist out there who wants to become an entrepreneur but thinks that they're not expert enough at something to look at what they have. Even at the most basic level, you have a voice, and that is something you can leverage. You can become a medical writer; you can become a voice actor like me; you can become a podcaster.

I have a podcast called *The Pharmacist's Voice Podcast*. I share my journey from pharmacist to voice actor. I also interview a variety of people who use their voices to advocate for something, educate in some way, or entertain. And the goal is to inspire people to use their voices too.

The podcast has really been a joy; it has also been a helpful branding tool. It has really served my business. People know through my podcast that I am a pharmacist and voice actor. Because I positioned myself that way, I can network and increase my influence by meeting people and then bringing them onto the show. I absolutely love it. I really encourage anyone that wants to have a podcast to start one. Dr. Erin L. Albert told me in 2019 that I should look into starting a podcast since I already knew how to record, edit, and produce audio. She was right, I looked into it, and it has really helped me position myself as a go-to pharmacist podcaster.

In 2021 I went to the Medipreneurs conference, and it really brought to my attention the need to create some sort of podcasting service. In the future, this is something I would like to do, and by creating a podcasting service, I mean render MP3s. I want to help anyone in the pharmacy realm become a podcaster: women pharmacists, pharmacy students, technicians, everyone. It really can be as simple as stepping into the booth. I'd like to offer a service in which people can use my booth. I would record and edit the audio and give you the final MP3 for you to upload to your own podcast.

There are a lot of women out there who are afraid of tech. They don't want to buy a mic or learn how you use it. They are afraid of learning how to record, edit, and produce audio. And I don't blame them. But if you would just start, just jump into the pool, you might be surprised by how quickly you can learn. You can make some MP3s and be out on the airwaves using that as your branding tool. At Medipreneurs, I learned that this was something a lot of people were interested in, having someone assemble the MP3s and handle the tech side of podcasting.

People will find my website and then listen to the podcast and reach out to hire me for a job. I have been hired to do audiobooks by two of my guests. Both of these people I actually met at Medipreneurs and have done books for this year. It can definitely be used as a means of marketing yourself. People tend to think the only way you can do that is through advertising, like getting paid to promote brands, but that is not the only option.

Often when I have conversations with people before or after the podcast, they will ask me, "What is your company? Can we work together on something?" While I don't get any money from the podcast itself, I form relationships with the people I interview, and things happen from there.

I also want to continue creating online courses. I'd like my next one to be more affordable, only like $20. And it would allow people to see what goes on under the hood of a podcast. They can hear it from a pharmacist and podcaster who speaks their language. I'm nothing special, I'm not the most tech-savvy person, but I know how to podcast. I have done this 122 times as of this weekend. I know what I'm doing. I think it can be really valuable for people to see what it is like behind the scenes, what the time commitment is, how uploading works, and all of that stuff. The course would also serve as a funnel to booking me for one-on-one coaching or helping them render their MP3 files.

For many people, rendering an MP3 file is the hardest thing. That is the step that is limiting them from becoming a podcaster, so if I can help people get around that, I want to.

Advice for Aspiring Entrepreneurs

My advice to anyone looking to become an entrepreneur is to think about their Ikigai, their reason for being. Entrepreneurs need to look at what they love, what the world needs, what they can get paid for, and what they are good at. Dr. Erin L. Albert told me this on my podcast, "You need to also look at what you value. With that in mind. Entrepreneurs need to do soul searching before they go into business." You have to read a lot, listen to podcasts, and do that soul searching so that when it comes to forking over money to a coach or learning a skill, it's not going to hurt so bad because you have the passion.

CONTRIBUTOR
CONNECTION

**Kim Newlove,
RPh**

🌐 www.thepharmacistsvoice.com

in www.linkedin.com/in/kimnewlove/

ANGELA ORR

Biography

Angela Orr is a certified life coach, certified HeartMath practitioner, pharmacist of 36 years, and serial entrepreneur. She was fortunate to experience many different settings in pharmacy. After working in hospital pharmacy, she went into home infusion therapy in the early 1980s. She had worked part-time in community-based pharmacies that were independently owned. She then transitioned and worked for an insurance company as the executive liaison with the pharmacy benefit managers (PBM). It was there that she began to see how pharmacies were treated by the payers and chose to leave and go back to retail. It was there that she felt she could truly make an impact and help make a difference for people in their life. Along her journey, she opened and owned, for a total of 15 years, two of her own pharmacies in Maine. With increasing regulations, tightening reimbursements, and a breast cancer diagnosis, she decided to change my focus to offering non-dispensing care. She sold my pharmacies and transitioned to becoming a certified life coach, certified HeartMath practitioner, and business coach.

Entrepreneurial Journey

I am a serial entrepreneur. I went to college and graduated in 1985. I've been a licensed pharmacist for 36 years. Part of why I did that was because I wanted to be in healthcare, and I wanted to make an impact on the world. Back then, nurses weren't paid well, and they weren't respected. I really wanted to be a physician, but I didn't feel I had the money to do that. A mentor of mine's husband was a pharmacist. I went to pharmacy school, and it was the best thing that ever happened to me. I love being a pharmacist. I've had times where I have experienced burnout, but all in all, I feel that pharmacy has been a really wonderful career.

I was the first person in my entire extended family to graduate college. In some ways, I feel I forged the way for the next generation of pharmacists or pharmacy influencers. I helped pave the way for that. I grew up very poor; my family lived in a housing project, I never knew I was going to be a pharmacist. Not only was I the first to go to college, but I really wanted to break the cycle of generational poverty. That is a big part of why I do what I do. One of my mentors always says, "Make more to give more so that you can really make a difference in the world." That has always guided everything I have done.

I owned two multimillion-dollar pharmacies in Kennebunk and Walterboro, Maine. In 2013 I was diagnosed with breast cancer. And although it looked like I had everything, I was very overweight, I was very stressed, I was experiencing burnout, and now I had a cancer diagnosis. The business model we have today is very different from what we had in 2007; there was a lot of stress. I don't think pharmacy ownership is a bad thing. I was very glad to see new pharmacies open up in my community in the past few weeks. But I had to build up the courage to sell mine.

Since then, I have been focusing on staying healthy and developing my coaching business. I really believe pharmacists have so much to offer. For myself personally, I have helped hundreds of thousands of patients over the last 36 years, mostly in my community. What I see myself doing now is helping other pharmacists who are burnt out, feeling stressed, and having anxiety. A lot of people really want to make a career change but don't know where to start. I think a part of that is when you are in a state of burnout or stress, it is really hard to have the clarity you need to move forward. I work to help pharmacists address that and move past it so they can start working with clarity and energy.

Methods to Monetize Your Knowledge

As far as monetizing my knowledge, I have a plethora of programs that I offer. My signature is one-on-one coaching programs; I am a certified life coach and a certified heart map practitioner, which specializes in heart-mind intelligence. That is more of a mindset coach.

I like to be called The Pill-less Pharmacist. You have likely heard other contributors discuss the pill for an ill method. I am really interested in looking at other modalities of healing. I don't think a pill is always the way to go. Studies have shown there is a placebo effect in many categories of medications, especially antidepressants. I believe in medication. I pinched a nerve a couple of weeks ago and had to take cyclobenzaprine. It's not that I don't believe in medicine. But I think we should reserve medication for after we have explored other modalities.

I do one-on-one coaching. I have a program that runs for three to six months. I also host retreats. My first retreat was in Maine in October. It's called 'The Magnificent You Time To Meet Her Again.' It is all about taking time out of your busy schedule for yourself. It was held at a former bed and breakfast, now VRBO overlooking the ocean. It is called Willows. That retreat is all about resiliency and being strong. We are ten minutes away from my favorite place, Noble Lighthouse. We are going to practice meditation and breathing. I am even going to get a photographer who can take pictures of us while we walk on the beach.

I also have affiliate programs that I offer. That is an important point; if you have products that you recommend to people, having an affiliate link is a great way to have people refer you. I also have what I call the 'Inner Oasis.' It is a power hour with me to help jumpstart breathing and meditation, and that is $99 and is an hour-long guided meditation with me.

The Epigenetics of Balancing Your Heart, Mind, & Body

As pharmacists, we know about genes and genetics. But I am interested in epigenetics. The Center for Disease Control and Prevention (CDC) website defines epigenetics as "the study of how your behavior and environment can cause changes that affect the way your genes work." And that's how most drugs work. Your genes are either turned on or off. But what often happens because of your environment is your genes are inappropriately turned on.

What do I mean by your environment? Food, water, exercise, thoughts, perceptions. Your thoughts and perceptions matter just as much as your food intake. Really basic epigenetic changes occur when the genes are turned on or off, and you can affect how those turn on or off. What I specialize in is the heart-mind connection. HeartMath is an organization that has been around for decades. They have over 400 published articles on the heart affects the mind. There is more information sent from the heart to the brain versus the vagal nerve, which sends information from the brain to the heart.

When you are out of coherence, when your parasympathetic and sympathetic nervous system is out of balance, that is when you begin to suffer from diseases. The more balance you can create internally, the more you can reduce the conditions that cause inflammation, which I believe is the root cause of most chronic diseases. The goal is to have your heart and brain balanced. This can be accomplished through meditation, breathing, and life coaching.

All of this research is science-based; I have studied it. Research has proven that these tactics affect how you think and feel, and how you think and feel affects your health. Balancing your heart and mind within your autonomic nervous system can increase your health. I use simple techniques through advanced technology. We have a simple device that you wear inside your ear while you sleep, and it measures your heart rate variability. Your heart rate variability is a naturally occurring beat-to-beat variation in your heart. The analysis of heart rate variability serves as a dynamic window into the function and balance of the autonomic nervous system. The device connects to an app so I can have access to all of my client's readings and identify things that may have impacted their heart rate variability.

The balance comes from meditation and breathing. And again, this is not new science. Yogis have known about this for centuries. But there is scientific evidence to back this up. There are studies on HeartMath itself about heart center breathing. There are Harvard scientists who have evidence proving that clearing your mind for 15 minutes every day impacts how your genes operate. I teach people that you don't have to have an hour-long morning routine. A lot of people get scared off from the idea of morning routines because they don't have an hour. But what I tell my students is that if you can take 15 minutes for yourself, you can receive the benefits. This kind of regular practice also helps increase your emotional intelligence. That really is what it's all about, raising your level of awareness so that no matter what is going on around you, you can still feel centered and grounded. When you are stressed out, when you are worried or are experiencing burnout, you don't even breathe.

It is in moments like when your breathing becomes shallow that really affects your physiology. If you can learn to breathe regularly throughout the day, you not only get the benefits of that practice but the ongoing benefits throughout the day. If you do that consistently, you keep raising the bar of your emotional intelligence. There have been studies that show how breathing and meditation decrease blood pressure and help you with your health, especially in regard to diabetes. The evidence has been built up here.

Phil Mickelson, who won the Professional Golfers Association of America (PGA) tour at the ripe age of 50, one of the reasons he cited for his increased performance was a very strict diet and meditation. I am happy to see this mindset becoming more normalized. I think a lot of people didn't believe this was scientifically based. Deep breaths help voluntarily regulate your autonomic nervous system; it has many benefits. It helps you relax; it helps you decrease stress, the hormone cortisol is released into your system.

With all that being said, as pharmacists, we all have particular areas we enjoy researching, learning about, and passing along to others. I love being able to use this gift and turn around and help others. I'm at a point in my career where I just want to help other pharmacists so they can help your patients. If you're rushed, upset, and out of balance, your patient is going to feel that, the doctors you work with are going to feel it, your staff is going to feel that. When you come from a more founded area, it gives you much more power. That's what I help people do.

Advice for Aspiring Entrepreneurs

My advice for aspiring entrepreneurs is that the only way not to win is to quit. It is okay to fail as long as you fail forward. I have felt this many times. I felt this after I sold my pharmacies. I still work for the company that bought my pharmacy; I am hopefully transitioning to retirement next year. I have tried a lot of things, and I have failed miserably at some of them, but I always learned something. You have to keep going forward.

I also recommend that aspiring entrepreneurs hire a coach. I have three coaches right now, and I would not be where I am today without them. When you think of people like Oprah and Tony Collins, these people all have life coaches. If you feel like you are overwhelmed, look into getting a business or life coach. I have a business coach. I have a tech coach who taught me about the tech part of my business. I have a mindset coach right now. My mindset coach is helping me with my relationship with food. I need to lose the weight I gained after my breast cancer diagnosis. I have actually already lost about 100 pounds, but I have more to go. I have a coach who is helping me with my mindset surrounding food.

Hire a coach. Invest in yourself. It is not an expense; it is an investment.

Angela Orr, RPh

CONTRIBUTOR
CONNECTION

🌐 www.angelaorrconsulting.com

in www.linkedin.com/in/angelaorr

SUE PAUL

Biography

Sue Paul is a pharmacist, entre-preneur, and small business owner with over 20 years of experience in the industry. After journeying through the traditional pharmacy avenues of retail, nursing home consulting, and hospital, she founded SyneRxgy (pronounced si·nr·jee) Consulting LLC©, a concierge pharmacy service that is registered as a Limited Category 2 Pharmacy in the State of Ohio. SyneRxgy assists patients and physicians in managing chronic disease states, including medication adjustments and education, implementing and analyzing pharmacogenomic and nutrigenomic testing for patients, and compiling/reviewing current medication lists for patients. She enjoys educating clients on all aspects of medication to empower them to take control of their health. Current worksites include physician offices, employer worksites, and in-home patient visits. In 2018, Sue co-founded PGx101 LLC, along with Dan Krinsky, RPh, MS, which offers pharmacists 20 hours of ACPE approved continuing education and a certificate in Pharmacogenomics (PGx). She has been using PGx in her clinic and with home patients to implement patient-centered medication modification in conjunction with their providers since 2016. Sue is Co-Founder, along with Michelle Fritsch, PharmD, BCP, BCACP, and Anna Garrett of Medipreneurs LLC, an international conference and community for pharmacy entrepreneurs, which was founded in 2017. She gets a kick out of empowering other pharmacists to dream about how they would practice if there weren't any barriers. She is active in local, state, and national professional

organizations, including a board member and Vice President of the Ohio Pharmacists Foundation. In her spare time, she enjoys spending time with her husband and four adult children—Megan, Emily, Ian, and Evan, reading, walking with friends and brainstorming with others about action plans to get from where they are to where they want to be. Recent awards include the 2017 SCORE (Service Corps of Retired Executives) Client of the Year Award, 2019 Top 25 Women Pharmacists of the Year Award according to the Talk to Your Pharmacist Pharmacy Advisory Group, and the 2020 Upsher-Smith Excellence in Innovation Award by the Ohio Pharmacists Association.

Entrepreneurial Journey

I never had the desire to be an entrepreneur. I had ideas about what should be done in healthcare to fix some of the gaps but never thought I could do something about it. I recognized that America is overmedicated, and it took me 16 years to act on it. I worked in nursing homes as a consultant for 16 years, but the idea to find a way to help patients decrease their medication burden kept following me. I worked part-time in several different locations; I worked three days a week in the nursing home and two days a week in retail pharmacy, so overall, I worked more than the typical full-time 40 hours a week. Once I stopped doing nursing homes, I spent those other days in the hospital. And the thought kept running through my head that if pharmacists had gotten to these patients earlier, they might not need this level of care.

The thought kept occurring to me, so I started taking little steps towards building my own business. The first question I asked myself was, "Where can I make a difference? Where can I find an adequate amount of time to sit down with patients and thoroughly go through medications?" I actually explored opening my own independent pharmacy for a year. I was partnering with a different person at the time, and we ended up having different priorities. But I am grateful for that year and having that journey because it allowed me to become more clear on what I actually wanted. And I realized that I didn't want to open a brick-and-mortar pharmacy; I wanted to go where the patients were. I looked up how to get an LLC.

From there, I joined a business mentoring group, and it was awesome because there weren't really any other healthcare professionals in the group. That helped me learn how to simplify my language. If you're speaking to a bunch of other pharmacists, you can use language like pharmacogenomics, and everyone knows what you are talking about.

But if you use a word like that with a patient, they're like, "pharma what?"

Back in 2013, I was working in hospitals, and I noticed none of the doctors were using clopidogrel. I began investigating why they weren't using that specific medication. I came to learn that there is a variance in people's genes, about 30% of people cannot metabolize clopidogrel in its active form. Patients may then have another event after their heart attack or stroke. I pitched it to the cardiologist, and that didn't go anywhere. They said it wasn't standard operating procedure. But I learned how to develop a pitch; I learned what their objections were and how to answer those.

Eventually, I got to the practice I am now, mostly through networking. And I am an introvert; I don't necessarily like to do things like that. Going to networking events was not something I necessarily wanted to do. But what I would do, is I would set an intention, something specific. I would decide I want to meet somebody else who knows patients who need help with their medication. Well, I would walk into those events forget all about my intention, but by the time I would leave, I'd realize I had met three people who needed help.

I was able to keep going with that, and the more I networked, the more I gained confidence. I just kept pushing myself to get out of my box. I was prepared; I learned all I could about pharmacogenomics. I learned all I could about creating a business plan and working in a physician's office. I set up the LLC so that when the opportunity finally came, I was ready. It took me a while to get all of those pieces in place, but when the opportunity came, I was prepared.

I have been doing it now for five and a half years. Through SyneRxgy consulting, I work three days a week and see patients in the physician's office. I have 30-minute appointments. It is so rewarding. I actually had a phone call this week with Scott Knoerat, the American Pharmacists Association (APHA); it was in the middle of my workday. I just let the physician who I was working with know, "Hey, I have this meeting. I'm going to talk about my business model. Can you give me a quick quote I can give him?"

She said, "Oh my gosh, Sue, I will never work in an office again without a pharmacist. The amount of stuff you take off my plate is immeasurable. It has immensely reduced my level of burnout. You bring a totally different skillset and body of knowledge. I'm not meant to know everything, and I shouldn't have to. You can tell him I say that you're indispensable."

It's incredibly rewarding for me, the patient, and the physician. I've been working with that particular physician for about a year and four months. And it does really help the patient to see these changes. There is a lot of inertia when it comes to prescribing, where if a patient has been on medication for a long time, and they aren't getting worse, we just leave them on it. But they aren't getting better either, and sometimes we can make it better. Oftentimes I am even able to get the patient off medication. My favorite day is when I tell patients I am going to take them off insulin. It happens pretty regularly.

Methods to Monetize Your Knowledge

The way that I monetize my knowledge is by using a daily rate. I charge the practice I work at a daily rate for eight hours. They are responsible for filling up my schedule, which is always either booked out for the next month, or there are no shows. The reason I did it that way is to keep it simple for me.

Many people call me Dr. Sue Paul, but I have a BS in pharmacy, I don't have a residency. I'm not board certified. It's just a matter of having the knowledge and foundation that is needed. It's constantly maintaining a growth mindset. You can't learn everything you need in pharmacy school and then never learn again. In order to expand my business, I have created ways to take appointments. I spoke at a conference last month with one of my physicians about how she uses a pharmacist in her office.

It truly started with hypertension, diabetes, anticoagulation management, and it has grown into everything from code genomics to mood, anxiety, weight, and everything else. I was actually the one to introduce pharmacogenomics to my practice in 2016. We're now starting a pharmacist-run Hep C clinic. I was able to speak at a particular conference that has 333 clinics throughout the nation. That is where I am going to concentrate. I have a meeting with their CEO later this month. That will start my steps toward expansion. I have already hired a COO Chief Operating Officer, and I've got an educational officer also, so that's exciting. Many of us are planning on turning into full employees, having W2 employees under us as we grow our entrepreneurial business. We will have intrapreneurs working for us who are being paid directly. It is exciting to be creating these jobs and businesses.

I have also worked to monetize PGx in a number of different ways. I could never have envisioned myself on this journey, but it was just a matter of taking that next step. I think it was Martin Luther King Jr.

who said something like, "You don't need to see the whole staircase. Just take the first step." I really try to sit and concentrate my mindset around that every day. I think to myself, "Okay, I just need to take the next step." I don't need to have this multi-level pharmacy company running by tomorrow.

In PGx101, we have a 20-hour certificate training, and I felt I wasn't getting what I wanted out of this training. We worked on embellishing it. I brought one of my providers on, and she talked about how she uses pharmacogenomics, how it has changed her practice, and affected patients and prescribing. We also give customers a low-cost option for a personal PGx test, so you can see what the patient is going to see. We do lots of case studies from our own personal experiences, and we expanded it because the people who were going through our training were asking for more and more help. We opened up a year-long membership on June 28. We call it PGx201 since it is the next level. We offer templates like those you get in a physician's office and a collaborative practice agreement that we developed along the way.

I used PGx in nursing homes prior to working in the physician's office; I have used it in multiple settings. We have done walk-throughs for independent pharmacists who wanted to implement it into their practice, so we have a bunch of different methods to monetize it.

What Do You Do with an Idea?

What do you do with an idea? We all have different kinds of ideas. If it disappears really quickly or you run into too many obstacles, maybe it wasn't meant for you. But if you start gaining some traction and it's something you're passionate about, you should pursue it.

I try to work on my mindset every day, and this morning I read something that totally encapsulates my philosophy and what I want to share with people. It said, "Challenges draw something out of us that easiness could never ignite. If the reason behind our vision lacks purpose, if it's to become famous or earn approval, we'll get discouraged. The moment we face rejection, we'll likely throw up our hands and walk away because we believe we missed the mark. But if our vision is tied to a clear purpose, we won't be discouraged when times get tough." Turn the volume down on your doubts and stay focused on your purpose. Set aside the belief that the end goal will come clear quickly. Because it won't, you're going to run into lots of obstacles.

This is from Ryan Holiday's *The Obstacle Is the Way*, and it really helped with my mindset. It helped me get past my doubts which were saying, "Dang. Maybe I'm not supposed to do this." or "Maybe there is a better path." But there is always a better path. Focus on the process, with all the ups and downs, triumphs, and missed starts that will ultimately get you there. You are learning along the way. Start with the idea first, surround yourself with people who encourage you, who can support you.

Kimber Boothe has been very influential for me because she sees things differently than I do. She will say, "Why don't you do it this way?"

I'm like, "Oh my gosh, I didn't even think about that. That is so easy."

I also have a free book club. We just finished *Atomic Habits*, and prior to that, we read *You Are Badass* by Jen Sincero. We will be starting up another one soon. I really do believe in the power of books to help develop these ideas.

I would also recommend people look into the PGx101 guidelines; even if you don't elect to use PGx in your practice, it can be very helpful to see and learn what other entrepreneurs are doing.

I encourage you to take the next step; build your confidence. I don't have complicated evidence-based stats to share with you, but it really is that easy. It will be challenging; people are going to think you're crazy, but becoming an entrepreneur is the most rewarding thing. There is never a day I don't want to go to work, whether I am working on my business, developing new content for PGx101, or working in a physician's office and seeing the patients I love to see. I also take students; I have a student intern right now who helps me with prior authorizations. This is incredibly helpful to doctors when it comes to prescribing patients the medications they need. If we can work to make that easier or switch it to a formulary myth, they want us to do it. We take a lot off their plate. It's so inspiring.

Advice for Aspiring Entrepreneurs

For those who don't know, an entrepreneur is somebody who creates something unique on their own. An intrapreneur is somebody who develops a new service within their current salary job. I have done both. And it's nice to be able to make hundreds of thousands of dollars for your employer, but it's even nicer when you can do it on your own.

My last piece of wisdom comes from Brene Brown; she is someone I read often. She says, "We can choose courage, or we can choose comfort, but we can't have both." That's it. If you're happy with going to the drug store or hospital every day, and you're satisfied with your salary. If it is easy for you and you are comfortable, you probably don't need to be very courageous. But if you want to do something on your own, face some new challenges and find a career path that is incredibly rewarding, take some courage. It really will change the path of your life and your level of enjoyment in your work.

Sue Paul, RPh

CONTRIBUTOR
CONNECTION

www.synerxgy.com
www.pgx101.com

www.linkedin.com/in/sue-paulrph/

RAJINDER RAI

Biography

Rajinder Rai is an entrepreneur and business owner with over 25 years of experience in community pharmacy, looking to expand interest in medication management. As a longtime advocate and public speaker for holistic healthcare, she is dedicated to educating patients throughout their medication journey. With dueled experience as a pharmacist (PharmD) and multi-store pharmacy owner, she has strong knowledge of internal and external functionalities in running an effective business in the healthcare field. With years of creating relationships with my customers, she has found a strong need for humanistic approaches to pharmacy. As Founder and CEO of SunRaisRx Health & Wellness Inc.©, she aims to optimize patient therapeutic outcomes with one-on-one consultations on comprehensive medication management. Her transitional care service works to ensure patients understand their medication, simplify patients' medication regimens, and identify less expensive medication alternatives. She is a strong advocate for the pharmacist community and always looking for ways to empower fellow healthcare professionals. She works locally as President of Ventura County Pharmacist Association (VCPhA) and directly with California Pharmacists Association (CPhA) at a state-wide level to ensure our voices as pharmacists are heard. She has successfully mentored future generations of pharmacy students as a preceptor and pharmacists who have ventured to own pharmacies of their own.

Entrepreneurial Journey

I would like to share my story with you because there are so many pharmacists that are on the fence trying to figure out what they want to do. I think that my story might be helpful because I have really come full circle. I followed the traditional path of pharmacy entrepreneurship; I owned my own pharmacy. But it was more than that.

My entrepreneurial journey really began when I was 15 years old and got my first job at Wendy's. I never really thought of myself as one day being a business owner, although my family-owned businesses. But whatever position I had, I always moved up. I think people see something to me that perhaps I didn't see in myself. I married a pharmacist as well; he is very ambitious and wanted to have his own pharmacy. When my son was three, and I was pregnant with my daughter, we bought our first pharmacy. We took out a loan on our house, and we went from there.

The plan was that my husband was going to work in the pharmacy. I would continue to work part-time and take care of the kids. Unfortunately, my husband had a heart attack at the age of 40 and needed to have surgery. That basically propelled me into the role of running the pharmacy, whether I was ready or not. So I am familiar with being a pharmacist, but I have never run a business. Overnight, I had to learn to manage the things my husband was doing and manage more responsibilities while still balancing kids. But once I took that role, I never looked back.

I have assumed the role of being a problem solver, of putting out the fires. We continued to grow as a company and add more pharmacies. Eventually, we were up to owning about five pharmacies. We had pharmacists that worked for us, and we were building relationships along the way that really allowed us to grow.

It was the relationships with our customers, patients, providers, vendors, employees, and the community that made us successful. Each of our pharmacies was different, but they all had the same standard operating procedures and policies. Each pharmacy had its own personality in a way; they all had different demographics and different employees. I had to learn the personality of each store and cater our services based on the needs of those patients and the capabilities of those employees.

As I am sure you have heard before, understanding your patient's needs and meeting them where they are is key to being successful in your business. That is the kind of knowledge you can only get through experience. As pharmacists, we have to be listeners; we have to be able to get that information and use it. We have access to so much information and data, but sometimes we hesitate to utilize it because we are concerned about patient privacy or infringing on a patient's rights.

But I thought I had found my key to success. I was living the American dream. I went from making $4.25 an hour to owning multiple pharmacies. I checked all the boxes of being a successful entrepreneur. But that is not where my story ends.

Methods to Monetize Your Knowledge

I thought that I would move away from pharmacy. I felt that I had done everything. I've done Institute for Functional Medicine (IFM) and Fellowship in Anti-Aging, Metabolic and Functional Medicine (A4M), which is an anti-aging fellowship. I was moving from being at the end of people's lives, when they're already at a higher disease state and taking a lot of medications, to being on the other side when they first get diagnosed. I really wanted to make those interventions and give patients the tools to make a difference and realize that their condition is not a death sentence.

With my passion for pharmacy, I wanted pharmacists to be trained in wellness, for them to know how to become health consultants. I have created programs to train pharmacists, programs for independent pharmacies to put into place to train their staff so that they can raise extra revenue and become a resource in their communities. I want to help pharmacies become the places people go when they are seeking the tools to be healthy. It's about changing the whole image of where, why, and when you would go to the pharmacy.

I obviously have a bias towards independent pharmacy, but I really believe that independent pharmacies could be the hub of healthcare. I think they could really help our system move along and be a service to vulnerable people who need the most medical care. Pharmacists are the best guides to give unbiased information. We have a vast knowledge of medication; we can learn more about supplements and alternative treatments. We can distribute knowledge about lifestyle modifications. There are always ways to put your background to use and monetize your knowledge, while at the same time helping people be healthy.

If we have healthy people, we have a healthy community. There is no better legacy to leave for your children and grandchildren than helping to improve the health of their communities. So for me, it is helping me become a better person, it is helping my colleagues become better people.

▪▪

Introduction to "Reclaim your ROARR"

I have spent over half of my life in pharmacy. It is really important to me. And to be honest, I was busy running my own business, doing what I needed to do to make sure that my family was successful, and my community was doing well, that I didn't notice what was happening in the outside world. There are so many changes that are happening in pharmacy; the industry is changing, the level of job satisfaction is dropping, people are experiencing burnout.

My real mission as a Pharmfluencer is to help as many pharmacists find joy in what they do. Sometimes we may blame the job, we may blame our boss, but we often have to dig deeper to find what is really going on. What is causing the dissatisfaction? What are your expectations? Is it our own health? Sometimes it can be hard to know. It is easy to have a target and blame the current situation that you're in.

I want to help pharmacists get paid for their services. I am extremely passionate about what we do. Even the role of a traditional retail pharmacist, what we do matters. You are helping patients with their medications where they otherwise would not have access to the care you give. Some things are not in your control. But all of you should get a round of applause because what you do every single day does matter.

I also think it is important that we change the image of the pharmacist. I don't want to see commercials on TV. The only time we see pharmacists is when somebody is waving a coupon to show that you can save money at the pharmacy. I want to see all the different things pharmacists are doing. I want to see pharmacists making vaccines, making a difference in the community, being advocates. There are so many different kinds of pharmacists doing such important work.

I believe that as pharmacists, we have to be the ones advocating for ourselves. We have to show what we're doing. Nobody else is going to do that for us.

At this point, I had done it all; I felt pretty successful in that I was following my trajectory. I was running a traditional pharmacy, adding services like compounding point of care, testing, vaccinations to having pilots with health clinics. I was doing it all. I had helped people at the end of their life in hospice care. I used to get up in the middle of the night and help babies come into the world. But it wasn't until I had a personal experience within my own family that I realized what I was doing.

If you give a dog a bone, that dog will always go chasing after the bone. It doesn't matter how many times it sees the bone; it is going to go chasing after it. It doesn't matter whether it's a real bone or it is made of plastic; as soon as the dog sees it, he's going after it.

A lion is different. When a lion sees a bone, it doesn't really care about it. It sees the person that is holding the bone. It has a very clear vision of what it wants and needs. I read somewhere that lions can sleep 20 hours a day. But when there is something that needs to be done, they are still king of the jungle. My point in all of this is that I was the dog chasing the bone. I was going after things simply because I thought that was what I needed to do. That was what I was conditioned to do, to people, please.

Everything I did was to make sure the doctors and patients were content. I wanted to make sure I wasn't ruffling feathers with the insurance companies. I was successful, but I wasn't fulfilled. And then, my daughter was diagnosed with Hodkin's lymphoma, and I realized how much the system needed to change. She had been talking with her doctor, and the doctor was going over her treatment one day. And she asked the doctor; specifically, she said, "Why did this happen to me? I'm only 18 years old."

And the doctor said, "I don't have an answer for you, but I do have treatments."

And at that moment, I had a flashback of every single patient I have said something similar to over the years. And I felt like I had done them a disservice. I was not completely there for them as a provider, as a health professional, and as a person. I felt at that moment that not only had I failed as a mom, but also as a pharmacist, and honestly, even as an individual.

That is where my quest began. I wanted to learn the "how" and "why" of healthcare. I began studying functional medicine, wellness, and prevention, but in the process, I had to go through my own personal journey to find out what it was that I needed to do to really show up. Now, as a pharmacist, not as somebody's wife, or somebody's mom, or somebody's daughter, but as me.

This is what ROARR means: Reflecting, Observing, Awakening, Releasing, and Restoring. One night I was in the hospital with my daughter. It was the same hospital I had been going to since I was 15 years old. I had worked practically every day of my life until that time; everything I had done was working. And I think it was one of the very first times that she and I sat together and just watched the sunrise. It was at that moment that I realized that I hadn't given myself time to breathe. I hadn't given myself the opportunity to reflect on what I do and the contributions that I had made.

I believe that everything we do is an exchange of energy. Energy is currency. If you're thinking about creating a program, bringing something of value to somebody else, you need to have a clear understanding of what that is. You need to be clear on what your talents are and where your passions lie. From there, you just have to bring it together and create something that somebody will pay for.

If you spend your time chasing the bone, you're going to end up running in circles. You realize that you're not actually pursuing what you want, just expending energy and not bringing anything back. Hopefully, with this process of reflecting, observing, awakening, releasing, and restoring, you can find what your passion is and learn to improve those skills. Because sometimes we simply may not have had the training that we need.

Advice for Aspiring Entrepreneurs

I have three tips for new entrepreneurs. Firstly, you have to be clear to clarify. You really need to know what it is that you're doing and what it is that you are offering your clients. Who are your prospective clients? What do they want? Secondly, you have to make sure that you are taking action. This doesn't have to be perfect; it just means starting, having some kind of plan.

When I was a young entrepreneur, I invested in my business, but I did not invest in my personal growth. The most important lesson I can think of to offer is that you are your biggest investment. The biggest investment you can make is growing and becoming a better person and pharmacist. Whatever it is that you are trying to do to make the world a better place, either directly or indirectly. You need to work towards that goal in yourself as well.

But you don't have to do it alone. I think as pharmacists; sometimes we forget to connect. Regardless of your industry, regardless of whether you are in hospital or retail, we should all know what we are each doing. Knowing what other pharmacists are doing can help us in our own individual growth. When we lean into those connections and develop relationships we can trust, you are showing up for yourself and your community. Find other pharmacists to follow on LinkedIn, comment on their posts, send them a direct message (DM). Don't be afraid to start building relationships.

CONTRIBUTOR

CONNECTION

Rajinder Rai, PharmD

🌐 www.thrivewithdrrai.com

in www.linkedin.com/in/rajinder-rai-pharmd/

SIMONE SLOAN

Biography

As Founder and CEO of Your Choice Coach©, Simone is an accomplished business strategist, executive coach, and DEI consultant. She has held senior roles at Fortune 500 companies across marketing, communications, medical affairs, sales, and global business strategy. Her tenure includes successfully launching and leading products and services, implementing programs for key stakeholders across the globe, and developing and training sales, medical, and technical teams.

Simone's mantra is "Voice, Power, Confidence." As an emotional intelligence executive coach, she changes the way leaders and their businesses engage their employees and clients. Simone emphasizes the human element with a focus on diversity and inclusion.

Simone is a keynote speaker and has been featured as a thought leader in articles for *Huffington Post*, *Forbes*, and *Pharmacy Times*. She is an active member of the Tri-State Diversity Council and advocate for women, LGBTQI, BIPOC, people with disabilities, and cross-generations.

Simone holds a BS in Pharmacy and an MBA from Howard University. She is co-author of the books *Achieving Results* and *30 Days to Courage* and is certified in DISC, Emotional Intelligence (EQI) 2.0, IDI Cultural Competence, BlockChain, Behavior Design, and is also accredited through the International Coaching Federation.

Entrepreneurial Journey

I approached my career in pharmacy with an entrepreneurial mindset, and really looked at it as an opportunity to differentiate myself from others in this profession. This was before personal branding became en vogue. It was during my pharmacy rotations that I started asking myself what I liked. Where would I fit and how can I be different? These questions caused me to evaluate my career path differently and more strategically.

Differentiate yourself and find your value proposition

I have never stopped asking myself, how can I be different. It is a question that has constantly forced me to evolve and remain relevant. That question has really resonated throughout my professional career, from pharmacy school to industry, and as an entrepreneur. My career in pharmacy started in the long-term care industry and then transitioned into marketing, medical affairs, and global strategy. During my professional journey, I have never stopped asking myself, how can I be different. It is a question that has constantly forced me to evolve and remain relevant.

That question has really resonated throughout my professional career, from pharmacy school to industry, and as an entrepreneur.

Stepping outside of your comfort zone

My immediate role post-MBA was as a product marketer for consumer brands. Consumer marketing was fun because I learned how to tap into the heart of our targets. I conducted focus groups, attitude and usage studies, and regularly monitored the market to determine the health of the business. I learned how to manage inventory, work in matrix organizations, and partner directly with manufacturing, R&D, sales, and finance teams.

From a people perspective, it was challenging because I worked in a matrixed organization. As an individual contributor and people manager, you have to learn how to influence people. I quickly had to learn how to influence, motivate, and connect with others. Establishing trust with your co-workers is another skill to learn, especially when you need them more than they need you. Motivating others can be challenging. I learned that you have to understand their why and what is in it for them to get people motivated for one's cause.

Methods to Monetize Your Knowledge

My company, Your Choice Coach, offers executive coaching, diversity, equity, and inclusion consulting, training, speaking, and business coaching.

For my diversity, equity, and inclusion (DEI) consulting services, I help companies jump-start their DEI strategy and support them with their existing strategies through training, assessments, and inclusive leadership coaching. We also support companies by reviewing their marketing and communication collateral, collaboration practices to ensure they are inclusive for both their internal and external stakeholders.

For executive coaching, we provide emotional intelligence and performance effectiveness coaching to help managers increase their ability to develop trust, connection, and collaboration with their teams. We also offer on-demand learning services.

For entrepreneurs, we support them with their business strategy and foundational elements to help them be successful with their endeavors.

Trust in the Power of You

My mantra is "Voice, Power, Confidence." One common thread that I have noticed across organizations is that people's voices, regardless of titles, can be muted. Either we do it to ourselves, or it is done by someone else. The result is that we are not heard nor seen. We all have power. We need to harness, recognize, and own our power. The first stage in trusting the power of you, is by using your voice. Be seen and heard.

The second stage in trusting the power of you, is forging relationships. Business is all about relationships. Relationships are important for your business to grow and prosper. Forming connections and collaborations are what make us effective leaders. When running a business, there are ideas to harness and a vision to develop. Your ideas and vision are realized with a plan. If you do not have people to support you, and have relationships in place, then you can either veer off course or lose traction of the plan.

Your communication is important. The message has to be consistent, clear, and relatable. Your message can empower or disempower people in the way they engage with you.

Trusting in the power of you is about owning what you want professionally or personally and then stepping into it fully. It is your energy and passion that you are selling. People are choosing to buy you.

Advice for Aspiring Entrepreneurs

As aspiring entrepreneurs, do not keep your idea in a bottle. Build up the courage to flesh out your idea and test it. Don't be afraid to share it in the early stages. The earlier you can get feedback, the earlier you can pivot to evolve your idea. As you evolve your idea, bring others into your process. This is one approach to create users and advocates for your product or service.

If you are interested in learning more about me and what I do, you can find me on LinkedIn as Simone Sloan. You can also reach out to me via my website: www.yourchoicecoach.com.

CONTRIBUTOR CONNECTION

Simone Sloan, RPh, MBA

www.yourchoicecoach.com

www.linkedin.com/in/simonesloan/

NATASHA STAMPER

Biography

Dr. Natasha Stamper is a clinical pharmacist and online fertility coach. She found her love for all things fertility while living in a remote Alaska village, navigating her own IVF journey alone. After many miscarriages, two ectopic pregnancies, and one cervical ectopic, she had her two miracle babies. Now with over 12 years of clinical pharmacy experience and her own experiences, she is so excited to be helping families all over the globe fulfill the dream of making their family complete.

Entrepreneurial Journey

I never really thought of myself as an entrepreneur. That sounds silly, but for me, it was always simply having a plan in mind and putting it into action. I never thought of what I did as entrepreneurship, but I was on the phone with my mom the other day, and she said, "Natasha, you've been an entrepreneur since you were little." I was like, "What?"

But then I really began to think about it. I grew up pretty poor, and there was one instance in high school where I got invited to attend a trip to Australia. My family couldn't afford it, but I made it happen. I had sent letters out to all these different businesses to raise the money to go to Australia with my class.

My mom said, "Remember when you were a kid you would sell home-made Father's Day signs? You would pick up worms in the park and sell them to the bait shop. You sold chocolates that we made."

Looking back, we see these entrepreneurial skills all the time. Think about young children on the side of the road selling lemonade. We don't think of ourselves as entrepreneurs when we are young children, but we have the skills instilled in us.

From a young age, I had that drive and passion. I have always had that. I just never give up. I'm the oldest of four, so maybe that's why. I actually started my journey by getting certified with the Institute of Functional Medicine (IFM). On top of everything else, working and being a mom, I was in the IFM too. I was so excited to start learning about functional medicine.

Methods to Monetize Your Knowledge

I monetize my knowledge by offering one-on-one coaching when it comes to fertility. I love working one-on-one with people, but I am also noticing where things are going. I see online courses are becoming really popular. I recently did a VIP day with a coach who is helping me develop a course. I am in the process of building a course that will be launching soon.

I also joined a course called 'Rise to Reels,' which was amazing. It is run by these two girls from Australia, and it's all about networking. They hooked me up with a friend named Leah, who is a virtual assistant in Australia. We started getting together once a week just for fun. It's during the day for me and at night for her. Once a week, we get together and talk about the Reels course. Down the road, we are hoping to collaborate and work together to monetize our knowledge.

Right now, I have my one-on-one clients, and I am building an online course and currently trademarking. I filed my trademark for Online Fertility Academy, which is what I want to call my course. That was just in the last two weeks, so that was really exciting. I'm really passionate about this course I am building. I have a podcast episode with Dr. Christine Manukyan coming up, and I go deeper into my story in that podcast.

To tell the abbreviated version, I lived in a village in Alaska, and I coordinated my own InVitro Fertilization (IVF) program. I took all my knowledge, and I made guides for patients and clients. I assembled this guide to IVF that they could purchase. Things like what to ask your insurance and questions to ask at your first appointments. It's all there for them. For me, offering that kind of service really made sense and is something that I'm passionate about. It has been really healing for me on my journey.

Tips to Grow Your Instagram

To give some background on my history with Instagram (IG), I started an IG account this past December. I had no knowledge of monetizing social media. I had social media accounts for years, but it was mostly pictures of my children, food, pharmacy school, and things like that. I knew Reels were important, but I was afraid to do them; I let this limiting belief stop me. I obviously don't look like an IG model. I'm 40 years old, and I just had a baby a year ago. After she was born, she was in the NICU with COVID, so I haven't lost the baby weight.

I'm hard on myself for the way that I look, so the idea of posting photos of myself on IG was hard for me. I can't dance, and I worry about what others think. But I knew I had to stop doing that. I started researching TikTok reels in March. My husband is also a pharmacist; he is more traditional, very detailed, super professional. I was trying to explain TikTok and Reels to him, and it was difficult because they're not very professional. We went back and forth for a while, and eventually, he helped me with my first TikTok.

We did an instructional video about drawing up progesterone and oil. I had an old bottle from my own IVF journey, and it went viral. It got 32,000 views, and I only had 11 followers at the time. For me, that was super viral. I posted the same video on Instagram, and it got 100 views. I was curious as to why the same video did so well on TikTok but not on Instagram.

It was through there that I stumbled into the world of IG Reels. I took that course on Reels and started researching. I wasn't sleeping a lot, so I just read about Reels all of the time. Today I want to go over how the IG algorithm works and how you can make it work for you.

What most people don't realize is that there are steps to it. There is a method to the madness. It can often feel like the algorithm is working against you; I know a lot of people complain about that. But just because it feels that way doesn't mean it's true. I don't think there is a magic trick; sometimes, it is just luck. But there are steps, and I am going to go into how you can implement certain strategies and be rewarded by the algorithm. I also have three tips on how to create viral-worthy Reels. If you ever feel frustrated, understand there is a method to the madness.

Step one: When you go on IG, you have the option to post a picture, a carousel, or a Reel. Step two is once you post, IG will show that to your hot and warm followers. That is my term for the people that like and share your stuff the most. You have people in your life who are your favorite people in the audience; they are always cheering you on. Whether it be your mother, sister, or best friend, these are your hot followers.

Step three is when likes, saves, shares, and comments start to come in. For this, there is not much to say other than slowly building it over time.

And step four is when your post is shown to a warm or even cold audience. Step four relies on step three, so this may not happen if you're not getting the likes, saves, shares, and comments. Your post may stop there.

Step five is getting more likes, shares, and comments, building up your audience.

And step six is when your post is promoted to the Reels page, the hashtag page, or the explore page. On the IG app, there is a button in the middle of the bottom bar that takes you to the Reel page. Or if you follow a certain hashtag like #fertility, for example, your page might be at the top if it is the most searched, if your post is the most popular under that hashtag.

Hashtags could be a whole other conversation in and of itself. But our main goal is to be on the explore page. The explore page is where we are discovered by our cold audience. Your cold audience means people who don't currently follow you; they don't know who you are or what you do. If we can land on the explore page, and that leads them to seeing our account, they may become a follower or even a client.

As I said, step six is your cold audience. This is how you actually grow your page by getting cold followers in. If you look at these steps, you can begin to see how the algorithm works. You can begin to learn how to grow your account. If you pay attention to your hot and warm followers, you know what they like. You can tweak the content to meet their needs. And if you give them more of what they like, they are going to keep sharing and saving it. That is going to cause you to grow and get more engagement and a bigger audience.

Step seven is new people seeing your profile.

And step eight is that they will either follow you (which is what you hope they do) or they will leave the page.

What do you do in order to move through these steps and build your audience? I am going to give some tips I have used to build my following. My first tip for mastering the algorithm is understanding the way in which Instagram has changed over the years. In the past, likes were all anyone wanted. Likes had value and were sought after. But now, saves and shares are more valued by the algorithm. If somebody is saving and sharing your post, it means they have it. It has enough value to them where they are putting it in a place where they can either access it later or share it with others. It is important to understand what kind of follower interaction is the most meaningful.

Another way you can add value to your posts is through your captions. Your captions should provide valuable information that allows people to share and save your posts. Your captions need to serve a purpose. Some people refer to the captions as microblogging, and what that means is that the captions can serve as a mini blog post, a little story. I have heard rumors that if you can get people to click on the "more" button on your post or Reel, you get more points with the algorithm.

I don't know how true that is, but it shows that there is a longer engagement time. The more time someone spends on your posts shows IG that they like that post, and it is going to push it further along those steps.

Tip two is to use infographics. This is especially important in carousels. You can really get people's attention with infographics. It could be a pie chart, a bar graph, whatever you want. I like to do mine in Canva.

You also really want to make your Reels relatable. My audience is more the mommy groups type of people. I like sharing videos of my baby doing something silly to make the content relatable. Carousels are a great opportunity as well because this is where you can really put your education to use. My most saved post is a carousel I made that was a guide to fertility medications. I did a whole guide on egg freezing, and I listed all the meds and side effects. I did like six different slides, and it got quite a few saves and shares.

Tip number three is to engage with your audience. They call it social media for a reason. We need to actually be there and be social.

Instagram weights the depth of your relationship with your followers. They know if you're just going to comment on a post and say "love it" or use a heart emoji, that isn't going to get them as far as if you write, "Thank you so much for this post. It's so helpful. I'm going to save it for later." You can show you care more by writing more.

I learned that from my friend Jerrica at *PharmaSis Magazine*. She said your comment should always be a certain number of words. Don't just say, "Great. Thanks. Following." Actually, put some thought into it, try to pay attention to what you're saying, and actually give some good feedback. Another piece of advice; do not post and ghost. What that means is do not post and then log off IG. You should at least stay on the platform for 30 minutes after posting to engage with your community scroll through comments and likes.

A good tip I've read is to find five big accounts in your niche, five medium accounts in your niche, and give small accounts in your niche. Set notifications for when they post and leave some really nice comments on their post. That kind of interaction is not only good for them but can help you gain followers as well. I've gained followers through this method. I even gained a potential client from commenting on others' posts. We had a discovery call, and she never ended up hiring me, but now we're friends and talk all the time.

You can get a lot out of interacting with your followers. I'm always answering DMs. It's like if you walk into a JC Penney's and ask for customer service if the sales lady doesn't answer you, you'd consider it rude. It's not good customer service to ignore people. Another nice touch is to leave a voice message, or to answer back with a cute little message is kind of cool. I've been trying to research more about marketing in DMs and how to ask prospective questions. Always answer your DMs. These are all tips you can use to boost your engagement and make connections.

Next, I want to talk about growing your business using Reels. If you haven't heard the news, a few weeks ago, the head of IG, Adam Mosseri, revealed that IG is no longer a photo-sharing app. If you don't already follow him, I would highly recommend it because he shares a lot of valuable tips. But this is huge news, and a lot of people are wondering what that means. My initial thought was, "Are we not going to be able to post photos anymore?" And I don't think that is true.

What I'm reading is that because TikTok is huge, and YouTube Shorts will be coming out soon, IG is trying to stay competitive. Right now, TikTok has the market, so IG is doing the best it can to stay appealing. I've been reading that they are actually paying people to make Reels.

There are caveats with that; I know you can get paid to go on IG live. You can get paid $150 to $250, but you have to have the capability to go live often. I've heard that in the next year, they are going to roll out more opportunities for creators to monetize on video, whether that be IGTV, Instagram Live, or Reels. That is definitely something to think about.

They even recently came out with IG Shopping. There are new ways you can attach links in your Reels. Not everyone has those features, and I think that's IG's tricky way of keeping us going by not giving everyone access to those features. It is important to remember that their focus is to keep us on the platform, to keep us entertained, educated, and inspired. And it seems like they are now prioritizing short, engaging videos as a way to do this. If you have been waiting for the right time to start filming Reels, now is the perfect time. I think now is the most opportune time for growth.

There is a girl I follow; her name is Pink Sparrows Social. In 42 days, she reached 2 million followers. She didn't even use ads; she just posted a Reel a day and tried to educate people every day using those Reels. I think it is a great opportunity. This is a time period in IG's history that we have never had before. It's the perfect opportunity to organically grow your business, but you have to be willing to get on camera and commit to building your content, to educate and entertain people.

I have developed three tips for creating viral Reels. As I said before if you haven't started, you just need to start, take that step. It is very intimidating; I completely understand, I am still intimidated myself. But you just have to get out there and practice, practice, practice. It does get easier.

My first tip is to use a hook at the beginning. There are so many people scrolling through so many videos right now. You want them to stop and read what is on yours. You want to stop the scroll, and there are a number of ways you can accomplish that. The first thing you can do is create visual interest. A good tip for the ladies: you can wear bright red lipstick or big sunglasses. You see them in every video, the big blue-light blocking glasses. I've seen ones where people wear cute hats. Another is movement; transitions are really big right now. You'll see people wearing a white shirt, and they flip a towel, and they have changed into a beautiful ball gown, or they'll do head turns. All those are transitions. There are also a lot of great tutorials that teach you how to do these trends on TikTok or Reels.

Another is text. You can learn to put different texts, colors, and fonts on your videos. This text is really important to reel your audience in. Some other things to keep in mind: you always want to know what your audience's pain points are, write them out and keep these in the back of your mind.

Now I want to discuss some Reels I have seen as positive examples. There is one that I've seen where a girl in a dress says, "switching up my bottoms this summer." She's already told us what her hook is. We know in our mind when we're scrolling that she is not wearing pants. That knowledge is going to make us want to stop and see what is happening there. Then we see a transition, and she changes into jeans.

Another one I have seen that is really well-done talks about "five tools for Instagram Reels" That is her hook; that is her client's pain point. When I saw this, I thought, "I need to learn what she knows. I need to know what she is doing." She's very successful, and so I make a point to stop and watch the whole thing.

The last one that comes to mind is about "reasons why your reels aren't converting." These are all pain points. These last two Reels use those pain points to draw in their audience and get them to stop the scroll and actually watch the video. There are different rules regarding how long a video has to be watched to consider it "viewed," but I do know that right now, shorter videos are doing better. I've heard seven seconds or less. This seems kind of counterintuitive because IG has recently changed the maximum length of Reels. You could do 15 seconds back in August, and then it became 30. Now I believe you can choose. Some people have the capability to even film 60 second Reels.

In my mind, at that point, you are essentially doing IGTV. I say it's best to keep it short because these days, people's attention spans tend to be shorter, and they don't want to focus for that long. In order to keep people's attention spans going and keep them entertained, it's best to keep it very short, seven seconds or less.

The best Reel I did was just a slideshow of my daughter; it had pictures of her from an embryo to being in the NICU and finally being bigger. It ran on a loop, so you couldn't tell where the beginning or end was, it was only 11 seconds, and it got 10,000 views.

Tip number two is; Do your research, adapt your trends to your niche, and find the trends. I spend 15 minutes a day going through the Reels tab, and I set a timer so that I'm not wasting a whole bunch of time on my phone. But over time, you start seeing the same trends or the same music over and over again. Right now, there is a Missy Elliot trend that is popular, the "give me your number so I can call ya." trend. When I see a trend I like, I'll save it in a folder. I have a Reel folder and a Carousel folder. I also recommend you look at TikTok;

most viral trends will start on TikTok and two weeks later become popular on Reels.

A helpful resource is a free website called talkboard.com. What it does is it tells you the popular songs for the week. It's not always updated; last I looked, it was two weeks behind. But it can still be a valuable tool to know what is trending. They also have apps you can download, but they do cost money.

Tip number three is to always end with a call to action. I know as entrepreneurs, you have this down. This will prompt your followers to take action. Here are a few examples, "Share your story in the comments," "tag a friend," "DM for likes," "follow or comment below," "click the link in my bio." I could make a Reel of this right now. I could get on and say, "Five calls to action that you may not know," and play my Missy Elliot song. That would be a perfect Reel right now.

There is an IG guru that I follow, and I urge you to look at his account. His name is Lucas O'Keefe, and he has roughly 500,000 followers. He said that he recently had a call with a team member from IG, and they talked about the hashtags, Reels, and the algorithm. And he got a PDF from them saying that they want Reels that make people's day, that are surprising, that make people laugh out loud, and are timeless. They also want it to be relatable, inspiring, and culturally relevant. I thought these were great tips straight from IG's mouth about what is needed in order to go viral.

I hope that these tips, tricks, and resources help you build your audience or inspire you to use Reels to spread your knowledge.

Advice for Aspiring Entrepreneurs

Some takeaways I can offer you, do not let the fear of being on camera stop you. I am still working on this myself. I think it is just a messy action; you just have to jump in there and do it. It's like throwing spaghetti at a wall and seeing what sticks. You just need to have fun and smile. I had my daughter help me make one. I was saying, "The funniest things I have heard in my 12 years of pharmacy" That was my hook. I took a little pill bottle and zoomed in; I made a visual, she dropped it. It was not great, it was shaky, but we had fun making it together.

This is a really special time on IG. I don't know how much longer you will be able to grow on Instagram organically without paid ads. You can reach 2 million people in 42 days. The girl I follow was on every day, posting Reels and educating. You can get on there every day and talk about your niche. You can focus on how to make the algorithm work for you. And again, focus on saves and shares; that is what is most important. Don't worry much about the likes anymore.

Think about how you can provide value. You want to give value to your clients and your customers, and you always want to include a hook and a call to action. You always want to say something like, "five tips for how to increase your visibility on Instagram. Comment below." And this is hard; I know it's hard. We have many jobs and wear many hats. But if you can take a timer and give yourself 15 minutes to scroll through the Reels page and see what's popular, or the TikTok page and save the audio that you see over and over and think, how can I put that towards my niche?

How can I make this a Reel and make a game out of it? It becomes like a little adventure; it becomes addictive once you post, once you put yourself out there and see how many people look at it. The funny thing is the lifespan of your Reel is crazy. Take the one I posted with my daughter; when I first posted, it only had 200 views. Three weeks later, I kept getting pop-ups, people weren't liking it, but it made it on the hashtag page. And all of a sudden, it blew up to 9,000 views.

It was crazy. I got over a hundred new followers from it.

I was taught during the Rise to Reels course to film my content in Shot, so I have been using that. I also use Splice Splices, which is a little harder to use if you don't buy the paid version in shots. I have also read that IG will favor your Reels if you build them within the app rather than using editing software. I don't know how true that is.

Instagram is one of the only remaining platforms where you can really grow without having to pay ads. You can do it for free with Reels.

CONTRIBUTOR
CONNECTION

Natasha Stamper, PharmD

🌐 www.fertilitypharmacist.com

in www.linkedin.com/in/fertilitypharmacist/

KEN STERNFELD

Biography

Ken Sternfeld is a lifelong dreamer who believes that there is more to get out of life when you focus on helping others. As a son of a pharmacist, he was inspired by the way his dad was "Doc" to his patients when he visited the store he had in Jamaica, Queens, called Merrick Pharmacy. Customers were always looking to him for help with their medications and the management of their health even before they went to the doctor. Ken said as a child and as an adult now, "Why can't we do that as Pharmacists today?" Realizing the challenges and hurdles presented daily by the business giants of retail pharmacy, he decided to transform his career by developing RXVIP Concierge in 2015 as a new standard of patient care. That business model evolved over the years to become an experiential education online e-learning solution called "The RXVIP Cares Academy" in 2020 when the Covid-19 pandemic changed the landscape of our profession and our world. The Academy has affiliate relationships with close to forty (40) colleges of pharmacy and universities where we mentor the next generation of PharmDs on how they can practice at the height of their diploma and professional license as Providers, Ken's father never got to see him graduate from St. Johns in 1979, but today, he is happy to say that he has made his father and mentor proud.

Entrepreneurial Journey

I became a pharmacist because I wanted to help patients. I am not going to take the time to talk about chronic illness in traditional retail pharmacy, but I refer to it as CRAPS, chronic retail acute pharmacy syndrome. It makes your feet hurt, your back hurt, it makes everything hurt. But for me, I put up with all of that as a retail pharmacist and put up with working in a big box retailer. I put up with it because I wanted to focus on the patient. The patient and the people you work with are what move the numbers. I was not a number driver, and I did not live in that world. But I excelled at it; I was a back-to-back two-time Paragon winner and emerging leader.

Eventually, though, I had to tell them that the baby was ugly. I told them that moving pharmacists away from clinical work was not what pharmacy was all about. And more importantly, it was not what the pharmacists I worked alongside wanted. I decided to try to do something else and get more out of my career.

When people ask me why I do what I do now, I tell them about an adverse drug reaction that my father-in-law suffered. This was eight years ago, and it didn't kill him, but it put him on a path where the rest of his life was extremely challenging. I began researching care coordination and medication risk management by studying Pharmacogenomics and advocating for PGx Testing. I believe that pharmacists are caregivers, and pharmacists need to take care of patients with all the tools they have, so I have been working to raise awareness with students and pharmacists that we can and need to do more for our patients. When you take care of people, it inspires you, and that is how I want to practice as a pharmacist who cares.

My first inspiration was my dad, who worked in retail pharmacy. As a young child, I would love to see him in his long white coat, not the short ones or the scrubs they put you in now. His patients went to him before they ever went to the doctor. I wanted all aspects of my life to be like that. I am going to be talking about family practice. I believe as a profession; we are a family of pharmacists. Sometimes we get away from that and think of ourselves as cynical pharmacists, specialty pharmacists, or nuclear pharmacists; you're PharmD or PGY1 or PGY2. Well, I'm a PGY66. I'm 66 years old. All I want is to be a pharmacist who can care for patients.

Methods to Monetize Your Knowledge

I have some physical disabilities, and I don't get around very well. Taking this into account, I knew I needed to monetize my brain rather than my body. I did that in three ways.

I began by collaborating with Greg Alston, who, as you all read, is a very dedicated pharmacist. He helped create a telepractice toolkit for pharmacists, and it really is an engine to success. Everyone wants the education and knowledge we can give to them. But without the actual tool, the technology to allow people to practice at the height of their diploma, there is a gap. The first thing I did to monetize my knowledge as a healthcare provider was trying to innovate in order to provide the tools to the pharmacist who needs it.

The second thing I did was a personal decision, and that was choosing to commit to helping diabetic patients. I lost my brother to that horrific disease 25 years ago. I know that if remote patient monitoring and outreach and the technologies that monitor blood glucose were available, then he would be alive today. I am dedicated to creating a nationwide network of students of pharmacy and licensed Pharmacists to mentor them as CareSync Concierge Diabuddy RemoteCare Providers. I chose the new CareSync Concierge brand as it is an international trademark that defines what I believe a pharmacist can do by dispensing care, compassion, and empathy, instead of dispensing prescriptions at retail pharmacies. The DiaBuddy Club has already launched, and I am proud to say that we have partnered with the Diabetes Foundation to bring this to market with us for the next generation of PharmDs from universities all across the country.

The third area I used to monetize my knowledge is our CareSync Concierge efforts with non-profits and cause-related groups and organizations. We donate our services by creating support groups and then identifying the needs of patients who want to work with us going forward. We have developed WellnessRx Care Plans that mirror the monthly membership subscription programs that Concierge Physicians use. Everyone needs more information and education on how they can deal with their disease state; our remote care and ongoing outreach allow us to practice as care providers and set a new standard of patient engagement. We are all new to this pandemic world, and there is no blueprint that we can rely on, so we created this PharmD In A Box business model where we teach remote care and medication risk management to the next generation of pharmacists and students of pharmacy who can then share their expertise with patients. Whether you are just entering the profession or you have been in it for a long time. This is a new world. It's a more advanced professional practice experience.

We can deliver this knowledge because we have been there. It's like the commercials for Farmers Insurance. We know a thing or two because we have seen it. That is how we monetize our knowledge by delivering the education, and once the educational process is complete, we deliver the tools.

I started RXVIP at the office of an MD, VIP Concierge physician; he was my own personal physician. I really recommend this, and it doesn't have to be a concierge physician. For anyone who wants to engage in a physical pharmacist relationship, start with your own doctor. People can say, "Oh, he isn't part of the healthcare system," or, "There isn't an independent pharmacist position in my town." But there are physicians out there who you know. You know, because you see prescriptions going through when you're working at Walgreens or CVS. Don't call them when you're on the bench.

But you know who the physicians in your community are, who are providing quality care. Reach out to them. Do the first outreach call. You're not calling them for prior authorization; you're calling them on your day off. It is an opportunity for you to say, "I am a pharmacist who cares. I work in the community, and I would love to have an opportunity to speak to the doctor about how I can help your practice deliver better patient outcomes and additional revenue." Every physician is looking for additional revenue.

But if you go in saying, "Well, you need to pay me $120,000 a year" or, "How much am I worth to you?" You're not addressing their needs first. You need to determine what their needs are. You have to ask them those questions. Say, "I am here to help you. What are some areas where I could help you?" It could be medication management, it could be prior authorizations, it could be anything, but you become a provider by asking them what they need. You already know what you want, you want a job, but nobody is going to hire you unless you provide measurable results. That is how you do it.

I want to dive a little deeper into the concierge physician market because this isn't a new concept. If you don't know what concierge medicine is, do some research, don't be misinformed. It's not only a cash pay model; there are also hybrid situations. The physicians I work with use cash pay. In that case, you deliver your services in the way they want, as cash pay services. There are others who take insurance or charge an additional membership fee to their patients in order to cover the cost of your services.

I realized a few years ago that I needed to have personalized care. I ended up having four surgeries in 14 months for my knees and back. People need those things. Our concierge approach is to match the personalized approach to health care that has been proven successful with companies like MDVIP and dozens of concierge physician groups from around the country. MDVIP now has 1,200 individual practices. That wasn't the case when I started. If someone is interested and they tell me what state they're in, I'll make the call to a physician for them. They make the introduction, and I'll do the heavy lifting.

I don't have to travel to whatever state you're in. I'm going to be speaking to an MD VIP practice in Hawaii on Sunday. I wish I was going in person, but I'm not. At least I can connect with them.

Creating a Family Practice as a Concierge Pharmacist

Because I am going to be talking about family practice, I also want to talk about my family. I love my family and am committed to them. I've had a lot of happy days in my life. My younger daughter Emily got married to my son-in-law Aaron. I have four grandchildren. But three weeks after my daughter got married, my father-in-law, who is also my mentor and best friend, passed away. He had been dealing with the challenges I mentioned earlier, and I had worked with him for the last hundred days before the wedding to make sure he could be with us to celebrate.

When he passed, it was like I was a child again. I cried like a baby, and I had to find a way to fill the void. I didn't want to take any drugs or be on any anti-depressants. I didn't want to have to stand in line at CVS for refills or this or that. I had to find a way to help myself. I had been receiving knowledge about personalized care from my doctor, Dr. Michael Goodman. I thought I would take that knowledge and apply it to a pharmacy environment to change the landscape of traditional retail. As much as there are great pharmacists in every domain of retail who are doing great work, that doesn't mean there aren't needs that are going unmet.

I felt that pharmacy should be moved to a point of care, which is the physician's office. Now with the pandemic, we have pivoted our entire business to REMOTE CARE via telehealth. That is where the decisions regarding the patient are being made. By the time the patient gets to the retail store, decisions have already been made, you get them in and send them out, and it's all transactional. But to be clinical, you have to go where the patient is, and today that must include telehealth, so we partnered with a leader in delivering all we need with BodySite.

My vision was a RemoteCare Provider Solution, and now we have it. Todd Eury, who you read earlier, said, "pharmacy is the hub of healthcare." Guess who told him that? Me, six years ago. The two of us even started a podcast about it. I wanted to prepare our industry for an opportunity to change. And believe me, I didn't expect a pandemic to make telehealth what it is. But my attitude has always been one practice at a time, one pharmacist at a time. After I opened up my practice with Dr. Michael Goodman, all of a sudden, I had pharmacists telling me, "We love what you're doing."

After a short period of time working at the grassroots level, doing podcasting, talking the talk, and walking the walk, we had 15, 18 practices emerge in New York and across the country. People heard about what we were doing and were inspired. There is no cost to the physician; we work collaboratively with our physicians to increase their revenue. And trust me, physicians love to know they can get a pharmacist on their care team without it costing them anything. How can anyone not want someone on site who can increase their revenue and increase their patient outcomes with no out-of-pocket expense?

Around this time last year, the pandemic was in full force in my neighborhood. There are about four local colleges of pharmacy that I serve as a mentor for, and all of a sudden, they have all of these young professional students who need to graduate and no place to send them. I called my alma mater St. John's, and I told them, "We have two students who are scheduled to come. They obviously can't come because the office of Dr. Michael Goodman is closed. I'll take them, and we will do it remotely."

"Great!" they said, and the lady from St. John's called me back ten minutes later and said, "Can you take eight instead of two?"

"Sure," I said.

She called me back the next day. She said, "Tina Kanmaz, who is our experiential educator, knows of 17 educators who are calling her to ask what we're doing. Can you take them all?"

I said yes.

In a matter of 35 days, we went from four universities to 34, and in the last year, we have mentored over 490 happy students and helped them graduate, continuing into 2021 and 2022. We are continuing to grow, with the Class of 2023 coming soon.

I ask my students all the time, "What do you want to do with your career?"

And they'll say, "We want to do something clinical."

I'm like, "What does that mean?" And they don't know. There is so much stress over what to do for a career they don't know. I said, "Well, why don't we just try to create an environment that you love?" And that is what the health hub is. We have some students who are getting married and having kids, so we created a mommy PharmD program so that mom can work from home and do remote patient monitoring. Everybody was interested in mental health, so we did mental health. Some people wanted to do clinical trials, so we did that. I also made self-care a priority. I had my sister in Israel do a dance class for our students every Thursday so the students could have some time to take care of themselves.

I created the CareSync Concierge Diabuddy RemoteCare Providers to help take care of diabetic patients who really need it. There was suffering before the pandemic; they are suffering even more now. There are comorbid conditions that are just horrific. It is a horrific disease. With this disease especially, it kills me not to be able to help patients.

Telehealth is the toothpaste that has come out of the tube. It's here; it's not going back. It's convenient for patients; they can stay at home and not have to go into the office. It's affordable. Medicare is putting incredible revenue reimbursement models into place to take care of patients because they can't afford for them to come back to the hospital. They can't afford it. Medicare is spending its money on people who deliver value-based care; pharmacists deliver value-based care. We have also created a huge Cash-Pay Model as well.

We work collaboratively with the physicians, and we work directly with the consumers because not everyone who has diabetes is 65 years old. We work on building a relationship to increase adherence because if you can't connect with them through outreach, they're not going to take their medications properly. If they don't test their glucose level when they have diabetes, then you don't know how they are doing. We have real-time access to monitoring parameters per our technology. There is incremental revenue for pharmacists and students of pharmacy who deliver that remote care to patients. They want us, and they need us. We need to be the providers who deliver it.

Last year, 16,000 practices closed because of the pandemic, and the ones that stayed open needed revenue. Clinical Services can be added by pharmacists, and we can bring in revenue. I believe this is the new standard of patient engagement.

The Center for Medicare & Medicaid Services (CMS) just announced that they are introducing three more codes for remote patient monitoring. They're not just for data analytics but pain management, medication management, and other physical aspects that could tie into it. It's moving to where pharmacists are. If you want to wait for provider status, that's fine, but I'm not waiting. I want to collaborate; I want to be in consideration of all aspects of patient care. We can improve these things today. I can't wait for legislative reform when people are dying.

We all know about fast food pharmacy. It's horrific. The current state of community pharmacy is in shambles; we need to create a model of healthy, non-dispensing consultation for any pharmacists who want to raise the bar of their practice. Pharmacy students are struggling to meet the standards set by big-box retail chains. Patients are dying due to a lack of personalized care. Pharmacy interns in stores are not given the time and mentoring they need to advance their careers.

I want you to participate in mentoring students. I could never have worked at CVS if my interns and technicians weren't there. It is a collaborative process of putting like-minded individuals in an environment that is perfectly aligned to patient care and practicing at the height of your profession. It could be either a Medicare reimbursement model or a cash pay model hybrid.

People who join us as DiaBuddy RemoteCare Providers work from home; they make their own schedules and have the freedom to schedule around their lifestyle. They work with the physicians they want and like-minded pharmacists and colleagues, or they work directly with patients. You get to know the person next to you in your practice as he or she is from the same culture as you are as a health care professional. That doesn't happen when you get put into an environment that you didn't choose at a big box retailer when your supervisor or staff members aren't of the same culture. Our culture is care, compassion, and empathy every single time we work with a patient.

Find a partner and create your own Diabuddy RemoteCare Virtual Clinic. I'll give you the opportunity to try it. Take a patient or two; take someone in your own family. We can show you how to get started with your only expenditure will only be on technology, which is incredibly inexpensive if you want to own your own virtual care clinic. We want to share it with like-minded pharmacists who want to be part of this culture of delivering telehealth, remote patient monitoring, pharmacogenomics, medication risk management, all at the height of your professional skill set. You can start getting paid as a provider today.

There are many opportunities for revenue in Diabuddy RemoteCare. You can earn revenue from medication management and remote patient monitoring. I've created something I call a WellnessRx Subscription Based Program where patients work with a pharmacist to do a wellness prescription checkup. Come in when you're healthy, and we can talk about avoiding adverse drug reactions plus lowering the cost of your prescriptions. If you're a provider who can save patients' money on prescription medication, I promise you will have as many patients to work with as you want.

If you're interested in learning more, speak to someone at CareSync Concierge. This book is all about talking and sharing ideas. There are many pearls of wisdom in this book that Kimber has put together. Take advantage of it. Networking and connectivity is the pathway to success. This book is such an amazing opportunity to learn how to advance your career. I don't know if I have ever been involved in such an amazing opportunity.

If you're interested in working with a physician and setting up a DiaBuddy RemoteCare Virtual Wellness Clinic, then reach out to me. I'll talk to you any day, seven days a week. I am a concierge pharmacist; that is what I do. If you set up the time, I'll be there to make the appointment. If you want to reach out to your local physicians, I'll make that call with you. I had a student who introduced me to her physician. On a Friday night at 6:30, I helped close the deal for her. Now, when she graduates, she will have a practice to work in, and she can even start working there today as an intern under the supervision of a licensed pharmacist.

That is what I do. That is my story, and I'm sticking to it.

Advice for Aspiring Entrepreneurs

My advice is to just do it. By now, you have read about many people who have changed their profession after 40 plus years. If they can do it, so can you. Get started, begin putting the work in, and take the time to review it.

I have a plush stress toy I like to squeeze; it's shaped like a pill, and I call it the only pill in our industry that can cure CRAPS. If you squeeze it 30 times a day and still can't figure out how we as pharmacists can work together, something is wrong. I would love to work with you and help you in advancing your career in concierge pharmacy.

Ken Sternfeld, RPh

CONTRIBUTOR
CONNECTION

www.pharmacist.care

www.linkedin.com/in/ken -sternfeld-a96b4614a/

BLAIR THIELEMIER

Biography

Blair Green Thielemier, PharmD, is a business development consultant specializing in pharmacist-led billing models. She consults on and produces e-learning programs for state and national organizations, pharmacy wholesalers, payers, and technology start-ups. She has books and online courses available for individuals looking to leverage their pharmacy knowledge into monetized clinical programs at PharmapreneurAcademy.com. She speaks internationally about trends in leveraging pharmacists to improve value-based care.

Entrepreneurial Journey

I didn't intend to become the CEO of my own company, but a series of choices led me to pursue nontraditional routes in my career. Now I help pharmacists leverage and monetize their knowledge in new ways.

When I was pregnant with my oldest in 2014, I was actually let go from a clinical hospital position. It was a surprise to me, and I didn't know what to do. I didn't have any other skills; I didn't have a side hustle going; I hadn't built a safety net. In this book, you hear so much about the power of networking, but I hadn't done any of that. I didn't have those relationships. I didn't think I had the skills to brand myself as an expert either.

I began picking up some shifts at local independent pharmacies because my heart has always been in independent community pharmacy. Looking back, my great-grandfather was an independent community pharmacy owner in the Chicago area in the 1940s. To me, my pharmacy roots were always in entrepreneurship. My roots are in this balance of being a healthcare service provider while also dispensing a product.

I think that directly relates to what I do now, which is helping pharmacists to make the shift from being closely tied to a product and a business that is rooted in dispensing that product to, at the very least, diversifying their streams of income. Whether it is through things like functional medicine services, pharmacogenomic testing, or different innovative types of clinical services, I want to help people see that they have a viable business model and are providing something that can not only help patients but add income to their careers.

Methods to Monetize Your Knowledge

There are a couple of ways I recommend to my clients about monetizing their knowledge. There has been a lot of talk about predictions for the direction that pharmacy is going. We see that things are changing. Many of us no longer have the luxury of sign-on bonuses and are being forced to look for other ways of making money outside of traditional pharmacies. One way you can do that is through cash-based services.

There are three main paths in what we have come to call Pharmapreneurial practices. I lay this out in my beginner's business blueprint. These are basic business models that pharmacists can follow. The first path is the physician's office path. This means going into a physician's office and offering something like an annual wellness visit. This is pretty similar to a comprehensive meds review. If you have ever done Medication Therapy Management (MTM) through the Outcomes MTM platform, it is pretty similar to that. You're doing things like a health risk assessment; you are asking the patient the medicine that they are currently on, all of these things that pharmacists are the best option when it comes to providing these services because we are an extension of the provider. The physician's office path is the first one.

The second path is the pharmacy-based path. This might look like someone who owns a pharmacy and is looking for additional streams of revenue. This could be long-acting injectable administration, vaccine clinics, point of care testing, or rapid COVID testing. There are all of these opportunities to generate revenue through a clinical service that isn't necessarily tied to dispensing a medication product. Now sometimes, if you're living in a state where there is a collaborative practice agreement or some kind of blanket protocol, you can do testing for influenza and dispense Tamiflu, or something like that. That is the pharmacy-based path.

Now the third path has some overlap with the first two, and this is the patient pay path. This is a cash-based service model. I know lots of people who do this, and they focus on a specific area. It could be functional medicine that is rooted in gut health; it could be a homeopathy consultation; it could be pharmacogenomic and nutrigenomics testing. The benefit of this path is that it is flexible. It can be implemented in different locations: in a chiropractic office, in a pharmacy, wherever. But the whole idea is marketing. A cash-based service is very different from simply marketing your services. You have to position yourself as an expert and really create relationships with providers and organizations.

When you think about these three paths, you have to keep the end client in mind. Think about who is your ideal target market for this service. How do you speak about your value? I help my pharmacists create an elevator pitch. I help them create their personal story that resonates with the people they're going to be working with. If you're pitching to a physician about the value of pharmacist services, you're going to be talking about the Medicare Access and CHIP Reauthorization Act (MACRA) and quality metrics. If you're pitching to a health system, you're going to be talking about payment, reimbursement, and decreasing hospitalization. If you're speaking directly to the patient, you're going to talk about how they can live longer and fuller lives, get off some of their medication, becoming the healthiest version of themselves. The way you market to a patient is going to be really different from the way you go about having that relationship with the physician.

In terms of how I monetize my own knowledge, I have a number of different ways for people to experience what I do. I have free resources as well, and I'm actually teaching people how to do webinars as one of the ways they can learn more about consulting. I also have a book which is on Amazon, titled *How to Build a Pharmacy Consulting Business*. I also offer courses in which I talk about the Beginners Business Blueprint, information on Current Procedural Terminology (CPT) codes, chronic care management, and annual wellness visits. I also provide the latest information about MACRA since the technological elements change every single year.

I provide a ton of content, so I don't suggest people enter the academy and go through every single module because it would take forever. There are 30 to 50 hours of lectures, past summits, training, and other events we have done. I recommend people look through it and pick out what interests them; it is sort of like Netflix for pharmacy services. If you're interested in transitions of care, you don't need 50 hours of courses on transitions of care. Learn the things you need to learn so you can begin moving forward quickly. That is our Pharmapreneur Academy, it is a membership program, and it is open 24/7. You can join any time and start working your way through the models.

We also have a forum, which has proven really helpful. When people get stuck, they can just go on the forum and ask questions. There are paid expert consultants in the forum because I'm not an expert when it comes to health systems or pharmacogenomics. I am not an expert in every single one of the modalities, but we're building a community of experts and leaders who can help take pharmacy to the next level.

The Inner Circle Mastermind is our accelerated group program; it is a six-month program. We actually have another retreat coming up; this year, it is going to be in Orlando, Florida. I'm excited to have it in Florida because then people can bring their families or spend a little extra time at the spa. We do our content on Thursday and Friday and dedicate Saturday for community fun and relaxing. To me, that is what building a business is all about. It's about being your own boss, building the life that you want to have. The Inner Circle Mastermind is really for those people committed and ready to take it to the next level. If you're interested in learning more about that, I'd love for you to join our community.

There are many pharmacists, especially those on the patient pay path, who are marketing to patients across the country. They really focus on a specific disease state, so if you're doing something like health coaching, you can develop an audience pretty quickly. It is much easier to brand yourself as an expert if you focus on a single niche. That is something we discuss a lot in our webinars. We have a lot of great stuff available for those who are interested in consulting.

Evolution of the Pharmacy Business Model: Three Predictions for the Next Ten Years

The three predictions I have for the next ten years in pharmacy are what get me up in the morning. This is what gets me excited.

Because we all feel it, pharmacy is not going to be the same ten years from now. It was already so different ten years ago; what is it going to look like in 2031? I am already using artificial intelligence (AI) in my business right now. We have no idea what that technology is going to look like in the next ten years.

But if I am going to make predictions, my first prediction would be that dispensing is going to decrease. We're going to focus less on making revenue from dispensing. Pharmacy Benefit Managers (PBMs) are kind of a bad word, but they are taking over with decreasing reimbursement with Direct & Indirect Remuneration (DIR) fees or with Amazon getting into the mail order pharmacy space. My first prediction is that we should start to focus less on dispensing volume because I believe that is going to decrease significantly in the years to come. I have talked to a lot of pharmacy owners, and they feel like the more they fill, the more they lose. Why should we keep focusing on filling prescriptions? We need to start making that shift. We need to start asking, what are some other things that patients are going to be looking for? Especially people in our generation, as our generation ages we are going to become patients. We need to ask ourselves what kind of things we will want out of pharmacy.

For me personally, genetic testing has changed my life, functional medicine, taking supplements, changing my diet. All of these lifestyle modifications that we talk about, what if pharmacists could be the ones at the forefront of bringing them to mainstream healthcare, bringing the herbal supplements, bringing the different ideas surrounding functional medicine and nutrition back to patients. I really think that is going to be the thing that takes pharmacy to the next level.

My second prediction is that preventative services are a fantastic opportunity for pharmacists to get involved. I know so many pharmacists who don't want to take medicine unless they have to. I am the same way. I have a healthy respect for medicines, but part of what that means is not reducing them of their value by using them when you don't need to. I don't even want to take an antibiotic unless it is serious. We know there are other opportunities to improve our health.

I did a genetic test a few years back. It was a Nutrigenomics test on a patient's child. The child had attention deficit hyperactivity disorder (ADHD) and was experiencing some major side effects. They had no appetite, they weren't eating, they were experiencing anxiety, and they began having trouble sleeping at night. I came up with a list of about ten different things, including diet, natural supplements, and herbs that this mother could try before adding additional medication to the child's regimen. Patients don't realize just how much value we have to offer as pharmacists and healthcare providers. We're so good at talking to each other about how much we know and how much we help people, but we need to get better at tooting our own horns to people outside of the pharmacy industry. That is my second prediction; that pharmacists can be the ones to bring preventative medicine, nutrition, lifestyle, and herb medicine to the mainstream.

I'm really interested in Ayurvedic medicine. We understand how those chemicals work at the biological level. Biochemistry is our space; Pharmacokinetics is our space. That is our area. How can we take what we see in Eastern medicine and holistic medicine and combine it with Western medicine so that we can give patients what they want? I think we can take that from the fringes into the mainstream.

When I tell people that I don't really take a lot of medicines, they will ask me for recommendations. I'll give them five things that aren't medication recommendations. They are surprised; they expect me to give them an over-the-counter pill, when really, I'm asking about how much fiber they are consuming, how much water they are drinking, how much physical activity they undergo. I always think we should try these other things first. To me, medicine is a last resort. And I think a lot of pharmacists see it that way. We have nothing against other providers, but they are trained in a specific way. They don't have the time to sit down and have these conversations. Deep prescribing is a huge issue. How can we be the healthcare provider that really listens to the patient and gives them opportunities to change their health in ways besides just medication?

My third prediction is that in the years to come, we are going to be working a lot more closely with providers to help them with preventative services and help their patients get off medications and find better outcomes.

Advice for Aspiring Entrepreneurs

One question I am often asked is how to convince patients to pay for lab tests or functional labs on top of their consultant fees and supplements. My answer is, it's all about niching down, individualizing the care as much as possible. When patients realize their care is personalized, even if it is not within the traditional demographic of patients you are used to working with, they will pay for the care they need. And like I said, these may not be the patients you are used to seeing five times a month in your pharmacy. It could be a younger group of people; it could be women over 40, but find that demographic that you want to cater to and focus on them.

The whole idea is to be an expert in a particular niche so that the people you are speaking to instantly realize you are the person who can help them because the care is specific, it's personalized, and customized to their needs. It is not about convincing patients that they need to be on supplements. They are coming to you as the expert. They are saying, "Please help me. This is what I need." There are different labs you can work with; there are different opportunities for pharmacists. Some states require a collaborative practice agreement to order testing from labs, but it depends on what labs you are trying to order from.

Again, the opportunities are out there. Find a mentor or a coach, even if you need to pay for their services. When I first started my business, I had no idea what I was doing. I had no business or marketing skills. We don't get taught that in pharmacy schools, but it can be taught. Look for opportunities to be taught how to market yourself, how to speak in front of a group, how to host a webinar. You are smart people, but everyone has things they need to learn in order to get them where they want to go. Figure out where you want to go first and identify the skills you need to get there.

Blair Thielemier, PharmD

CONTRIBUTOR CONNECTION

🌐 www.pharmapreneuracademy.com

🔗 www.linkedin.com/in/btpharmacyconsulting/

TIM ULBRICH

Biography

Tim Ulbrich is the Co-Founder and CEO of Your Financial Pharmacist (YFP)©. Founded in 2015, YFP is a fee-only financial planning firm and connects with the YFP community of 12,000+ pharmacy professionals via the *Your Financial Pharmacist Podcast*, blog, website resources, and speaking engagements. Tim received his Doctor of Pharmacy degree from Ohio Northern University and completed postgraduate residency training at The Ohio State University. His academic career included nine years at Northeast Ohio Medical University and, most recently, a role at The Ohio State University College of Pharmacy as a clinical professor of pharmacy and director of the Masters in Health-System Pharmacy Administration (MS HSPA) program. Tim is the host of the *Your Financial Pharmacist Podcast* and co-author of *Seven Figure Pharmacist: How to Maximize Your Income, Eliminate Debt and Create Wealth*. Tim has presented to over 100 pharmacy associations, colleges, and groups on various personal finance topics, including debt management, investing, retirement planning, and financial well-being.

Entrepreneurial Journey

My entrepreneurial journey really begins with my individual and personal 'why.' I'm sure some of you reading this are familiar with

Simon Sinek's work: *Start with Why*. That book was really transformational for me and led me to spend a lot of time thinking about what "why" means and what it looks like for me individually. It also caused me to ask what does that lead to in terms of my pharmacy career. Where do I want to go professionally?

First and foremost, I am a husband and father of four boys. But they are also integral to my why, which is that I want to make sure I am focused on living a rich life. When I say that, folks often think that because I am a financial pharmacist, I am talking about dollars in the bank account. But I'm really not; I'm talking about living a rich life in terms of identifying the things that mean the most to you and deriving the greatest value and significance for you. Balancing those meaningful things while also making sure we are taking care of the future in terms of finances as well.

I have a passion for helping others identify what the rich life looks like for them and balancing it with financial planning. As I look back on my academic and entrepreneurial career, I can see some of those dots connecting. I often found myself in roles and situations where I was helping other students, residents, or colleagues identify their goals and what it looked like for them as individuals to lead a rich life.

That passion also grew into personal finance as well. I really point the origins of my entrepreneurial journey back to growing up in a small business. My grandfather opened a nursery farm in Alden, New York. I grew up in the Buffalo, New York area. My grandfather opened a tree farm in the Adirondacks that he would later move to Alden. My father and uncle continued to grow his legacy in this work as they took over the business when I was a small child. I grew up working in a family business and was always intrigued by what was involved (the ups and downs) of owning your own business.

My parents, however, encouraged me towards a very traditional career path. They had some negative experiences that came with owning a business and, more specifically, owning a family business. There is some drama that can come with that. While they may not have said much about it out loud, going to get a doctor of pharmacy degree when I was 18 years old and then entering a profession where I would have a very "stable" six-figure income was very reassuring to them.

I went on that path and graduated from pharmacy school at Ohio Northern University in 2008, and after that, I completed a PGY1 ambulatory care residency. But I always felt like I had this need to scratch the entrepreneurial itch. Ironically, I tried to scratch it within the career that I had and the academic environments I found myself in. I was always starting new programs new residency initiatives, and I found myself actually starting a company at one of the institutions I worked with.

In 2015, I really fell into this passion of personal finance, I had paid off a couple hundred thousand dollars in debt, and I felt like there weren't any resources or support out there for other pharmacists struggling with their finances. This was something I heard over and over again; pharmacists were making a six-figure income but still felt like they were living paycheck to paycheck. That was exactly what I felt when I was going through that journey, and I felt like there wasn't a community; there wasn't support and resources that were designed to empower and motivate pharmacists on their financial journeys. And I know how important that is when it comes to your relationship with your career.

That was the beginning of Your Financial Pharmacist (YFP). I started a blog and eventually evolved into a podcast and books, and fast forward five years later to an entire business. I look at how to put a dent into the financial topics and issues that are front and center for pharmacists.

Methods to Monetize Your Knowledge

I would like to be clear and upfront by saying I am not monetizing my clinical knowledge. I have not been involved in direct patient care since 2011. I always tell my family, "If you have a question that is pharmacy-related, you need to talk to your local pharmacist." I am not the person to answer those clinical questions.

I do, however, feel I have an indirect impact or at least a different kind of impact on the profession. I firmly believe that by getting our financial houses in order, we can be better clinicians. We can bring better things to our business; we can approach our ideas with more confidence. When our financial houses are in order, we are better partners, better parents, why not be better professionals too? That is the impact I want to have on our profession as a whole, as well as individually, on folks' lives. I operate as a financial pharmacist specifically in terms of monetizing my mission to help pharmacists achieve financial freedom, period. That is it. That is what we are about. That is everything we do.

We have two main arms of our business. We have an education and media arm of the business, which makes about 20% of our revenue, and we have the financial planning arm of our business which makes up about 80% of our revenue. I suspect as we continue to grow, the latter will become a larger percent simply because of how those services are priced and because it is recurring revenue. The former will likely become a smaller percentage, even as it continues to grow because it's not recurring revenue. It's also just not at the same price tag as you would see for the financial planning side of the business.

However, that first arm is still incredibly important to our mission, as well as the overall marketing of our business. We need to make people aware of what we do and the financial planning services we offer. I firmly believe from personal experience, and this points to the mission, that one-on-one coaching when it comes to your financial plan has a huge impact when it comes to transforming individuals. Our goal is always going to be to transform individuals by helping them meet their financial goals.

We now have 12,000 plus folks in our community and ~250 pharmacist households engaging in 1:1 planning. We do one-on-one comprehensive financial planning, which, as I said, makes up about 80% of the revenue of our business. But the media and education arm of the business handles things like our podcast. We are 234 episodes into our podcast and have launched two additional podcasts on our channel. We have also published four books. Our four main revenue sources in the media arm of the business are affiliate revenue, book sales, sponsorships, and speaking engagements. We have worked with 40+ colleges of pharmacy doing speaking engagements as well as an ongoing relationship with the American Pharmacists Association and several state associations, all of which have been producing revenue. This is how we extend our mission while also pointing people to the services that we offer. That is, at a high level, what we do.

We have a team of 14 individuals who really help us accomplish this. We have a team on the media side that I would be lost without. They handle content creation, podcasting, promotion, editing and generally help me stay on track. Our financial planning team executes that side of the business, as well as some administrative folks as well. Going from being a solopreneur to leading a team has been one of the greatest learning curves for me. I suspect it is for other entrepreneurs going from being a solo content creator to trying to run a business. Those are two very different things.

0 to 10,000 Followers: Lessons Learned Building the YFP Community

I want to cover a number of milestones we hit as a company to give some more context as to who we are and what we do. In November 2015, I wrote the first blog post for Your Financial Pharmacist. I had just finished my journey of paying off $200,000 in student loan debt, and I published the first post, which was called, "I was a Confused, Trapped Pharmacist Living Paycheck to Paycheck." When I go back and look at it, it is far from what I would consider the quality of work that we put out today. But that is one of the lessons I hope to convey; get started, get off the ground, and get going. You will go back and refine it over time. That post was the beginning of the YFP brand.

Fast forward a little over a year and a half, in April 2017, we released our first book, *Seven Figure Pharmacist*. I co-authored this book with Tim Church, PharmD, BCACP, CDE, and we decided to self-publish this book, and I am always encouraging others to self-publish. It was very important for us not only in terms of validating our work and seeing what interests there were but also in terms of really putting a stake in the ground. We wanted to make it known that we were the entity that was going to focus on this intersection of personal finance and pharmacy.

In June of 2017, Tim Baker, CFP® and launched the YFP podcast. It is entirely self-produced and self-published. The first episode was called "The Genesis of the Your Financial Pharmacist Podcast." Similar to the blog post, I'll go back and listen to it and say it was okay, but far from where we are now, a couple of hundred episodes since.

April 4, 2019, was a game-changing moment for us as a business. When I had started the business in 2015, really on the content educational side, I always had it in the back of my mind that in order to fulfill the company's mission, we were ultimately going to have to figure out a solution to one-on-one planning and coaching. Whether you want to call it luck or fate, events happened that really helped make those decisions clear and come to fruition. One of those events was meeting Tim Baker, CFP®, who is now my business partner at YFP. At the time, he was a fee-only financial planning firm (Script Financial) focused on pharmacists. Meeting him was important because going into that meeting, I had been incredibly frustrated with what I was learning about the industry. I was seeing a lack of transparency, a lot of hidden fees, and companies not acting in the best interests of the client. I was very frustrated with the way these companies were doing business and how that was going to intersect with my mission at YFP. Learning about fee-only financial planning and how Tim was building his practice was exactly what I was looking for.

In April 2019, we (YFP) merged with Tim Baker's company, YFP Planning, formerly known as Script Financial, so YFP Planning is a wholly-owned subsidiary of YFP. We merged their financial planning with our educational activities. This was a huge accelerator to our growth and really laid the groundwork for where we are going in the future. As of December 2021, we've got about 250 pharmacist households in 40+ states for whom we do comprehensive planning. We have 12,000+ people on our email list, over 750,000 podcast downloads, and we've got 14 YFP W2 employees (12 full-time, two part-time) that make up our team and allow our engine to run well.

There are five big lessons I have learned in growing this business. These obviously have taken a lot of time and reflection, and there are certainly more than five. But looking back from that first blog post to where we are today and perhaps where we are going in the future, these are the five big things that really stand out to me.

The first is to lead with value and monetize second. One of the really integral influences on me when I was getting started was Pat Flynn. Many of you may be familiar with his work over at Smart Passive Income. Pat runs a smart, passive income podcast and has a platform with great content. He really drilled into my mind that if you focus on providing good value, the business will grow from there. If you have a problem that needs to be solved, and you have a solution that people care about, and you bring value to the table, the business will follow. Now that business might look bigger or smaller than what you have in mind. It may grow to something that is beyond your wildest dreams or take you in a different direction, but you have to stay true to the value.

Thinking back on my journey, much of the foundation we laid was in the education on the podcast, speaking events, and the blog. So many folks are now coming through the door as financial planning clients, and when we ask, "Hey, how did you hear about YFP and what piqued your interest?" They will say, "I've been listening to the podcast, I've attended webinars, I felt like I got something of value out of these sessions." And sometimes it just takes the right intersection events where suddenly this is something they need in their life and something they want in their future.

My second lesson is to focus on community. One of the things I constantly say to our team is that we are building a community that is passionate about empowering one another towards that mission of achieving financial freedom. This business is not about Tim Baker or me. This business is about pharmacists achieving financial freedom. We are the facilitators of that freedom through empowering individuals and bringing together a community to help encourage, inspire, and motivate one another. Two books that were foundational to this idea are *Tribes* by Seth Godin and *Building a StoryBrand* by Donald Miller. These really emphasized to me that YFP is not my story. It's the story of the pharmacists that have been impacted and influenced because of the work we do and the community we have created. We try to translate this into all of our content and how we focus on fostering the building of community. A good example of this is where someone may be asking a question in our Facebook group, and before I can hop into the conversation, 10, 15, 20 other pharmacists are answering those questions and encouraging one another. It is that sense of community that keeps people engaged and coming back.

My third lesson is to embrace the role and value of being a CEO. This is something I have struggled with. I recently made a transition from my full-time pharmacy academic career; up until this point, I had been half-living in the CEO role. I realized that now it was time to get serious. I had somebody share with me that there are three great values you can bring as a CEO. Those are the vision of the company, having the right people in the right roles, and making sure you have the resources and finances to move the company forward. The tasks that may have been integral early on in the journey as a solopreneur may no longer be the things you need to be doing. As your company evolves beyond just you, the growth and mission you are aiming to achieve are dependent on you empowering others to make those things happen. I know this is easy to say out loud and incredibly difficult to execute in person, especially when you have been in all those other roles along the way, but it's necessary.

Another thing I will say for those of you who are task-oriented doers such as myself, sometimes these things require a lot of sitting and thinking; creating the space to do that is really hard. Maybe you want to check something off the list, knock out those emails, or do other small tasks. But sometimes, the best thing you can do for your company is to take two hours and think about where things are going, beat those ideas, and see where they go. Vision, people, and resources are things you need to focus on as a CEO. This is what helps keep me centered when I feel like there are too many things just floating around.

My fourth lesson is that every great business is built on having a strong personal finance foundation. For those of you who are in the early stages of this, where you have an idea and believe in it firmly, the stronger your personal financial situation is, the more you're going to be able to approach your business with confidence. Having a strong financial situation will allow you to run your business without living in fear of having some cracks in your financial foundation.

This looks different for everyone. It could be debt repayment, building an emergency fund, or building out your investment plan. Having good savings will allow you to approach your business with confidence and feel like you can really accelerate your business without having to take steps backward or limit your growth because of your personal financial situation not being where you want it to be.

The fifth lesson is to evaluate risk appropriately. This is something that I am challenging myself to learn in real-time. I told someone this week that one of the greatest blessings and challenges we have had in our early business journey has been to cash flow the business and its growth without debt. Why is having no debt a potential challenge? Sometimes there are risks you have to take which may require debt. You need to understand whether or not that risk is appropriate so you can achieve the goals you want your business to achieve.

Tim Ferriss' *4-Hour Workweek* really taught me how to evaluate risk appropriately. A challenge I have for you is to fill in this statement and reflect upon your answer. "If I pursued my business idea and I failed, what is the worst thing that could happen?" Ask yourself honestly, what is the worst thing that could really happen? I think for many pharmacists, the worst thing that can happen is changing course and pursuing the other opportunities you have been thinking about; perhaps it is going back to a previous role. You can get out and further network with your colleagues to pursue those ideas. Identifying what the worst-case scenario is and putting that fear down on paper can actually help mitigate some of the negative feelings that come with that.

Another challenge I would encourage you to do is to think about if you fast forward five years and don't pursue your business, how would you feel? For me, that meant making the hard, but important and necessary, decision to leave my academic career and all the goals and accolades that accompanied that career for 12+ years to give my full time and attention to being the CEO of YFP. I felt like if I didn't pursue that opportunity to fully engage in my business five years down the line, I would have regrets. It became clear that my passion was for helping pharmacists when it came to personal finance.

Think about your life in five years; imagine what it looks like. In what ways is it the same as it is now? In what ways is it different? If you don't pursue your business, your dreams, and ambitions, what does that mean for how your life looks? What does that mean for how you feel? Now think about how that would change if you start taking steps to work towards your goals.

Advice for Aspiring Entrepreneurs

There are a number of steps you can and should take to make sure you have a strong financial foundation. These are the building blocks. If you think about building a home, you need to have a good foundation before you can even think about the addition. I often talk about five things you can do to ensure you have that strong financial foundation.

The first is having a debt repayment plan. This does not mean you have to immediately become debt-free; it just means having a debt-re-payment plan. Secondly, you have to have a good system in place that you can automate your goals and budget. Third, make sure you have the insurance part of the plan tidied up, not too much, not too little. Insurance is a big topic, but here I'm really focusing on the areas I see pharmacists often being over- or under-insured, which would be term-life, long-term disability, and professional liability insurance. Fourth, you need to have an emergency fund, and fifth, you need to have a strong investing plan in place. These are five things you can do to start building that strong foundation, and having that foundation for me means I can approach my business with more confidence.

I dropped this hint earlier, but the biggest piece of advice I can give is to just get started. If you haven't read *Start* by Jon Acuff before, I would highly encourage you to. That book was instrumental to me the summer before I started YFP. Really, it was the catalyst for me to release the blog and begin reaching out to folks with my ideas. I reached out to hundreds of people and said, "Hey, I'm starting a personal finance blog. What do you think?" And once I did that, I had to actually do it. I told them it was coming so I had to write it. That was really important in helping me get over that edge mentally and begin pursuing my dreams.

Tim Ulbrich, PharmD

CONTRIBUTOR
CONNECTION

www.yourfinancialpharmacist.com

www.linkedin.com/in/timulbrich/

JAMIE WILKEY

Biography

Dr. Jamie Wilkey is a pharmacist who loves what she does and brings passion and happiness to the pharmacy profession. Dr. Wilkey grew up in a small town in Wyoming, where she got her start in pharmacy working at the local City Drug. She attended the University of Wyoming School of Pharmacy for her Doctor of Pharmacy. She was active in student government while at UW and also served as President and later Vice President of her pharmacy class.

For ten years post-graduation, Dr. Wilkey worked in community pharmacy while having and raising her four little boys. Frustrated by the stress and schedule of that position, she created her own job that better suits her talents, passion, and family's busy schedule. She abruptly jumped out of the world of retail and into the world of entrepreneurship and has found her true calling in life. She is the founder & CEO of Arches Health, LLC. She serves patients in her community as a consultant pharmacist focusing on pharmacogenomics. After getting her practice up and running, she began to empower other pharmacists to do the same. She teaches pharmacists in her online program and active network called PGx Consulting Confidence Academy. She teaches participants to confidently champion PGx and create their own consulting practices that bring the flexibility, freedom, and satisfaction they are seeking from their careers. Just this year, she has taught over 126 pharmacists how to change their careers. Dr. Wilkey is a member of CPIC as well as the nonprofit organization GTMR. She has been featured on over 15 podcasts in the last year and was recently voted as one of the Top 50 Most Influential Leaders in Pharmacy.

Dr. Wilkey is optimistic about the future of pharmacy and knows great things are in store for those who are willing to push boundaries, think big, and use the full extent of their education.

Entrepreneurial Journey

It still feels quite unreal to be published in this collection and have you out there reading my words because my entrepreneurial journey was quite fast-paced. Not that many months ago, I was stuck in Walgreens and feeling very frustrated with the potential for my career. I felt like I was probably going to have to quit Pharmacy because there just wasn't anything I liked in it anymore.

I had been in retail Pharmacy for ten years, and I felt like there was nothing I could do other than retail. I have a doctorate in Pharmacy, and yet I was stuck. I couldn't even think about doing another year in retail, let alone another ten, twenty, thirty years. I really underwent an entire career transformation in order to be here. Being able to tell you my story and have you read it is really thrilling for me.

I want to help other pharmacists experience a lightning-fast change in their careers, the same way I did. If you're feeling frustrated in your career, I was you. I feel you, but if I can do it, you can too. I hope that you gain something from reading this and you learn from all these fantastic contributors. There is nothing but positivity and encouragement out there. There are so many opportunities for you to find a career that feels fulfilling. Even though it may be scary, you're actually in a really exciting place because you are in a place to take action.

This is your opportunity to do what you have always wanted. Just do it. Try it and see if it jives, and if it does, put some gas on it. If it doesn't jive, that's fine, pivot. I felt stuck for so long. I just didn't know what to do, and I kept trying to create the perfect scenario in which to leave, and I ended up just paralyzing myself. Finally, I just said, "Forget it. I'm quitting Walgreens, and I am going to open my own consulting practice."

I didn't even know if this was something that pharmacists could do, but I just decided to go for it because, at that point, I was so frustrated in my career that I had nothing to lose. In my mind, Walgreens was probably going to fire me anyway and hire someone they can pay half my wage anyway; I might as well leave on my own terms.

Methods to Monetize Your Knowledge

My main method of monetization initially was creating my own consulting practice. I saw many patients out here in Utah in a local clinic. We focused a lot on PGx, but for me, PGx (pharmacogenomics) is just the beginning of an amazing pharmacist/patient relationship. And so, even though I focus on PGx, I really use it to get in the door with clients. For me, it serves as the entryway to other pharmacist-led services, which are pretty awesome.

I had patients I saw in my clinic, but I have now pivoted into bigger consulting ventures and now work with corporate clients. What I am most excited about, however, is the PGx Consulting Confidence Academy.

I am the CEO and founder of the PGx Consulting Confidence Academy, in which I coach pharmacists who are building their businesses from scratch. It is such a great space; we share all of our knowledge with one another and empower each other. It is empowering to know that you are not on this journey alone, but you are doing it alongside pharmacists from all across the country, and you are building your knowledge together. That is what is so rewarding about what I do and what gets me jumping out of bed to get to work in the morning.

How Pharmacists Can Leverage Pharmacogenomics to Create Their Own Consulting Practice

Pharmacogenomics is the combination of genetics plus pharmacology. But for me, pharmacogenomics is not a siloed branch of pharmacy. It is not simply pharmacists doing pharmacogenomics and helping their patients make sure they get the right medication for their DNA. I believe that every pharmacist needs to master PGx because it is really a deeper dive into pharmacokinetics and pharmacodynamics. I think it should be treated the same way we treat drug allergies or renal dosing.

This is genetics-based dosing, and it takes the guesswork out of prescribing. We have been talking about this for over twenty years now, the technology is not new, but it is still not a mainstream part of our practice. Labs have historically reached out to doctors and really pounded in the message that doctors need to be doing this for their patients. But what happens is it becomes overwhelming; it is just too much for doctors who are already stressed out. Their practices are filled, they don't have the time to master this new science and treat their patients appropriately.

This is why I believe that pharmacists are the best champions for PGx, especially as the industry continues to change at such a rapid pace. We are getting out of dispensing and adjudicating roles and into the jobs of the future. But in its simplest form, pharmacy is all about forming relationships with patients and using your mind. As uncomfortable as these changes are, we need to learn to connect with parts of our practices that are going to become automated. This technology will be the standard in the near future; we need to become comfortable with these changes. We have doctorate-level degrees. We are more than adequate for taking on these new roles.

When I was working at Walgreens, I was not providing doctorate-level service. I was checking pills. I would tell patients to call me back if they had any questions because I couldn't actually take the time to counsel them, working in a 24-hour store with a drive-through filling up and the phone constantly ringing.

PGx has so much potential for creating a really valuable career in your future. It can also provide you with a safety net as more jobs become automated because when you have valuable knowledge, you cannot be replaced. I see our profession being the best fit to champion this level of personalized medicine and really take our patient encounters to the next level. For so long, I felt like I was med-icating my patients when really I wanted to de-prescribe them. That is how you truly help people. Most pharmacists want patients to get off medication, so just sending patients home with ten, fifteen, twenty medicines a month and a big old bill doesn't feel like you are serving them in a meaningful way.

Not only was it a frustrating job, but it didn't provide me with the inter-actions I was craving with patients. Doctors know that PGx is good for patients, but they are so overwhelmed they just don't have the capacity to deal with it. And it makes sense; even when pharmacists look at a sample report for PGx, it looks like an alien language, let alone doctors, nurse practitioners, PAs; nobody else can deal with it in the same way we can.

I am excited to help champion our profession and get pharmacists out on the front lines and at the grassroots level to create PGx-based practice and service. While I don't only focus on PGx, it's truly sensational to be able to say to my patients, "If we do this lab and talk for an hour, you will know for the rest of your life what medications are ideal for you and which ones are not going to work." It is so meaningful to take the guesswork out of prescribing. Nobody has even heard of this kind of relationship before, let alone experienced it in their life. For me, it feels like a slam dunk for pharmacists. Especially considering how many of us are feeling burnt out and dealing with competition in the space.

Patients want this. Patients want this so badly they are going without their doctor or pharmacist and ordering direct-to-consumer PGx tests online because they want to know how to achieve true health. If patients are doing all of that by themselves, think about how we, as pharmacists, can treat them.

Within my academy, I show you all of the different business models that are open to you. Whether you want to build something on the side to provide a little extra income, build your nest egg, or pay off your student loans, you will have the security of growing something on the side while having a full-time job. Or you can jump in and create an entirely new career for yourself full-time with a bang, which is fantastic too.

There are so many different paths. Whether you are seeing patients individually as a concierge pharmacist, working with doctors, or adding value to the services you provide at your existing job, there is no cookie-cutter model to implementing pharmacogenomics. I felt frustrated that there wasn't anyone helping me as I was building my practice for pharmacists specifically to champion this science and know how to actually do it. It is time for a change. I was able to make that change, and I am excited to help other pharmacists along the way. I want to create a community where we are putting all of our knowledge together because I don't know the answer to every single question being posed across the country. But when there are a hundred pharmacists all doing this, we can share and grow our knowledge together.

That is a really exciting space for me. I love the community that we are building and that we are cheering one another along. Too often, I see pharmacists trying to guard their knowledge like a dragon guarding its gold. They don't want to share what they have learned with others because they are afraid that other people will have an advantage. I'm not trying to create a competitive space. I want people to succeed and be excited, and get to celebrate with others. There is enough opportunity for everyone out there. To grow that opportunity and be able to create a community of support and encouragement has been pretty awesome.

There is so much power in personalized medicine, and it's completely under-utilized. If you have patients who take medicine or will ever have to take medicine during their lives, PGx can help them. It really is a bright spot in the future of pharmacy. I have a pharmacist in my program who started with us three months ago. On Monday, she had her first day of patients and made $1,600 in one day because she transformed from an independent community pharmacist who had no experience in other places to mastering PGx. She ran with it, told people in her community what she was doing, and she already has customers lining up.

This is an exciting place to be. There just are not a lot of "W2 jobs" in the PGx space, and any time there is a job listing, a hundred people apply to it. Whenever a new PGx job listing is posted, I'll get emails saying, "Hey have you seen this? Is anyone else applying for it?"

I'm like, "Yeah, I've got 30 other people emailing me about it."

It's just because there are so few official jobs in the PGx space. As an industry, we need to start having conversations with patients and doctors and say, "I'm a pharmacist, I can do quite a few things, PGx among them, how can I help you?" You'll be amazed at the opportunities in your community. It's a fun place to not only grow your career but to develop that creative process that I never experienced in retail or pharmacy school. We're just so technical. We are trained to study and take tests, but creating something is a completely different thrill.

One of the big things I teach my students is how to convince doctors that PGx is useful for their patients. I always tell my students that they need to form those relationships because if you just go in trying to sell PGx without a prior relationship with the doctor, nothing really sets you apart from the lab reps who are trying to do the same thing. The goal is not to sell them on PGx; the goal is to ask questions.

When I speak to doctors, I bring a notepad, and for the first conversation, I just ask questions: How is their practice going? What are their pain points? What is working and what is not? And I just listen, listen, listen. Once you can understand where they are coming from and what their pain points are, you can provide a solution. They are much more willing to listen when you are providing a solution that relates specifically to the problems they are facing. But if you come in with a handful of articles and say, "Look, this is a clinically valid science, here is the study." it becomes a very different conversion. When you approach someone from that angle, it is very difficult to convince them that they are wrong.

You have to put in the work to grow and develop that relationship first. You have to show the value of a pharmacist, and then you can speak from personal experience and tell them about the patients whom PGx has helped. It sets you on a totally different trajectory than just going in with an agenda to sell your service, whether they like it or not.

There are so many options out there for consultant pharmacists; it's not just in a prescriber practice with a collaborative practice agreement or in a traditional model like we learned in pharmacy school. I've spoken to many different behavioral health clinics, addiction centers, pain centers, even chiropractic offices that are focusing on wellness. They are excellent places to collaborate with outside of the traditional model. I promise there are clinics and opportunities in your community that are looking for you as a pharmacist to come and help them, whether they know it or not. Thinking outside the box, attracting people who you can provide services for and expand their offerings is a great way to go about implementing PGx. People are always surprised to learn what is in their community that they had no idea existed.

Advice for Aspiring Entrepreneurs

I know everyone says to just start, but it really is true. Pharmacists often feel insecure; they feel they can't create business because it's something they've never done before. If you don't take action, you'll be exploring forever. Take action even if you don't know where it is going to lead you. I've seen from pharmacists in my program that those who have the most success are the ones who just start. They have conversations with potential clients or patients. If you are motivated to take action, you are going to find success.

It's okay to be scared; I'm scared a lot. You just have to do it anyway. Take action and get started. Committing to action is what gets the ball rolling; the first domino falls, that is when the action begins to take effect. It's a simple thing, but really, action will cure all your worries. In the past year, I have done nothing but action. I've been able to transform my career. Now my mission is to help all the pharmacists who are miserable in their careers to get out there and create something they love.

CONTRIBUTOR
CONNECTION

**Jamie Wilkey,
PharmD**

🌐 www.drjamiewilkey.com

in www.linkedin.com/in/dr-jamie-wilkey/

AFTERWORD

Congratulations on finishing this book. I cannot wait to see what you do with all of the inspiring messages you have gained from our amazing contributors.

I wanted to spend a moment discussing the final module of the Pharmfluencer Business Course, and one of the most important. Celebration! As entrepreneurs, we tend to always be focused on the next thing: the next step in our business plan, refining our product, expanding our clientele, and don't get me wrong, it is necessary to be aware of the next steps we want to take. But we should also be taking the time to celebrate our victories, both little and big.

One way I like to celebrate myself for all the hard work I accomplish is by buying myself jewelry. I also love activities and experiences, taking a day off to do something special with my family or attending a concert or event. Sometimes even just an hour to spend with my kids feels like a wonderful celebration of all I have accomplished. There is so much for you to be proud of, don't forget to celebrate it!

If you are ready to go deeper on your entrepreneurial journey, then I have just what you need—the Pharmfluencer Business Course. This online course provides you with a clear path to start your side gig or transition an existing side gig to full-time entrepreneurship. You will learn to Influence, Multiply, and Impact Pharmacy through Entrepreneurship.

You may want to then schedule a session with me. I love learning what Pharmfluencers are out there influencing and impacting. Visit www.kimberboothe.com/contact to schedule an exploration call to see how I can support you. If you're stuck, frustrated, or just need a little guidance, I'm here to cheer you on and help along the way.

Join our growing Pharmovator Community at **www.kimberboothe. com/community**. You're not alone! There are so many other pharmacy professionals on this journey with you. Make connections, garner support, and ask questions to others who are in the same boat as you.

.

ACKNOWLEDGEMENTS

You are the sum of the people you surround yourself with. A strong inner circle is even more valuable on the rollercoaster journey of an entrepreneur. There are many people that I would like to acknowledge for being part of my inner circle and supporting me with tough love, advice, and cheering.

Family

Richard Boothe—Thank you for being my best friend and partner in life while being supportive of my career passions. You were there to encourage and balance me as I made the leap fully to entrepreneurship. You make life fun.

Evan, Ethan, & Ella—I love our family dinner games as I hear your innovative and thoughtful answers. I am excited to see how you will design the lives you want and use your entrepreneurial spirit.

Mom & Dad—Thank you for encouraging me to dream big and be myself. Your support at every stage of my life has been amazing.

Pharmacy Entrepreneurs "Pharmfluencers"

I am honored to know and share the inspiring stories of all the Pharmfluencers in this book. You are blazing trails to influence, monetize and impact pharmacy through entrepreneurship.

There are a few Pharmfluencers that I would like to highlight for their influence on my thought leadership journey.

Erin Albert—You are exemplary of the term you coined, multipational, having multiple passions in your career portfolio. You taught me the value of publishing for thought leaders and your advice that "books are the new business card."

Kelley Carlstrom—You have an amazing way of connecting with people, and I have benefited from your peer mentorship as you always ask insightful questions that keep me focused on my why and needle movers.

Jerrica Dodd—You are an inspiring pharmacy advocate and entrepreneur. Thank you for creating the *PharmaSis™ Magazine* and for encouraging me to put myself out there

Christina Fontana—Thank you for all you do to support pharmacist entrepreneurs. As my coach, you encouraged me to know my value and to give myself grace on this journey.

Todd Eury—You are a bold advocate and supporter of the profession of pharmacy. Thank you for supporting the move of my *Connector Life Podcast* to the Pharmacy Podcast Network© to increase the voice of innovation and health system pharmacy.

Michelle Fritsch—You are a master of goal planning and helped me to focus on what was most important. I value your collaboration and appreciate your ideas and support.

Anna Garrett—You showed me that this business model was possible in our profession. You are the first pharmacist I followed who was sharing your knowledge in diverse platforms for a greater impact.

Christina Madison—I have learned so much from you on the opportunities for pharmacists in public health and how we can raise the voice of the profession through the media.

Sue Paul—Thank you for your friendship and support. You helped me realize that my desire to support entrepreneurs in addition to intrapreneurs was fully in line with my overarching goal of advancing pharmacy.

Blair Thielemier—You are a highly successful Pharmfluencer and mentor. Your encouragement at your retreat propelled me to make my transition decision.

Tim Ulbrich—Your thought leadership and collaboration with our professional organizations, has inspired me. I appreciate your encouragement to own my niche as the "Strategy Pharmacist."

Pharmfluencer Mastermind

You are an amazing mastermind group that holds me accountable. I am in awe of what you are doing to advance pharmacy as entrepreneurs.

Other Influencer Entrepreneurs & Coaches

You have been an important part of my development as an entrepreneur, teaching me the foundation and mindset necessary for success.

Brendon Burchard
Catherine Dove
Marie Forleo
Michael Hyatt
Stu McLaren
Donald Miller
Bonita Palmer
Amy Porterfield
Anna Runyan
Jeff Walker

Supporters

Thank you to the pharmacy entrepreneurs who supported the work of the Pharmfluencer Summit.

Medipreneurs Summit©—Support—Innovate—Thrive: We guide professionals in healthcare to exit their comfort zone and create a business or lead their organization in a way that offers them freedom, money, and the ability to live a personal and professional life that aligns with their values.

Pharmacy Podcast Network©—Pharmacy Podcast Nation is our flagship show hosting all of the Pharmacy Podcast Networks 1400+ episodes. With 30+ different podcast programs and over 40 different co-hosts helping to develop audio content about different subjects in pharmacy, the PPN delivers a unique publication to all healthcare professionals with a specific focus on pharmacy.

PGX101©—Improving Lives Through Personalized Medicine: Educate healthcare providers on important concepts of pharmacogenomics (PGx) and collaborate with forward-thinking healthcare providers who want to establish a PGx testing

RPhAlly—Provides an exclusive platform for pharmacy professionals in the US to obtain and share vital industry information, network with other pharmacy professionals, grow their careers, and adapt to a rapidly changing industry in real-time, resulting in more productive, successful, connected, and compliant professionals.

RXVIP Cares—360 is an education and career development program for pharmacists and student pharmacists to enhance their roles as patient-centric providers. We provide direct patient encounters via telehealth to ensure that each patient gets the care they need to improve their life.

Clients

To my incredible clients, it has been an honor to be part of your intra-preneurship and entrepreneurship journeys. Your desire to learn more about the Pharmfluencer Business Model led to my creation of the summit, course, and now this book. I have learned much from you, and you have supported the achievement of my goal to advance pharmacy practice.

Pharmfluencers Book Team

Thanks to everyone on the Holon Publishing team who helped me to bring this book to fruition. Catherine Valerio, Nesha Ruther, Victoria Stingo, Rebekah Spivey, Brady Klueber, Jeremy Gotwals.

INDEX

Pharmfluencers' Topics

Pharmfluencers' Methods to Monetize

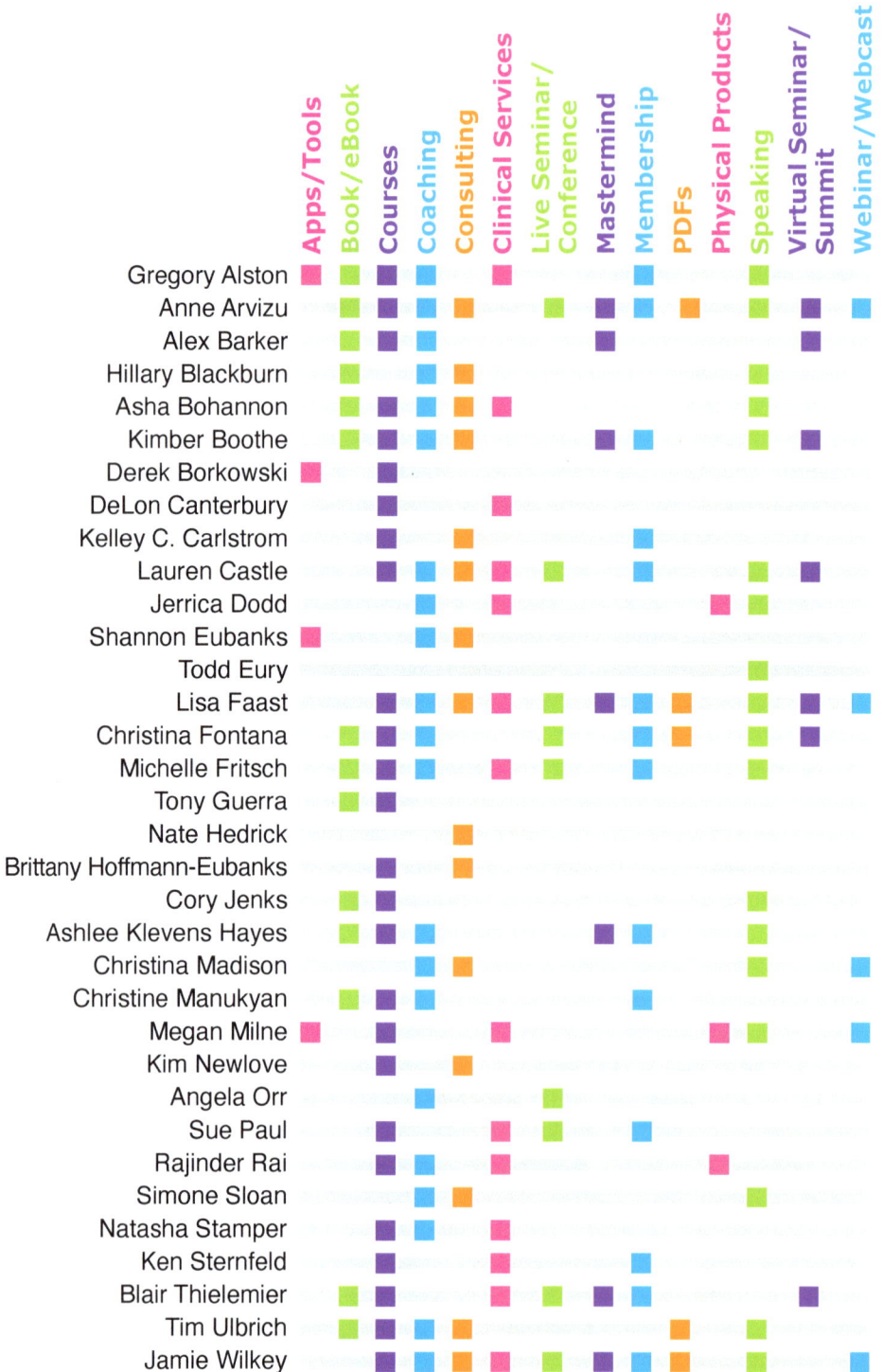

	Apps/Tools	Book/eBook	Courses	Coaching	Consulting	Clinical Services	Live Seminar/Conference	Mastermind	Membership	PDFs	Physical Products	Speaking	Virtual Seminar/Summit	Webinar/Webcast
Gregory Alston	■	■	■	■		■			■			■		
Anne Arvizu		■	■	■	■		■	■	■	■		■	■	■
Alex Barker		■	■	■				■					■	
Hillary Blackburn		■	■	■	■							■		
Asha Bohannon		■	■	■	■	■						■		
Kimber Boothe		■	■					■	■			■	■	
Derek Borkowski	■		■											
DeLon Canterbury			■			■								
Kelley C. Carlstrom			■						■					
Lauren Castle			■	■	■		■		■			■	■	
Jerrica Dodd				■		■					■	■		
Shannon Eubanks	■			■	■									
Todd Eury														
Lisa Faast			■	■	■	■	■	■	■	■		■	■	■
Christina Fontana		■	■	■			■		■	■		■	■	
Michelle Fritsch		■	■	■		■			■			■		
Tony Guerra		■	■											
Nate Hedrick					■									
Brittany Hoffmann-Eubanks			■		■									
Cory Jenks		■	■									■		
Ashlee Klevens Hayes		■	■	■				■	■					■
Christina Madison				■	■							■		■
Christine Manukyan		■		■					■					
Megan Milne	■		■			■					■	■		■
Kim Newlove			■		■									
Angela Orr				■			■							
Sue Paul			■			■	■		■					
Rajinder Rai			■	■		■					■			
Simone Sloan				■	■							■		
Natasha Stamper			■	■										
Ken Sternfeld			■			■			■					
Blair Thielemier		■	■			■	■	■	■				■	
Tim Ulbrich		■	■	■	■					■		■		
Jamie Wilkey			■	■	■	■	■	■	■	■				■

ABOUT KIMBER
CHIEF CONNECTOR & PHARMOVATOR

Dr. Kimber Boothe, PharmD, MHA is a pharmacist, healthcare leader, and entrepreneur with decades of experience in health systems and the pharmaceutical industry. Kimber is the founder and CEO of the Kimber Boothe Group where she helps pharmacists transform and advance practice to have a joyful engaging career. She serves by providing coaching, consulting, and courses on:

- Leadership & Career Development
- Pharmacy Strategy & Innovation/Intrapreneurship
- Pharmacy Entrepreneurship

She is known as the 'Strategy Pharmacist', calls herself a Connector and a Pharmovator®, and is creator and author of several programs and books to guide pharmacists to success. CONNECTOR CORE™ is a program on the Connector Framework™—Connectorability™, Connector Alignment™, Connector Foundation™, and Connector LIFE™. PHARMOVATION® is a course and system to Accelerate Your Pharmacy Career, Advocate for resources & Advance Pharmacy Practice, and PHARMFLUENCER™ is to Influence, Multiply, and Impact Pharmacy through Entrepreneurship.

Kimber previously led the pharmacy services for a four-hospital community health system where she drove innovative strategy for the pharmacy enterprise as the Chief Pharmacy Officer. She was also the Director of Clinical Pharmacy Services at Yale New Haven Health. She is a graduate of the University of Connecticut School of Pharmacy and Medical University of South Carolina College of Pharmacy, University of Phoenix Masters in Health Administration program, and completed residency training at Virginia Commonwealth University Medical College of Virginia Hospitals.

She is passionate about spending time on the right things to develop others and deliver strategic, focused results. She has supported the addition of over 250 health system pharmacy positions. Her motto is Pharmacy Can do More with More™ and her goal is to support the addition of 100 new health system pharmacy positions annually.

She is the recipient of the Connecticut Society of Health System Pharmacists Meritorious Achievement Award and her prior organization has been recognized with the Kentucky Society of Health System Pharmacists Innovative Health-System Pharmacy Practice Award.

For more information on Kimber, use this QR code or visit **www.kimberboothe.com/links**

WORK WITH KIMBER

I have created several programs based on the needs of my clients and trends in our profession to support pharmacists in advancing pharmacy through entrepreneurship and intrapreneurship.

The Pharmfluencer Business Course:

The Pharmfluencer Business Course provides you with a clear path to start your side gig or transition an existing side gig to full-time entrepreneurship. You will learn to Influence, Multiply, and Impact Pharmacy through Entrepreneurship.

PHARMFLUENCER™ BUSINESS COURSE
INFLUENCE • MULTIPLY • IMPACT
PHARMACY THROUGH ENTREPRENEURSHIP

CONNECTORx LEADERSHIP CIRCLE™

Connector Leadership Circle:

Membership community to support your goals joy & connection, practice impact, and career acceleration. Experience live group coaching roundtables, masterclasses, bootcamps, leader rounding, and more.

Connector Coaching:

Connector Coaching enables you to accelerate to a joyful and engaging career through one-on-one engagement. Gain clear direction and confidence applicable at any stage of your career. Connector Coaching offers personalized programs for transformation, acceleration, launch, strategy, or VIP days.

CONNECTOR COACHING

The Pharmovation Course & Book:

Pharmovation is the only implementation program of its kind that not only shows you exactly what to do to accelerate your career and advocate for resources but ultimately how to advance pharmacy practice to bring joy to your work and improve patient outcomes.

PHARMOVATION

ACCELERATE • ADVOCATE • ADVANCE

BY KIMBER BOOTHE

PHARMOVATION CONSULTING

Pharmovation Consulting:

Pharmovation Consulting helps you connect the dots from strategy to execution to advance pharmacy practice. I am available to help organizations as an independent contractor for short- and long-term needs. My main areas of focus and expertise are listed here:

- INNOVATION
- PHARMACY ENTERPRISE
- STRATEGIC PLANS
- BUSINESS PLANS
- PROJECT PLANS

Kimber "Speaks":

I give presentations about pharmacy leadership to help pharmacists strategically advocate for roles and resources to advance practice and accelerate joyful engaging careers. I am available for small and large audiences on a topic of your needs, or you can choose one of my keynotes.

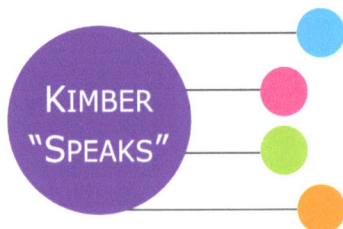

KIMBER "SPEAKS"

For more information on Kimber, use this QR code or visit **www.kimberboothe.com/links**

www.ingramcontent.com/pod-product-compliance
Lightning Source LLC
Chambersburg PA
CBHW041305210326
41598CB00011B/850